THE NORMAN CONQUEST

THE NORMAN CONQUEST

WILLIAM THE CONQUEROR'S SUBJUGATION OF ENGLAND

TERESA COLE

AMBERLEY

First published 2016

Amberley Publishing
The Hill, Stroud
Gloucestershire, GL5 4EP

www.amberley-books.com

ISBN 978 1 4456 4922 1 (hardback)
ISBN 978 1 4456 4923 8 (ebook)

British Library Cataloguing in Publication Data.
A catalogue record for this book is available
from the British Library.

Typesetting and Origination by Amberley
Publishing.
Map illustration by Thomas Bohm, User Design,
Illustration and Typesetting.
Printed in the UK.

CONTENTS

AUTHOR'S NOTE ON NAMES

Anglo-Saxon and Danish names will be found with many variations in spelling. In particular the 'Æ' at the beginning of the names of Saxon nobility, with no real modern equivalent, has commonly been rendered as A or E (Alfred or Edith). In general I have used the simplest and most commonly recognised version of a name, except where a multiplicity of Sweins and Ediths at one time can be distinguished more easily by a variation in spelling. The one exception to this rule is made in the case of the father of Edward the Confessor, who has been so damned by the name 'Ethelred the Unready' that I have preferred to use the alternative Athelred in the hope it might buy him a more sympathetic hearing.

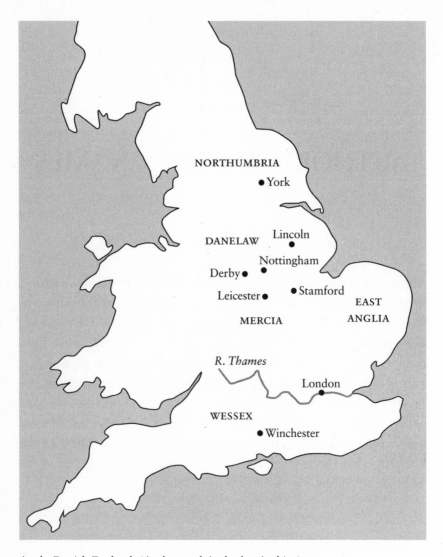

Anglo-Danish England. (Author and Amberley Archive)

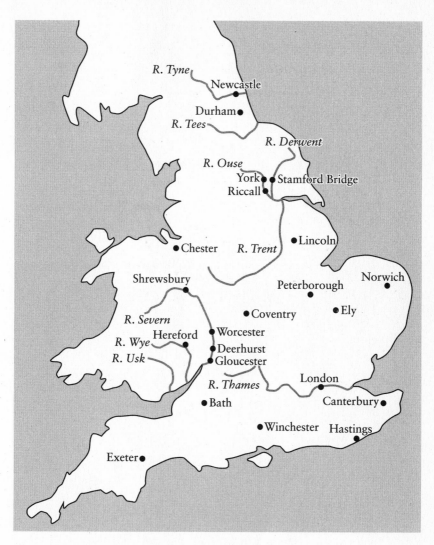

England in 1066. (Author and Amberley Archive)

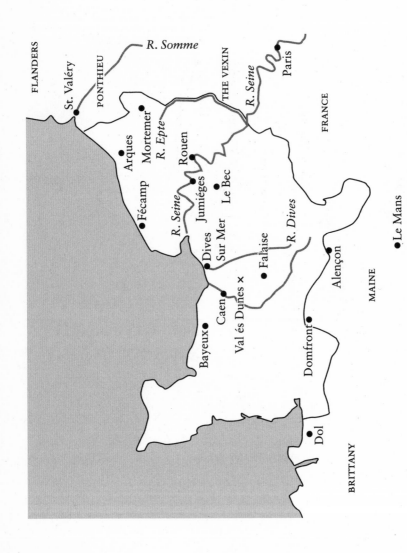

Normandy at the time of William I. (Author and Amberley Archive)

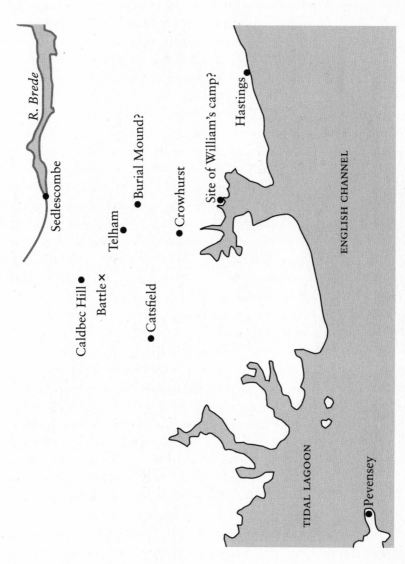

The Battle of Hastings 1066. (Author and Amberley Archive)

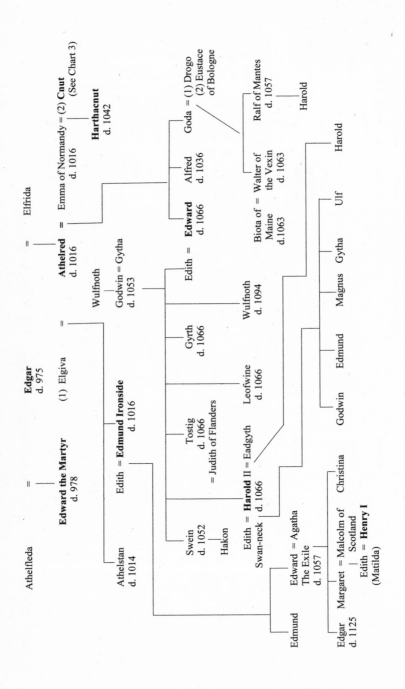

Selected descendants of King Edgar of England. (Author and Amberley Archive)

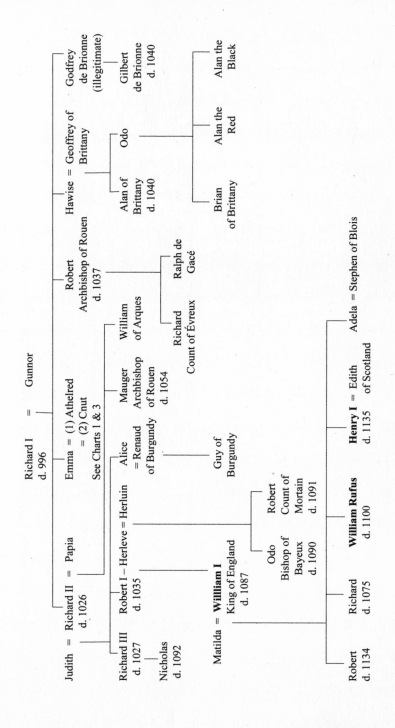

Selected descendants of Richard I Duke of Normandy. (Author and Amberley Archive)

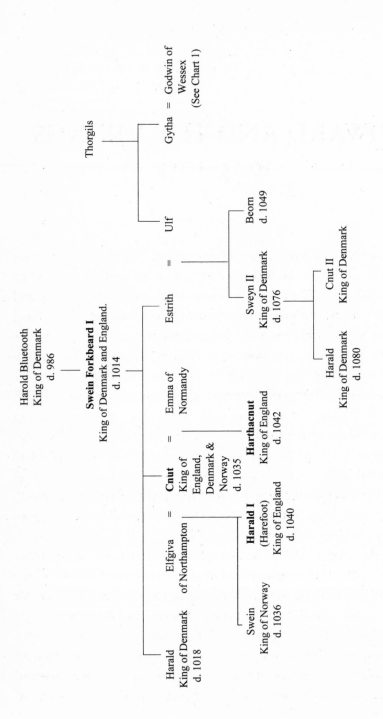

The Danish connection.. (Author and Amberley Archive)

I

EDWARD AND THE VIKINGS
1003–1017

The one fact that anyone can tell you about Edward the Confessor is that he died in 1066, perhaps adding that his death was followed by the Norman Conquest. If pushed they might be able to add that he was an old man when he died. How he might have filled the long years of his life, however, and what was happening to the country he ruled during those years, has long been a matter for the professional historian and a closed book to everyone else.

It has always been convenient to divide history into slices like a particularly long and rich fruit cake. Where the knife might fall in some eras has been argued over, but the division of the Norman Conquest is a very clear and obvious one. So in most histories Edward is either a footnote to the Anglo-Saxon era, or a brief scene setter before the bloodshed of the Battle of Hastings. 'That's not my period,' an historian will say of an event a few years before or after the time of his specialist study.

For the people who lived through those times, of course, there was no such clear division. Life might change dramatically but it was still life, fathers, sons and grandsons each leaving their greater or lesser mark on the years of their lifespan, and their own legacy for the future. This is particularly true of the years before and after the Conquest. To miss out the life and times of Edward is to miss the whole first act of the drama, and to risk leaving what followed without any really satisfactory explanation. For the events of

1066 involved not two players but three: the English, the Normans and the Scandinavians. The history of the Danes and Norse had been entwined with that of the English for centuries, and they too had a decisive part to play in that momentous year.

When Edward died in his bed in January 1066 he was securely King of England. That title, though, was of very recent coining. Most of his predecessors had claimed only to be 'King of the English'. Indeed the idea of England as a single entity was only gradually becoming a solid fact rather than a distant dream.

From the time of the coming of the Angles and Saxons, around the fifth century, the land we call England had been divided into a number of kingdoms, frequently warring among themselves and growing bigger or smaller as a result of those conflicts. Though traditionally referred to as the 'Heptarchy', there were often more than seven of them, and the peninsula of Devon and Cornwall was excluded from the count entirely, sometimes being referred to as 'West Wales', and holding on to pre-existing British traditions.

Gradually the lesser kingdoms became absorbed into the greater until, by the ninth century, there were three major powers, Northumbria, Mercia and Wessex, with a lesser kingdom of East Anglia surviving as a separate entity. It took an attack from an outside force to make people begin to think of themselves as English rather than Mercian or West Saxon, and that attack was the first coming of the Scandinavians.

In 793, according to the *Anglo-Saxon Chronicle*, the church at Lindisfarne off the coast of Northumbria was sacked by heathen men with much slaughter and brutal robbery. Fearsome omens were also noted for that year, possibly with the benefit of hindsight, including whirlwinds and fiery dragons seen flying in the sky. More likely the dragons came by sea, and soon the famous dragon-headed Viking longships were a familiar bringer of terror to those dwelling anywhere near the coast, or indeed a major river, as they raided up and down the British Isles. By the mid-ninth century, as Churchill noted, the Viking sailors had become soldiers, ready to fight and win battles against the armies of the ruling kings, and casting envious eyes at the prosperous and fertile land that appeared to be at their mercy.

The Vikings who came to invade and eventually become settlers were predominantly Danish. East Anglia fell to them, along with substantial parts of Mercia and Northumbria, and only the stubborn heroism of the West Saxons prevented the whole of the land being overrun. King Alfred, rightly titled 'the Great', succeeded in drawing a line which the invaders could not cross, and a peace of sorts was eventually established by what is known as the Treaty of Alfred and Guthrum around 884. This basically divided the land with a line roughly from London to Chester. An area of Danish influence lay to the north and east, with an area of English influence to the south and west.

The treaty established a framework for relations between English and Danes rather than a political boundary, but the kingdoms of Jorvik (around York), Danish East Anglia and the Danish areas of east Mercia and Lindsey (Lincolnshire) known as the Five Boroughs were for a time ruled by the leaders of the Danish settlers who now moved in to share the land with their English predecessors. Nor did it mark the end of hostilities.

Men of Wessex and Mercia had fought together to halt the Danes, and now united again in supporting the children of Alfred to reclaim the lost lands. Edward the Elder, King of Wessex, together with his sister Athelfleda, the so-called 'Lady of the Mercians', scored victory after victory, until Edward's son, Athelstan, who had been brought up in the Mercian court, could be recognised as overlord of all, for the first time bearing the title King of the English.

The lands he ruled were still divided but the Danish settlers had not come in sufficient numbers to displace the earlier population. Certainly some English lost their lives and their plots, but there was land enough to be shared by all. The Danish presence is shown by clusters of place names, the '-by', '-thorp' and '-thwaite' infilling among the Saxon '-ham' and '-ton' in the Danish areas. The rapid adoption of Christianity by the formerly pagan invaders also made interaction and intermarriage easier, and it was not long before children in the same families were being found with both English and Danish names. It should be remembered, too, that the Danish homeland was very close to the place from which the Angles and Saxons themselves had come a few centuries before. The royal houses of the English kingdoms, in the more fanciful parts of their genealogies, had all claimed descent from the Nordic god Odin. It has been suggested, too, that at this time the languages were still mutually understandable with a little effort.

This was a time of reorganisation prompted by the Danish wars. Wessex had long been divided into shires, for one or more of which an ealdorman was responsible to the king. Alfred had begun establishing a network of 'burghs' or garrison towns across the south which quickly became trading centres as well as places of protection. Within the Danish areas the process occurred the other way round. The Danes had established their administrative centres, complete with military garrisons, at 'boroughs' ruled by a jarl, each having its own sphere of influence. These included not only the 'Five Boroughs' in the east Midlands at Lincoln, Derby, Nottingham, Leicester and Stamford, but also others such as York, Cambridge, Bedford and Northampton. As this land was recovered it too was divided into shires based on these centres. The jarl, now owing allegiance to the English king but still drawn from the Danish community, became the equivalent of the ealdorman, and over time the names were blended into the new title of earl.

Clearly there were now two strong influences at work in the land. Christianity was a powerful force making firm connections with mainland Europe, in particular with the Low Countries, France and Rome. At the same time England has been referred to as an Anglo-Danish kingdom, and was similarly affected by events in the Scandinavian lands.

The cluster of petty kingdoms in Norway had been largely united under the rule of Harald Fairhair, and some of those driven out had found new lands for themselves in Ireland, Scotland and Cumbria. When Harald's son, the delightfully named Eric Bloodaxe, set about challenging his father's rule and disposing of his brothers and half-brothers, Harald sent a younger son, Haakon, to be brought up at the court of Athelstan in Wessex. Later Athelstan equipped the young man to go and expel Eric and take his place as King of Norway. Eric Bloodaxe then appeared in Jorvik and intermittently ruled there in defiance of the English king, until finally thrown out and killed in 954.

By the time of the coronation of King Edgar in 973 the authority of the King of the English seemed to be complete. Edgar had already ruled for more than thirteen years, coming to the throne at around sixteen years of age on the death of his unpopular brother, Edwy. Firmly guided and advised by the saintly Dunstan, whom he had appointed Archbishop of Canterbury, his reign was a time of peace and plenty. It witnessed the revival of art and learning, along with the reform and rebuilding of the Church, strongly influenced by similar reforms on the Continent.

His coronation at Bath was the climax. In a lavish ceremony devised by Dunstan and drawing on Continental models, the king was both crowned and anointed with holy oils, making clear Dunstan's belief that the king was both an earthly ruler and God's appointed protector of the Church in his realm. This ceremony formed the basis of all future coronations of English kings, and was also the first time a queen had been crowned and anointed along with her husband.

Later, during a royal tour of his kingdom, a strange form of submission to the newly crowned king is said to have taken place at Chester. According to some sources up to seven 'kings' – Scots, Welsh and Cumbrian – rowed Edgar along the River Dee from his palace to the church of St John and back, to demonstrate his supremacy over them. More contemporary records put the number at six or eight, and only mention the swearing of loyalty to the king as overlord. The message is clear, however, that Edgar was king of all the lands now known as England, and overlord of other territories as well.

He is described as 'the Peaceable' and the *Anglo-Saxon Chronicle* records that 'in his days it prospered well, and God granted him that he dwell in peace the while that he lived.' Furthermore, he 'bettered the public peace' more than any king before him in living memory, so that 'kings and earls gladly to him bowed and were submissive to that that he willed'.

This Edgar was the grandfather of Edward the Confessor, and, given the fulsome praise for his reign just recorded, it is hard to see what could have gone so wrong in just a couple of generations to leave his peaceful realm so open to war and conquest. The *Chronicle*, however, records 'one misdeed' which, with the benefit of hindsight, was clearly felt to have contributed to England's later woes.

Edgar's misdeed was to grant a large degree of self-rule to his Danish subjects living within the areas of his land that would later be known as the Danelaw. Provided they still acknowledged Edgar as their king, they could live under their own social and legal customs. The earls were still appointed by the king, as were the bishops, and, though it might be organised slightly differently, the militia was still expected to answer his call. Still there is no doubt that laws and landholdings developed along Danish lines in these parts of the kingdom, and made it attractive for many travelling from Scandinavia in search of a better life. As the *Chronicle* puts it, 'He foreign vices loved and heathen customs within this land brought too oft, and outlandish men hither enticed, and harmful people allured to this land.'

Two years after his magnificent coronation Edgar died and the peace of the kingdom died with him. A squabble broke out at once as to which of the two young sons he left should be rightful king of the English. It should be remembered that at that time the succession of the eldest son was by no means automatic. Several times since the days of Alfred a brother was preferred to the son of the previous king, especially if that son was still a child.

To complicate matters Edgar's sons had different mothers. The queen crowned alongside him at Bath was his second, or possibly third, wife. In his youth he had married Athelfleda, and their son, Edward, was around thirteen years old when his father died. However, some at the time claimed that Edward was not

Athelfleda's son, and was in fact the illegitimate son of a lady called Wulfthryth who later became a nun. Nor were matters entirely straightforward with Edgar's last wife, Elfrida, who was the widow of an ealdorman of East Anglia. There were stories that Edgar had plotted her husband's death in order to marry her. Their eldest son, Edmund, had died in 971, and the younger, Athelred, was around seven years old in 975.

Edgar's leading counsellors, including Dunstan, favoured Edward as king and carried the day, although a number of ealdormen and Queen Elfrida supported her son, possibly feeling that a younger king would leave more power in their own hands.

In his short reign Edward seemed by most accounts to offend almost everyone of importance, and then, on 18 March 978, at Corfe in Dorset, he was murdered. The story goes that he was paying a visit to his stepmother and young stepbrother. On his arrival he was offered wine to drink, and as he leaned from his horse to accept it he was set upon by members of the household and stabbed to death. We will never know for sure who was behind this, though later writers fixed upon the prototype 'wicked stepmother'. No one was ever punished for it. Edward was rapidly buried with no ceremony or regal honours at nearby Wareham, and within a matter of weeks the ten-year-old Athelred had been crowned king.

By some accounts Athelred was present when the murder took place and the event certainly shadowed the start of his reign. Soon miracles were being reported at Edward's grave, and the reputedly bad-tempered, offensive youth was being called 'Edward the Martyr'. The *Anglo-Saxon Chronicle* entry for the year devoted a long paragraph to his wrongs and how he was now being properly rewarded by God in heaven, and soon his remains were transferred to Shaftesbury Abbey and became a place of pilgrimage.

And now, with an unfortunate sense of timing, history began to repeat itself. England had never been entirely free of Viking raids, but from 980 onwards they began again in earnest. It is often tempting to see the Vikings as daring adventurers and the English as timid and spineless. This is far from the truth. In fact, in most of the set-piece battles that were fought, the English gave at least as good as they got. Perhaps it is better to view it as a contest between those who had nothing to lose and everything to gain, and those who had already won their kingdom and wanted only to enjoy it in peace.

There had been upheavals in the Scandinavian countries at this time. Harald Bluetooth, king of Denmark, had deposed and killed the king of Norway and installed in his place his own man, Haakon Sigurdsson. Those expelled or seeking equal fame spread out around the Viking world, which now reached from Iceland and even North America in the west to Russia in the east, and in coastal areas from the Baltic to the Mediterranean.

The sheer connectedness of this world is startling given the transport available. Fighters from Norway appeared in the Varangian Guard of the Byzantine Emperor. Brides for Scandinavian nobility might come from Ireland, Kiev, Poland or even England. It was every man's ambition to be a 'ring-giver', a leader of men who were bound to him by ties of personal loyalty. For that he needed wealth and treasures of all kinds to reward his followers, and these were there for the taking in rich, settled lands like England.

In 980 Southampton was sacked by men in long ships. The next year it was Devon and Cornwall that suffered and the year after, Dorset, while even London was not safe from the raiders, who could strike wherever water would carry their sleek, shallow-drafted craft. They raided mostly in summer and then withdrew to strongholds in Denmark, Ireland, the Scottish islands and, increasingly, in Normandy, that part of northern France that had been gifted to Rollo the Viking to settle barely seventy years before. By 990, so hostile was the relationship between England and Normandy over this harbouring of raiders that the Pope himself sent an envoy to calm things down and to persuade each side to sign a treaty – possibly the first between them – agreeing to give no shelter to the other's enemies. This treaty was eventually signed in March 991 but by then the game had changed. 991 was the year when Olaf came.

Olaf was Olaf Trygvasson, one of the heroes of the Viking age whose deeds were commemorated in the sagas. According to these he was a great-grandson of Harald Fairhair of Norway. He was born around 964 after his mother had fled from the violent upheavals in Norway at the time. Brought up in Novgorod in present-day Russia, he had led an adventurous life, fighting with the German Emperor Otto against Harald Bluetooth in Denmark amongst other things, before arriving in England in his late twenties. It is claimed that the death of his first wife had turned him to the life of a Viking raider, and he had been all around the British islands, and even been converted to Christianity by a holy man in the Scilly Isles, before appearing with ninety-three ships off the coast of Kent in 991.

This was a sizeable fleet, though not all would have been fighting ships, and it has been suggested that it carried between three and four thousand fighting men, many more than would have been needed for a raiding party. The *Chronicle* describes how, having raided around the Kent coast and sacked Ipswich, they moved to an island in the mouth of the River Blackwater in Essex and threatened the town of Maldon. Maldon was the site of a royal mint and had been attacked before, being successfully defended by the local ealdorman, Britnoth. It has been suggested that revenge for that defeat was one of the motives that brought Olaf and his men there on that day in August 991.

We have an epic poem, probably written soon afterwards, that tells us what happened next. Britnoth, it is claimed, was well over six feet tall and had in his time been a great warrior, though by 991 he was around sixty years old with 'swan-like' white hair. He now called out the fyrd, the local militia of the time, and set his battle line along the shore facing the Viking forces on their island. It is claimed that Olaf's men greatly outnumbered the English, but this may not be true since they began by demanding payment to go away. The reply was that they would have only spear points and sharpened swords as their tribute.

When first they came together to trade insults it was high tide, but as the waters ebbed a causeway wide enough for three men linked the island to the mainland. As this began to appear the Vikings started to press forward across it but it was easily defended on the shoreward side. Now, however, Olaf requested that his men should be allowed to cross onto solid ground so that the two sides might face each other more fairly. Astonishingly Britnoth agreed, but in the close combat fighting that followed he paid for his generosity with his life.

Nevertheless, despite the fact that, in the language of the time, the Vikings 'had the power of the battlefield', they had been pressed so hard by those remaining on the English side that, according to one account, they had scarcely enough fit men left afterwards to man their ships. They must have made a swift recovery, however, for by the end of the year they were in a position to drive a hard bargain in a peace treaty with the English king.

By this time King Athelred was in his early twenties and as secure as he was ever likely to be on the throne of England. His Saxon name means 'noble counsel', or possibly 'well-advised', and it is not known who gave him the nickname 'unraed' or 'badly advised' that in its corrupt form of 'unready' has survived through history. Unready he probably was for the trials that would face him during his reign, but he certainly seems, to us at least, to have been badly advised, and the events following the Battle of Maldon give a classic example of this.

As a young and possibly unsure ruler, no doubt Athelred believed he was doing the right thing to listen to his counsellors and follow their advice. The most important source of advice at the time was the 'Witanagemot', a flexible and rather ad hoc body made up of ealdormen, the higher thegns, archbishops, bishops and the heads of monasteries. For important decisions a whole council would be summoned, but probably some part of this moved around with the king, including his chief advisers. Among these at this time was Sigeric, Archbishop of Canterbury, and by all accounts it was he who first advised the king to buy off the Vikings by payment of what came to be known as Danegeld. A treaty was drawn up agreeing, among other things, to overlook all the killing and looting that had gone before, and to pay to Olaf and his men the huge sum of £10,000. In return they would agree to go away and never return.

Sadly, as Kipling noted in his poem 'Dane-geld',

We've proved it again and again,
That if once you have paid him the Dane-geld
You never get rid of the Dane.

And so it proved here.

The policy might be justified as a means of buying time, to assemble men and materials to repel future attacks, for example. Even the great Alfred had used it for this purpose and there is some evidence that Athelred intended this to happen. In 992 he tried to assemble a fleet of ships at London but, like so many of his plans, it all went astray, and the next year the Vikings were rampaging freely down the east coast of England.

Olaf returned in a 994 with a powerful new ally. Swein Forkbeard was the son of Harald Bluetooth and had become king of Denmark some years before after overthrowing his father. His sister became Olaf's third wife, and though they were not natural allies, together they brought ninety-four ships to attack London in September 994. It is not clear if this was an attempt at invasion and conquest, but the Londoners put up such a fight that they were forced to withdraw. Instead they took their revenge by cutting a swathe of destruction through the southern counties of England, from Essex to Hampshire, where they 'wrought the utmost evil that ever any army could do', until Athelred was forced to come to terms and buy them off again. This time it cost £16,000 and winter provision for the entire force that camped throughout at Southampton.

This, however, was the last they would see of Olaf. The *Chronicle* records that he was confirmed in the Christian faith at Andover with the king as his sponsor, swore he would never attack England again, and was as good as his word. Instead he took himself off to overthrow the Danish Haakon Sigurdson in Norway and make himself king in his place. It should be recorded that his reign was ended by his former ally Swein Forkbeard, leading combined Danish and Swedish forces at the battle of Svolder in 1000. With the battle lost, Olaf refused to be taken or killed and jumped into the sea, never to be seen again.

This was not the end of attacks on England, however. Within a few years the Danes were back again, and whatever plans Athelred made against them seemed always to hold some fatal flaw. In one year the English attacked too soon, before their full forces were assembled. In another when there seems to have been money and men raised to co-ordinate a fleet with land forces, there was so much delay with the ships that the enemy had already landed in numbers, and the 'ship force' was declared to be just a waste of money.

After a brief lull around 1000 the raids began again the following year. Strong opposition in Hampshire cost many lives on both sides, but still the Danes 'had possession of the place of carnage', and only turned aside to plunder Devon instead. This year, instead of going away they overwintered on the Isle of Wight, a statement of intent that led Athelred, early in 1002, to buy them off again, and now it cost £24,000. Clearly England was a cash cow that the Danes intended to milk again and again.

It was in the spring of 1002 that a rather surprising marriage took place. Until this time English kings had married English wives, usually the daughters of ealdormen from Mercia, Northumbria or East Anglia. Athelred himself had married Elgiva of Northumbria while still in his teens and had a considerable number of children. Now a widower, in 1002 he married Emma of Normandy.

It was certainly a political marriage, possibly sealing another treaty between the two lands. Emma was the daughter of Richard, generally accounted the first Duke of Normandy, and on her mother's side she was a granddaughter of Harald Bluetooth of Denmark. She was probably nearly twenty years younger than her new husband, and even in an age that produced a number of strong female personalities, her part in English history is striking. We have a first-hand account of this in a work she herself commissioned known as the *Encomium of Queen Emma*. This, while highly selective of the facts it narrates, at least gives us a flavour of the times, and the views Queen Emma wanted to put on record for posterity. Written around 1042, probably by a monk from St-Omer in Flanders, it is also useful in that it is almost contemporary with the later events it relates and so is less coloured by hindsight than many sources.

Unlike many queens, there was one role Emma was not required to play, that of mother to an heir. Athelred already had six sons who, in the normal course of events, would expect to secure the throne for some time to come. We don't know when Athelred and Emma's first son was born. At the earliest it would have been in December 1002, and at the latest some time in 1005 when he is mentioned in a charter. We do know he was christened Edward, later to be known as 'the Confessor'. It has been pointed out that Athelred had named all his earlier sons after predecessors on the throne of Wessex with the single exception of his murdered half-brother. Possibly this was a belated peace-making with that Edward, or, since the next son was named Alfred, it may simply have been a counting back to the glory days of his ancestors. If he was hoping for a return to those days he was to be disappointed, and by the time of Edward's birth he had already made the mistake that would cost him his throne.

On 13 November 1002, St Brice's Day, Athelred ordered that all the Danes in England should be killed since they were plotting against him and meant to have his life and his kingdom. Whether this was the result of pure paranoia or more bad advice we don't know. Nor is there any way of knowing how far this order was carried out. Certainly it would not have been enforced in the Danish towns of the Danelaw, but evidence shows that there was a massacre of Danes in the southern parts of the country, and a strong tradition declares that the sister of Swein Forkbeard was among the victims.

Whether that is true or not, it was a situation that the Danish king could not overlook. A series of punitive raids over the next few years showed how weak and divided were the English forces. Only in East Anglia in 1004 were the Danes seriously challenged, by one Ulfkell who, though defeated, gave them 'a worse hand-play' than they had ever met with in the land before.

A severe famine is recorded in 1005, possibly as a result of the fighting and plundering of the previous years leaving less seed to sow and fewer men to sow it. However, the Danes returned the following year, cutting a swathe through all of Wessex and being bought off with a further payment of Danegeld, this time amounting to £36,000.

The world into which young Edward was born, therefore, was a world in crisis where it seemed only a matter of time before a full invasion would come to take the throne itself. Among the claims attaching to his childhood is one that he was sent to the abbey at Ely to be educated, or possibly to become a monk himself. There is no real evidence for this and, given the upheavals of the time, the heart of the Danelaw would seem the very last place that Athelred would send his son. It is likely the story is simply a late bid for reflected glory when, years later, Edward was canonised as a saint.

Having bought a little time, Athelred again set about improving the defences of his kingdom. An apparently strong ealdorman, Edric Streona, was appointed to Mercia, and for the second time a fleet of ships was ordered. A tax was levied to pay for these, and by 1009 the king had assembled around 100 ships and their complement of crew and fighting men. Even this, though, turned to farce. One of the commanders, Britric, a brother of Edric Streona, denounced another of them, Wulfnoth, to the king. Wulfnoth was immediately banished but then took twenty of the king's ships and began plundering the south coast. The other ships were sent after to stop him but were wrecked in a storm, whereupon, the *Chronicle* records, the king gave up and went home.

It was shortly after this that the Danes returned in earnest. In August 1009 a new and impressive force arrived commanded by Thorkell the Tall, another mighty warrior who had fought with Swein Forkbeard in a number of campaigns. This force was reputed to contain a legendary group of professional fighters known as the Jomsvikings, whose base was a huge military camp at Jomsberg fortress, near the mouth of the River Oder in present-day Poland. These Jomsvikings are repeatedly mentioned in the sagas but for many years it was doubted whether they really existed, particularly since the size of their camps and the numbers of professional soldiers mentioned seemed unlikely. It was thought they were simply part of the complicated Scandinavian mythology. Recently, however, traces of such camps have been discovered in Scandinavia, the largest of them capable of holding 2,000 men, and these have been dated to around this time so perhaps the sagas are correct after all.

Whoever they were, they were more than a match for the English defenders. In tones of resignation the *Chronicle* describes how any part of the southern counties would be quickly overrun if they did not promptly pay up the equivalent of protection money. Only London held out against them, but then there were plenty of easier conquests elsewhere. Athelred called out all his forces, but whenever they came close to any kind of decisive action, something always happened to prevent it. The blame for much of this seems to have been laid at the door of ealdorman Edric Streona of Mercia.

Nor did this force withdraw for winter. Instead they based themselves on the lower Thames and lived off the counties on either side. Then, in the spring of the next year, they took up where they had left off, brushing aside Ulfkell's army in East Anglia and using the rivers to lead them to Oxfordshire in the heart of Mercia, ravaging and plundering, 'and ever burning as they went'. English morale was shattered. When they are eastwards, says the *Chronicle* despairingly, our forces are westwards, and when they are southwards we are northwards.

By the time Athelred attempted to treat with them in 1011 they had overrun all the area to the east of a line drawn from the Wash to the Dorset coast. Even as negotiations were going on, Canterbury was seized and Archbishop Alphage taken captive, with an additional ransom being demanded for his release.

It took until Easter the following year to collect the massive Danegeld of £48,000 to buy off these marauders, and then it appeared that the archbishop had refused to allow a ransom to be collected on his behalf from the already overburdened people. At the time he was being held at Greenwich, probably at a winter camp of the Danes, and this refusal was to cost him his life.

The *Chronicle* tells us that on Easter Saturday the men became very drunk on wine from southern lands, and, stirred to fury against the archbishop, they began pelting him with animal bones and cattle heads. What may have started as a kind of rough play quickly got out of hand. Thorkell apparently tried to intervene but the men were beyond his control. One account written much later says that Alphage was finally dispatched by a blow to the head from the back of an axe, delivered by a man he had baptised the day before. If this is true it could have been a swift repentance for the baptismal promises made, or alternatively a merciful ending of prolonged torment.

The Vikings have been noted through history for their cruelty to prisoners, but this brutality in beating to death an elderly priest seems to have literally revolted Thorkell. Possibly the insubordination of the men was also a factor, but at this point he and a sizeable number of his followers, forty-five ship's companies, left the Danish force and offered their services to Athelred as mercenaries. No doubt after the first suspicions were overcome they were gratefully received.

At this time we have no information as to the whereabouts of Queen Emma and her children. We know that by now Edward had a brother, Alfred, and a sister, Goda, to go along with all his older half-brothers and sisters, and the chances are that this younger family of Athelred were in London, since that seems to have been the most stoutly defended place in the country.

Outside of London the realm was in tatters. The *Chronicle* blames this on the bad advice given to the king. He never fought when he should or negotiated when he should, but always came too late to each of these possible policies. At about this time another voice gave an alternative reason for the plight of the country. The Archbishop of York, Wulfstan (who punningly signed himself Bishop Wolf, or 'lupus episcopus'), published a series of sermons and other writings on the evil days through which they were living. Known as the *Sermon of the Wolf*, they declared that England was being punished for its failings in upholding the Christian faith. No one, said Wulfstan, not the clergy or the lay people, had lived as they should. Desires were transformed into rules and God's law was despised. He lists an entire litany of wrongs from the despoiling of churches and murder of priests, down to the defrauding and enslaving of poor men and the enforced re-marriage of widows. As a result the country had suffered military devastation, famine, disease of men and animals and not least the burden of taxation. 'Nothing,' he said, 'has prospered for a long time,' and his long time seems to go back to the murder of Edward the Martyr more than thirty years before. Since Wulfstan was one of Athelred's close advisers and the drafter of his code of laws, this might be seen as simply deflecting criticism away from himself, but it was undoubtedly the opinion of many within the beleaguered kingdom. And if God was inflicting punishment on them for their sins, it must have seemed as if He had lost patience with them altogether, for things were about to go from bad to worse.

In 1013 Swein Forkbeard himself arrived at the head of an army that was now clearly intent on invasion and conquest. Tradition says his first landfall was at Sandwich in Kent, possibly to allow his full fleet to assemble or simply to sound out the situation in England at the time. His main thrust, however, was through the mouth of the Humber and south along the River Trent to Gainsborough in present-day Lincolnshire, and here he established his camp in the heart of the Danelaw. Immediately, as no doubt he anticipated, all of Danish England from Northumbria to East Anglia acclaimed him king.

He had with him on this expedition his son, Cnut, who by most calculations (though with little firm evidence) was around eighteen years of age. There is a tradition that, with his father regularly involved in consolidating his hold on Denmark and Norway during the boy's early years, Cnut may have been brought up with the Jomsvikings, with Thorkell the Tall for mentor and teacher. It is unlikely, however, that he would have been seriously involved with military action before this time, and nor was he expected to be now. When Swein Forkbeard and his host had been provided with horses and provisions, and set out to conquer the southern lands of England, it was Cnut's job to remain at Gainsborough in charge of the fleet, the camp and the hostages that had routinely been provided by those who had already submitted to the Danish king. At around this time he also acquired a wife. In the Danish 'handfast' fashion he became married to Elfgiva of Northampton, the daughter of a Mercian ealdorman.

Swein Forkbeard, meanwhile, had swept south through Oxford and Winchester, which both fell before him, and was attacking London where Athelred and his family were stoutly defended by, among others, Thorkell and his mercenaries. Rightly reasoning that London would not hold out long if the rest of the country had submitted, Swein then drew off westwards as far as Bath, and duly received the submission of all that part of the land, before returning to Gainsborough.

It was by now clear that Athelred could in no way turn back this tide of conquest. Using the breathing space he had been allowed, he made good his withdrawal from London as far as Greenwich where the English fleet lay. Then Emma and afterwards the athelings Edward and his brother Alfred, were escorted across the sea to the safety of her brother's court in Normandy. At this time Edward was at the most ten years of age and possibly younger. Athelred himself remained for a while at Greenwich, but when it was obvious London was about to surrender to Swein he withdrew to the Isle of Wight, spent Christmas there and then joined his family in Normandy.

That same 25 December Swein Forkbeard was formally recognised as king of England. The whole conquest had taken him something less than six months, and no doubt he looked forward to enjoying the fruits of his labours for many years to come. In the event he held the title for barely six weeks. On 2 February 1014, while visiting his son at Gainsborough, he died following a fall from his horse.

It was an outcome no one had expected and threw the game wide open again. Cnut was probably a younger son of Swein, and certainly his brother Harald immediately claimed the kingdom of Denmark. In England the Danes swore allegiance to Cnut, but kings of England were not made so easily.

According to the *Chronicle*, when the Witan met all agreed that Athelred should be sent for, 'for no lord were dearer to them than their natural lord, if he would rule them better than he had before done'. Although the younger children of Emma had fled before the Danes, there were three older sons of Athelred who had apparently remained in England and no doubt they used their influence to achieve this general acclamation. Athelred's response was to send messengers promising forgiveness and faithful service, and, perhaps as some sort of guarantee of goodwill, he sent with them the ten-year-old Edward. In a short time all was agreed between them. 'King Athelred came home to his own people and he was gladly received by them all.'

It was a decisive move, perhaps the only correct decisive move of his reign, and clearly took the Danes by surprise. Within a few weeks of his father's death Cnut had gathered a mounted force ready to continue with his work, but when unexpectedly he found Athelred and a full English army advancing upon him, he was rapidly put to flight. Abandoning the men of the Danelaw who had flocked to serve his cause, Cnut and his fleet sailed away home to Denmark, only pausing on the way to put ashore at Sandwich all the hostages that had been delivered to his father when he first arrived – each of them mutilated with hands, noses and ears cut off. Nor did Athelred spare those in the Danelaw who had taken arms against him, but ravaged and killed and burnt far and wide. It has been suggested that for some time he and Cnut were hated with equal force in that area for the destruction they had brought on the people. This, together with a suggestion that some of the Jomsvikings in his own service might also have been treacherously killed, might explain why shortly after this Thorkell the Tall withdrew his men and ships and went back to offer his service to Cnut.

There seem to have been divisions, too, on the English side. In June 1014 Athelred's eldest son, Athelstan, fell ill and died. On the day of his death he made a detailed will, generously disposing of his possessions among his family – but no mention was made of his stepmother or his young half-brothers. His place as heir apparent was taken by his brother Edmund, and it soon became clear that Edmund, though only around twenty years of age, was a more enterprising man than his father, and not afraid to disagree with him and pursue his own way.

In the early part of 1015 a great council was held at Oxford. Among those attending were two thegns, Siferth and Morcar from the Danelaw, coming to ask pardon for their involvement with Cnut the year before. Instead they were murdered by Edric Streona. Whether or not this was on the orders of Athelred is not certain, but the king certainly acted to confiscate their lands, and he also ordered that Siferth's widow, Edith, should be arrested. Edmund, however, acted even more swiftly. In a matter of weeks he had carried off the lady in question, married her, taken possession of the confiscated estates and been accepted as lord by the whole of the Danelaw, from the Five Boroughs up to York. It was against this background that in September 1015 Cnut came again to England.

The *Encomium* puts an interesting spin on the actions of Cnut after his father's death. He was not abandoning his men and fleeing to safety, but withdrawing to Denmark to consult with his brother Harald. When he got there the first thing he proposed was that they should share the kingdom of Denmark (which was not an unknown arrangement among the Scandinavians) and then together return to conquer England. After that he very generously offered his brother first choice as to which kingdom he would prefer, with Cnut taking the other. Whatever the truth of this, unsurprisingly Harald was not going to play. The *Encomium* insists Cnut was the older brother, but this seems very unlikely. In any case, Harald pointed out that Swein had given Denmark to him. Let Cnut go and get his own kingdom. He would help him raise men and materials, and there is some evidence he actively accompanied him to England at least for a time, but Denmark was his and would remain so.

In the event Cnut recruited some of the foremost fighters of the day to his cause. Thorkell had, of course, returned and with some apparent difficulty had satisfied Cnut that he was now prepared to fight for rather than against him. In addition Eric Haakonsson joined the expedition. With over thirty years' experience of fighting as far afield as Kiev and Estonia, he had recently been sharing the duties of viceroy of Norway with his brother Sweyn. A brother-in-law of Cnut, he was just the sort of seasoned warrior needed by the young, untried adventurer.

Cnut made no attempt to appeal to the Danelaw for support. Possibly he realised how unpopular his desertion the year before would have made him, or maybe he had news of Edmund's strength in the area. Instead he attacked the heart of Wessex, landing on the Dorset coast at Poole harbour. Immediately Edmund raised an army to oppose him, and Edric Streona in Mercia did the same. Almost as soon as these forces met, however, Edric, with an eye to being on the winning side, deserted the English cause and took his men over to Cnut.

Within a short time Cnut was master of most of the west, from the south coast up as far as Warwickshire. Edmund's army, perhaps realising what they were facing, refused to fight unless reinforced by troops from the south-east, and they also demanded the presence of the king. Athelred did indeed bring a force to join them, and presumably was reconciled with his rebellious son. It is likely, however, that at this stage the king was already suffering from his final illness and he soon withdrew again to London.

Making a new alliance with Uhtred, Earl of Northumbria, Edmund led their forces into northern Mercia, ravaging the land from Cheshire down to Staffordshire, and thereby attempting to deny Cnut all the Mercian resources he would otherwise have had through the treachery of Edric Streona. At once Cnut struck north through the Danelaw and into Northumbria, forcing the submission of those lands. Uhtred, returning to his own territory, was promptly murdered, leaving Edmund once more with no useful ally.

By now Cnut held most of England with the exception of the south-east corner, and London became his next target as he moved to transfer his fleet to the Thames. Before he arrived, Edmund had hurried to join his father in the city, and there on 23 April 1016 Athelred died.

Immediately those within the city acclaimed Edmund as king, but a few days later a wider gathering of noblemen and bishops at Southampton agreed to accept Cnut as their monarch. It seems likely that Emma and her children were also in London at this time, and Emma apparently gave her full support to Edmund, but clearly he would have a great deal to do before he could establish himself on the throne of England.

Soon after, Cnut arrived with his fleet at Greenwich and, encircling the city of London with an earthwork, began what is known as the Siege of London. Before this Edmund had slipped away westward to gather an army and fight for his kingdom. By some accounts the young Edward went with him and fought with him in the battles that followed throughout the year. Bearing in mind that he was at most about fourteen years old at the time, it seems a hugely fanciful story in the Viking saga that has him coming face to face with Cnut in battle and almost cutting him in half with a mighty sword stroke. Cnut was saved, apparently, by Thorkell who pushed him from his horse, but Edward's sword cut clean through both the saddle and the horse's back! This unlikely tale, incidentally, seems to be the only deed of combat ever recorded about Edward.

Edmund seems to have had no difficulty in rousing the people of Wessex to his aid, and, with Cnut following to deal with this challenge, indecisive battles were fought in Dorset and Wiltshire. Soon after, apparently taking the Danes by surprise, Edmund managed to briefly raise the siege of London, but the victory was so costly in men that he was forced to withdraw again into Wessex to raise fresh troops.

The tide seemed to be turning against Cnut. He made a huge effort to conquer the city of London, and when that failed drew off to the River Orwell to re-provision his army, before returning to Kent where he was defeated in battle by Edmund. At this point the slippery Edric Streona once again changed sides. It is hard to see why Edmund would accept his return, except that perhaps at that time he needed every man he could get. There have been suggestions that, in fact, Edric only made this move in order to betray his countrymen to the Danes, which he did at the next possible opportunity.

This came in the autumn of the year, on 18 October at Ashingdon in Essex. The Danes, who had been raiding in Essex and Mercia, were met by Edmund with an army drawn from 'the whole English nation'. A graphic description of this battle of 'Essandun' is given in the *Encomium*, with a claim that it lasted well into the night. Whether or not that is the case, the die was cast early on by the sudden withdrawal of Edric and all his men. The resulting victory for Cnut left a long list of English dead, including the valiant Ulfkell of East Anglia, but crucially Edmund escaped, although he was seriously wounded.

Once again he travelled west, this time to Gloucestershire, pursued by Cnut, and another skirmish took place at Deerhurst before the rivals decided to negotiate. Both the *Chronicle* and the *Encomium* name Edric Streona as the go-between, though why either side would put any faith in the man who had clearly only ever served himself is a mystery. Nevertheless, when the two kings met on an island in the River Severn, a treaty was agreed between them, dividing the land in the same way as Alfred had done before them. This time Edmund was to have Wessex while Cnut would have all the land north of the River Thames.

Whether Edmund contemplated a re-conquest such as Alfred's children had achieved we don't know, but in fact it was not to be. On 30 November, barely a month after the treaty, he died. Although it is more than possible that the wounds he had received at Ashingdon were the cause of his death, rumours abounded that he had been murdered, and certainly there was a sense of shock at this sudden reversal. It is only fair to relate that he was buried with all due honours at Glastonbury and that in later years Cnut is known to have visited his tomb to offer his own homage to a worthy opponent and a true English hero.

The *Encomium*, written a quarter of a century later following the largely peaceful years of Cnut's reign, expressed the view that Edmund's death was God's mercy towards the people of England, since, if both Cnut and Edmund had survived, there was sure to be renewed conflict and further devastation of the land. It seems highly unlikely that this opinion would have been current at the time.

Some have suggested that the treaty signed at Deerhurst had expressed the intention that whichever of the two kings should survive the other would inherit the whole land. This would certainly give a motive for the murder theory and might even implicate the treacherous Edric, but whether true or not there certainly seemed little alternative in the autumn of 1016 to the recognition of Cnut as king of England. Although Edmund's marriage in 1014 had already produced two sons, these were still babies at the time of his death. Of Edmund's surviving full brother, Edwig, we know very little, but clearly he had no sufficient following to mount a challenge, while Emma's sons were at most in their early teens.

It seemed, therefore, a matter of course that Cnut would be accepted as king by the people of Wessex, and, being duly accepted, he was crowned king of England at St Paul's in London on 6 January 1017.

2

EDWARD AND THE NORMANS
1017–1042

By the time of Cnut's crowning it seems that the sons of Emma and Athelred were already at least en route for Normandy again. There is some evidence that Edward was in Ghent on Christmas Day 1016 and this was, no doubt, a wise precaution. Though the bloodletting was in fact fairly limited, still it was unlikely Cnut would tolerate in his new kingdom any figurehead around whom a future revolt could focus.

A number of ealdormen and their sons were killed, though initially Eadwig, the last survivor of Athelred's first family, got away with being exiled. Later it is recorded that he too was killed on the orders of Cnut. As for the young sons of Edmund, the story is that they were sent away into exile in Sweden with their mother and the intention was that they should also be killed. In the event, with some sympathetic help they made their way to Hungary and grew up in safety beyond the reach of the new king of England.

It is doubtful whether Edward had ever had any great expectation of one day succeeding to the English throne. At the time of his birth there were six brothers ahead of him, though these had dropped away one by one, with Eadwig being the last. Similarly Edmund's babies, in the way of Saxon progression, could probably now be counted behind him, too insignificant at present to pose any real challenge. Still, the crown of England now rested on the head of a new royal house, and its wearer was a young man, probably less than a dozen years older than Edward himself. And in the way of new young rulers he was about to take steps to secure his dynasty and diminish even further any hope that Edward might have had of ever being king of England.

The initial reorganisation of England as a conquered country is recorded in the *Chronicle*. The land was to be divided into four regions with a strong commander in charge of each. Northumbria went to Eric Haakonsson, East Anglia to Thorkell, Mercia to Edric Streona, while Cnut kept Wessex, the likeliest source of trouble, for himself. In fact Edric's rule in Mercia seems to have lasted only long enough for Cnut to feel himself secure, for immediately afterwards his murder is noted. According to the *Encomium*, Cnut summoned his faithful commander Eric Haakonsson and instructed him to 'pay this man what we owe him'. Whereupon, taking the hint, Eric drew his axe and struck off the head of the serial turncoat, 'as an example to soldiers that they should be faithful to their kings'.

Then, says the *Encomium*, with all the country duly settled, all that Cnut lacked was a noble wife. This might have come as a surprise to the wife he had married 'in the Danish fashion' a few years before. Elfgiva had already given him at least one and probably two sons, but the *Encomium*, written by a Christian monk, refuses to regard this as a marriage at all, and refers to her only when absolutely necessary, and then as 'the concubine'.

It is similarly biased in the story of how Cnut acquired his noble wife. The *Chronicle* records bluntly that the king 'commanded' that Emma, widow of Athelred, be brought to him so he could have her as his queen. The implication, confirmed by one contemporary account, is that Emma had remained in England, been captured by Cnut and had little or no choice in the matter. The *Encomium*, reflecting Emma's own story, at least as *she* wished it to be recorded, is rather different. In this version the king sought far and wide for a worthy consort to become the partner of his reign. Finding in Normandy the wise and beautiful Emma, already a famous queen, he wooed her with costly gifts, but she refused to accept him until he swore an oath that, should they be granted a son, he and only he would become the heir to the kingdom of England. Thus, says the Encomiast rather sanctimoniously, she wisely made arrangements in advance to provide for her offspring. True enough she might be providing for future offspring, but by the same token she was deliberately disinheriting the offspring she already had, Edward and his brother Alfred.

Probably each of these versions has an element of truth in it. Despite his war-like background Cnut was, nominally at least, a Christian king, and seemed to realise quite quickly that his situation would be a good deal more secure with the backing of the Christian Church in England. If Emma was within his power he could have forced her to become his wife, but possibly reasoned it would look better if she appeared to have a choice in the matter.

Although she was some years older than him, there were distinct advantages for Cnut in the match, not the least of which was neutralising the threat posed by her brother Richard across the Channel in Normandy. By this time Richard would have had custody of Emma's two sons, each of whom had a strong claim to the throne now possessed by Cnut if their uncle had felt inclined to pursue it on their behalf. In addition to this the new king may have seen it as a means of smoothing over the rift with the previous regime if he presented his new subjects with a queen who had already held that position over them for more than a dozen years. There was a strong streak of diplomacy about the young Cnut.

As for Emma, as far as she had any choice it is harder to explain why she might want to marry the conqueror of her previous husband. Some have seen it as a betrayal, the action of a woman who was used to royal privileges and would grasp at any means to continue in that situation, rather than living the life of an exile and supplicant at the court of her brother. There is a story that she accepted Cnut as a means of purchasing the lives of her children, who were then allowed to depart safely for Normandy. However, since there is evidence that they were already out of England this seems a rather flimsy excuse.

The *Encomium* gives no reason at all for Emma's decision, but then it takes pains to omit Athelred from the story entirely. It gives a strong impression that this was the first time Emma had come to England, although its immediate declaration that this union would bring an end to the troubles of war that had torn England apart and cost so many lives makes little sense if that was the case.

It may be that Emma herself felt she could do some good for her former subjects by marrying Cnut, and that may well have been the case. On a purely personal note, too, it is possible that after fifteen years of marriage to the ineffectual Athelred, Emma, who was of Danish descent herself, found the youthful Cnut a more attractive proposition.

As far as the oath is concerned, that their child would be acknowledged as heir, this seems to be simply standard practice, or at least Emma's standard practice, at the time. A similar story is told in relation to the birth of Edward, though nothing seems to have come from it, or at least not until decades later when all other claimants were dead.

For whatever reason, the marriage took place in the summer of 1017, and, in the opinion of the unreliable *Encomium* at least, it was a huge success. England rejoiced, Gaul rejoiced, the armies rejoiced, even the happy couple rejoiced (Cnut 'unexpectedly'), finding a 'magnitude of joy' in each other. No doubt one who did not rejoice was Edward at his uncle's court in Normandy. It now seemed that Cnut was completely secure on the throne of England and the boy would have to resign himself to a long, possibly permanent exile from his homeland.

The place where he now found himself would have been a marked contrast to the country he had left. England, and Wessex in particular, had a fairly settled history dating back hundreds of years. Normandy as such had been recognised as a separate entity for little over a century.

At around the time Alfred in England was agreeing the division of his lands with the Danish invaders, the same pattern of raid and settlement was being repeated across the Channel in the Frankish kingdom still referred to as Gaul. The area targeted by this batch of Scandinavians was the northern coast, particularly the valley of the lower Seine, raided so repeatedly and savagely that it has been suggested it became almost depopulated. Here the Danish settlers moved in and proved so immoveable that in 911 the Frankish king Charles the Simple made the best of a bad job and granted the area around Rouen to these 'northmen' and their descendants. The conditions were that they, or at least their leaders, became Christian, that they paid homage to him for this land and held it as a buffer state between himself and further Viking raids.

The Viking leader, Hrolf the Ganger, after a successful career of raiding and plundering, seemed happy enough to undergo baptism, though how long he held to Christianity is open to dispute. He is generally known by the Frankish version of his name, Rollo, with the title Count of Rouen, but it should not be thought that all was then peacefully settled between the two populations. Though his son, William Longsword, duly pledged loyalty to Louis IV, his murder in 943 led to a pagan backlash and a messy war, with Louis seizing the illegitimate ten-year-old heir, Richard, and trying to impose his own rule on the area. In 965 a new treaty between Richard and the Frankish Lothair made a fresh start, and thereafter the 'Normans' gradually became less Scandinavian, adopting the language, religion and even some of the institutions of their overlords. By this time the original territory had been expanded across the Cotentin peninsula as far as Mont St Michel in the west and to the River Bresle in the east.

This consolidation and 'Frenchifying' did not mean that all links were severed with Scandinavia. Not only traders but also Vikings were welcomed and sheltered in the rivers and coastal waters of this new land of Normandy. Richard I was taken to task for this in 990, and even in 1014 his son, Richard II, was giving support to those involved in raiding other parts of Gaul.

This same Richard II was the first to whom the title Duke of Normandy could reliably be given, and, as brother of Queen

Emma, it was he who welcomed his young nephews Edward and Alfred along with their sister Goda to his court in 1017. The re-marriage of his sister and the birth soon after of a son, Harthacnut, to herself and Cnut removed any impulse he might have felt to take action on behalf of the boys, and, sinking into insignificance, Edward disappears from the record almost completely for some time.

Later Norman sources tell us he was educated at Richard's court, brought up as befitted a person of noble birth and had the air of a soldier; if he did there is no report of him ever acting as such. While we read of exiled sons of the royal houses of Denmark and Norway travelling the world, hiring out as mercenaries and amassing fortunes for themselves, there is no hint that Edward ever travelled further than the homes of various relatives from Brittany to Flanders, or ever raised a sword in anger.

The death of Richard II in 1027 was followed almost at once by a rebellion of his younger son, Robert, against the elder who now became Richard III of Normandy. Edward seems to have played no part. Nor is there any mention of Edward's participation in any of the years of turmoil that followed when Richard died (possibly murdered) the following year and Robert put aside his young son to become Duke Robert I. We know he had friends among the noble houses and higher clergy of Normandy, but there are no records of him being granted estates or even minor offices at the ducal court. He seems to have been the archetypal poor relation, content to sit and wait, watching for any developments in England that might be to his advantage. He would be waiting a long time.

Cnut was probably in his early twenties when he took the English crown and had the potential to turn into any kind of monarch, from monster to benefactor. His early disposal of potential challengers and those whose actions he disapproved of suggested the former, but in the event he proved a quick learner and remarkably open to the civilising influences of both Church and state institutions. The English were to find their new king most satisfactory. As early as 1018 he dismissed the great majority of the fleet that had brought him to power, though raising the £72,000 from the country and £10,500 from London to pay them off must have been a heavy burden on the people. Thereafter he retained only forty ships for his own use and the defence of the land, a smaller fleet than even Athelred had held.

In the same year a great meeting was held at Oxford with representatives from all over the country. It is likely that Archbishop Wulfstan had already gained influence with the king, and most have found his fingerprints all over the laws that were later written down following this meeting. The *Chronicle* tells us 'the Danes and the Angles agreed to live under Edgar's law' and in essence that is what it was with some modifications. The laws laid down the rights of king, Church and people, the holding of courts, the punishment of offences (often by mutilation or the payment of compensation), the treatment of widows and much more. An oath was sworn by all at Oxford to uphold these laws, and thereafter relations between conqueror and conquered seem to have become much more relaxed.

So much so that in 1019 Cnut was to leave the country for a prolonged period to return to Denmark. His brother had died and he went to consolidate his hold on the land, where there might be other challengers for the throne. It has been suggested that Thorkell was left as regent in England while the king was away, but even before this there had been a shift in Cnut's policy with regard to his new land. The deceased Edric Streona was replaced as ealdorman of Mercia not by a Dane but by the English Leofwine, previously ealdorman of the Hwicce, a subdivision of Mercia based around present-day Gloucestershire. At around this time too we find the first mention of Godwin in connection with the new king.

This Godwin was a man to whom we might apply the phrase first used about a modern American politician, that he 'rose without trace'. Although his daughter Edith later commissioned an account of the family specifically designed to heap praise upon them and to celebrate all their actions, she was surprisingly coy about their origins. All manner of later legends grew up, including one that he was the son of a cowherd who one day was called upon to give shelter to King Athelred, and that he tricked his way into the estates he later possessed. More probably he was the son of a thegn called Wulfnoth who was likely to be a South Saxon, and who may have been the Wulfnoth denounced to Athelred by Edric Streona's brother in 1009, who then took part of the king's fleet to plunder the south coast. Some property confiscated because of this action was returned to 'Godwin, son of Wulfnoth' in the will made by Athelred's son Athelstan in 1014. This raises the implication that Godwin was attached to the forces of Athelstan and Edmund at that time, and it has been suggested that it was his courage and loyalty to the cause that impressed Cnut and caused him to favour the man in his new administration. For whatever reason, in 1018 Godwin, who was probably about the same age as the king, was appointed Earl of Wessex.

It is likely that he accompanied Cnut to Denmark in 1019, and in the same year was further favoured by receiving in marriage the king's sister-in-law, Gytha, with whom he had at least nine children. When in 1021 the mighty Thorkell fell out of favour and was exiled, it seems to have been Godwin who filled his shoes as the king's right-hand man.

No convincing reason has ever been found for Thorkell's dismissal, which is even more puzzling when matched with his apparent complete reconciliation with Cnut two years later. Some have suggested the answer lies in the *Chronicle* entry which describes Cnut going out with a fleet of ships to 'Wiht' in the year 1022. Commonly interpreted as taking his ships to the Isle of Wight to intercept an invasion attempt by Thorkell, it has also been argued that this was a far more serious expedition to an area of the Baltic, possibly Jomsberg itself, to deal with some graver matter. All we know for sure is that afterwards Thorkell was confirmed as Cnut's regent in Denmark, and that, according to the *Chronicle*, the young son of Cnut and Emma, Harthacnut, who could not have been more than five years old at the time, was sent to be brought up by Thorkell, while in exchange Thorkell's son came to Cnut. If this was an exchange of hostages it did not last long, for shortly after Thorkell disappears from the record, probably having died, and the regency and guardianship of Harthacnut was transferred to Ulf, husband of Cnut's sister Estrith.

So quiet was England during this time that the Chroniclers have nothing to report but religious matters (to which, being monks, they were generally inclined in any case). In 1023 Wulfstan died, having served two kings at least as well as his God. In his place we find Godwin promoted to first place in the witnessing of charters. By now, though Cnut had fully embraced the Christian influence in his realm. He had already built a church on the site of the battle of Ashingdon and sent Stigand, his own priest, to serve it. He also arranged for the translation of the remains of Alphage, now St Alphage, to an honoured tomb in Christchurch, Canterbury.

A more warlike spirit was soon required, however, when King Olaf of Norway made a pact with Anund of Sweden to attack Denmark, and was surprisingly joined by Cnut's brother-in-law, Ulf. A joint force of Danes and English fought against them at 'the Holy River' in Norway, and lost with great slaughter, although this seems to have been only a temporary setback to Cnut's dominance in the area. Shortly after, we are told, Ulf was murdered on Cnut's orders.

The following year the king journeyed to Rome for the coronation of the German king Conrad as Holy Roman Emperor. It is not clear whether he travelled from England or Denmark. The latter is implied in a letter he sent back to England, but the monk writing his *Encomium of Queen Emma* lists Flanders, Gaul and Italy as the itinerary, suggesting he may at least have touched base in England on the way. He states that Cnut passed through the city of Saint-Omer, and 'I saw this with my own eyes'.

Cnut seems touchingly proud of the warm reception he got, not only along the way but also in Rome from the Pope and Emperor Conrad among many others. Nevertheless, like modern statesmen at a summit, he was prepared to drive a hard bargain for the benefit of traders and pilgrims from both England and Denmark. For the first time a Viking leader had become a Christian king, accepted as such through all the western world from the south of Italy to the Baltic. Relations with Conrad were particularly pleasing since Denmark and Germany had been traditional enemies, both having territorial interests around Jutland. Their friendship was later sealed by the giving of Cnut's daughter, Gunnhild, in marriage to Conrad's son Henry.

Immediately after this success Cnut extended his empire once more. Taking fifty ships from England, he drove Olaf Haraldsson out of Norway without even the need for a battle. In his place he installed as regent Haakon Ericsson, the son of his old friend the Earl of Northumbria, who had ruled in Norway previously. When Haakon was drowned the following year he then took the bold step of sending his own son Swein, together with the boy's mother Elfgiva of Northampton, Cnut's 'handfast' wife, to rule in his place. In fact this was a disastrous move, recalled with hatred in Norway centuries later as 'Elfgiva's time', a time of high taxes and the imposition of Danish customs and harsh rule on a proud and independent people.

For a time, though, Cnut could be referred to as 'Emperor of the North', king of England, Denmark and Norway, with a dominant presence on all the seas and trade routes from the English Channel to the Baltic. By and large it was a benevolent presence. Unlike some of his ancestors, Cnut seems to have been prepared to establish friendly relations with any European ruler who was prepared to do the same with him, and he corresponded with kings, princes and emperors over a wide area.

Not all were susceptible to his friendship, however, and one notable exception was Robert, Duke of Normandy. At least in the early years of his reign this duke seems to have had a talent for belligerence. The civil war he fought against his brother caused divisions and feuds in Norman society that would last a long time, and when he achieved his dukedom he immediately turned against his uncle Robert, Archbishop of Rouen, who was probably the most powerful man in the land. The archbishop had been trying to calm things down and exert some control over his unruly nephew but now he was first besieged and then exiled. His retaliation was to put the entire duchy under an interdict, a kind of religious ostracisation, in effect excommunicating the duke and all his subjects and cutting them off from the Church that played such an important part in the lives of everyone at the time. Duke Robert next attacked his cousin Hugo, Bishop of Bayeux, plundering Church property to reward his followers, and setting an example that would be followed by many lesser nobles in the duchy, until by some accounts a state of near anarchy existed.

Nor did he confine himself to his own lands, getting involved in conflicts all around his borders. When his cousin Alan of Brittany sought to take advantage of the disorder in Normandy he was quickly and sharply dissuaded. Similarly, taking sides in a dispute in Flanders, he returned Baldwin IV to power when he had been overthrown by his son acting together with his overlord the king of the French.

There is some evidence Robert also planned an expedition to England on behalf of Edward and Alfred, the sons of his aunt Emma. Certainly relations between England and Normandy had deteriorated with the death of Richard II. One story says that Cnut offered his sister Estrith, now the widow of Ulf, as a bride for Robert and considerable bad feeling was caused when she was rejected. If there was an expedition planned, however, it does not seem to have been very whole-hearted. The account that mentions it declares that, due to the wind being contrary, Robert abandoned thoughts of England and went and attacked Brittany instead. Possibly another hope dashed for Edward.

By 1030 Robert was being called 'Robert the Devil' and only when the Archbishop of Rouen was recalled and lifted the interdict was an attempt made to reconcile the different factions. Thereafter the archbishop seems to have been chief counsellor to the duke and brought a measure of stability and prosperity to the duchy, so that soon Duke Robert was surrounded by a strong group of noble supporters, and was being referred to as 'Robert the Magnificent'.

Nor had his wilder days done him any lasting harm. After his reconciliation, Alan of Brittany became a staunch supporter, as was Baldwin of Flanders, who married the duke's sister, Eleanor. Then in 1031 the young King Henry I of France was given shelter and support by Robert when his mother and brother tried unsuccessfully to deprive him of his throne. By the early 1030s, then, the Duchy of Normandy had become strong at home and was surrounded by a ring of neighbours, all of whom owed something to the duke and were well disposed towards him.

Robert, under the influence of the archbishop no doubt, even managed a reconciliation with the Church, returning property he had plundered and adding to it with gifts of his own. It may well have been this that led him to regularise his private life, at least to a certain extent.

The romantics would declare that Robert's spurning of Cnut's sister was due to the fact that he had already found the love of his life. Indeed the story, as told, is a romantic one, and may possibly contain more than a grain of truth. While opposing his brother in 1027 Robert was based at Falaise, and one day it is said, looking down from the castle, he saw a girl working at the dyeing trenches below. She was Herleve (sometimes called Arlette), daughter of Fulbert the Tanner. Barefoot and with skirts raised, she was trampling the leather into the coloured dyes. Robert sent a servant commanding her to come to him through a back door, but the girl refused. She would only come to him, she declared, riding on horseback through the main entrance to the castle. And so it was. She became his mistress and over the next few years bore him at least two children: a son, William, known at least at first as William the Bastard, and a daughter, Adelize.

How much of the romance is true we will never know, but the dyeing trenches were certainly in the right place. Strong, almost contemporary evidence says that Herleve's father was a tanner of hides (although the word used has also been translated as furrier or embalmer), and it is certain that William the Bastard was very sensitive on the subject of tanners. The difference in status between the duke and his mistress ruled out any possibility of marriage, although her father and brothers were apparently given minor offices at court. In 1031 Herleve was married off to Herluin, Viscount of Conteville, with whom she had two more sons, Odo and Robert, who would later prove extremely able supporters of William the Bastard. Perhaps we could just comment that Duke Robert himself never married.

The year 1035 was to prove a turning point in many lives. Towards the end of the previous year Duke Robert had suddenly announced an intention to make a pilgrimage to Jerusalem. This was not unprecedented. It was an age when religious belief was real in a way we probably cannot imagine today in our more cynical times. Pilgrim routes were already established across Europe, and counts of Brittany and Anjou had preceded Robert on this most arduous journey. It has been suggested that his pilgrimage was intended to obtain forgiveness for involvement in his brother's murder. Nevertheless, for the unmarried duke with no legitimate heir to leave his duchy at this time, albeit in the capable hands of the Archbishop of Rouen, must have caused dismay in some quarters – and possibly anticipation in others.

Before he left, Robert nominated as his heir William, his illegitimate son, who was probably about seven years old at the time. All the leading magnates were required to accept this and to swear oaths of loyalty to the boy, though no doubt some did so very reluctantly. A number of other nobles accompanied Duke Robert to Jerusalem, among them Drogo, Count of the Vexin, who was married to Edward's sister Goda. There is no evidence that Edward or indeed Alfred was ever invited to join them, which may suggest they were not that close to Robert at the time – or simply that, unlike their cousin, they felt they had committed no sins that needed such an extreme penance. Whatever the reason for Robert's pilgrimage, neither he nor Count Drogo ever returned. The duke died in the first week of July 1035 after falling ill in Asia Minor on his way home. Initially the accession of William the Bastard to the title was not challenged, supported as he was by both the

Archbishop of Rouen and by his overlord, Henry I of France, but a turbulent period was in store for him later on when the archbishop died.

In 1035, too, the people of Norway finally rose up and expelled Swein Cnutsson and his mother, causing them to flee for safety to Denmark. In their place, in the autumn of that year, the eleven-year-old Magnus was installed and accepted as king of all Norway. This Magnus was the illegitimate son of Olaf Haraldsson. He had gone into exile when his father was overthrown in 1028 and had been sought and found as far afield as Russia, and brought back as a focus for the attempt to expel Cnut and all the Danish influences from Norwegian lands. In the event Magnus, known to Norwegians as Magnus the Good, would have his revenge on the Danes, taking the fight to Denmark itself with considerable success.

It was a matter of a few weeks after the expulsion of his son that Cnut himself died on 12 November 1035. He died at Shaftesbury Abbey in Dorset, and was buried with the full honours due to a Christian king in the Old Minster at Winchester. He was probably around forty years old and we have no firm evidence as to what he died of, though there are suggestions that he had been ill for some time. If that is so he seems to have given little thought to what should happen in his various kingdoms after his death – or possibly his plans were thrown awry by the recent events in Norway.

There is no mention of a will or the nomination of one or more successors for the Witan to consider in the customary way. There were, if anything, rather too many of these to choose from, though most were not at the time in a position to press their claims.

His last and clearly legitimate son, Harthacnut, was probably around seventeen years old in 1035. He had already been given the kingdom of Denmark and it may well be that Cnut intended him to have England as well. If there is any truth in the story in the *Encomium of Emma* insisting on this before her marriage to Cnut, this would certainly be the case, and Harthacnut was clearly championed by his mother. Had he been in England at the time it is likely that his succession to the throne would have been immediately approved. But he was in Denmark, and with a threat of imminent invasion by the newly strong and united Norwegians, he would not be able to leave that kingdom for some time.

Since the *Encomium* was written specifically for Queen Emma it might be thought it would immediately declare Harthacnut as the rightful heir. However, by failing to mention that Emma had been married before, the writer had put himself in the awkward position of implying that all three sons of Emma were Cnut's, and that, while Harthacnut had been sent to be brought up in Denmark, the other two, Edward and Alfred, had similarly been sent to Normandy. Thus he talks of Emma being alone in England and alarmed at the absence of all her sons, and implies that their claims would rank alongside that of Harthacnut, although, like him, they would not be present to urge them for themselves.

The sons of Cnut by his 'handfast wife', Elfgiva, had also to be accounted for. Swein, in fact, never gets a mention. He had been given and had lost a kingdom, and never seems to have come into the reckoning at all. Some twenty-one years old by now, he would die of unspecified causes the following year.

The one son who was in England was Elfgiva's second son, Harald, usually known as 'Harefoot', presumably due to his prowess at running. He seems to have been living in Mercia, possibly Danish East Mercia where his mother's family came from, and his claim was taken up at once by Mercian and Danish factions in the country. He would have been about nineteen at the time and his logic is impeccable. Cnut had three sons. One had been given Norway, another Denmark, and therefore England should go to the third.

It was not quite as simple as this, however. While some claimed merely that he was not a legitimate son, since Cnut and Elfgiva had only married in the 'Danish fashion', the *Encomium* tells a story that Harald was not in fact the son of Cnut and Elfgiva at all. The *Chronicle* states simply that he 'said he was the son of Cnut ... though it was not true', but the *Enconium* gives full spiteful detail, presumably supplied by Emma herself, a bitter opponent of Elfgiva.

In this story Elfgiva was herself barren and the child Harald was the son of a servant, secretly introduced into her chamber to allow her to claim he was Cnut's son. And this, declares the *Encomium*, is the truth of the matter.

Whether true or not, the appearance of Harald with supporters caused the country to split once again on traditional lines. Possible Mercian loyalty to one of its own was involved, and quite likely a resentment on the part of older noble families at the speed with which Godwin had arisen and assumed superiority over them.

The Witan met for its traditional role of selecting a king at Oxford, on the border between Wessex and the Danelaw. At this meeting Leofric, Earl of Mercia, all the thegns north of the Thames, and the London 'shipmen' who had served Cnut spoke up for Harald as king, while Queen Emma, Earl Godwin and the men of Wessex wanted Harthacnut. It is interesting that the Danelaw was opting for a king that was at least partly English, while Godwin and Wessex were backing an entirely 'foreign' candidate. Most likely, as the counsellor who had been closest to the deceased king, Godwin felt he was carrying out Cnut's wishes, though it should also be noted the Scandinavian interest ran strongly in Godwin's own family. Not only was his wife Danish but the majority of his children had Danish names.

In the end a temporary compromise was agreed. Harald would rule 'with his brother Harthacnut', at least until that brother returned from Denmark. This was a kind of co-ruling that was not unknown in Scandinavian countries but it was a novelty for England. Following the Oxford meeting Harald was regarded as at least the 'protector' of the whole country, while Emma, with the support of Godwin, was to have charge of Wessex. The relative strengths of each, however, were to be established by an incident that took place soon after.

Emma and Godwin had retired to Winchester, traditional capital of Wessex but at that time generally regarded as the capital of England as well. It was the place where the royal treasury was kept. It may well be that the queen hoped to control this and deny the use of it to Harald, maybe even using it to buy support for her son. That possibility was swiftly ruled out when a force sent by Harald arrived, seized the treasure and carried it away to London, where he seems to have been based.

A story in the *Encomium* that Harald tried to force the Archbishop of Canterbury to crown him as king finds no support elsewhere, though the detail of the archbishop's refusal – putting crown and regalia on the altar of his church and forbidding any other bishop to touch or move them – is the kind of sharp out-manoeuvring that delighted storytellers of the day. More serious are the allegations concerning a letter sent at this time to Edward and Alfred in Normandy.

The *Encomium* claims to quote this letter verbatim, though how accurately we have no way of knowing. It purports to be from Queen Emma, describing not only her plight in England and her need of their support, but also, apparently for the first time in many years, recognising that they too might have an interest in England. They were being deprived of their kingdom and their inheritance, it says, by the actions of Harald who was apparently going round ceaselessly canvassing the support of important men by gifts, threats and prayers. According to the letter the people would really have preferred Edward or Alfred as their monarch, and one of them was requested to come quickly and secretly to consult with the queen at Winchester, sending back word of how they intended to come via 'whoever' should bring them the letter.

The *Encomium*, however, says that the letter was a forgery, sent by Harald Harefoot to persuade two of his possible rivals to walk straight into a trap. A certain vagueness in the terms supports this interpretation. The people would prefer 'one of them' – was this a ploy to get both to try their hand, or did Harald not know which might have precedence? Also the failure to name a known and trusted messenger could be suspicious, though there may have been so little previous communication between mother and sons that no such person existed. The time-honoured direction to 'tell me in advance what you are going to do' is the classic set up for a trap, but may equally well imply a gathering of support and protection.

For many years this was accepted as true, and at this distance in time it is impossible to be sure. Most now, though, believe it more likely that the letter is absolutely genuine, that Emma, feeling helpless in Winchester and seeing all possibilities of retaining power slipping away from her, did turn to the sons she had more or less abandoned some eighteen years before. If so, the story in the *Encomium* is simply a cover-up, an attempt to dissociate the queen from all that followed. Commissioned by Emma, directed by Emma, in praise of Emma, the *Encomium* had to make clear that not only Emma herself but other people still prominent at the time it was written were cleared of all blame for the consequences. For if it was an incitement to invasion the letter failed miserably, whereas as a trap to draw out rivals it succeeded only too well.

It seems likely that Edward did come to England, landing in the Southampton area in 1036. Later Norman accounts talking of a battle and plunder before he returned to Normandy are lacking contemporary evidence to support them, and it appears to have been a rather tentative expedition. Finding little in the way of backing and possibly more opposition than he had been led to expect, Edward returned immediately to Normandy and prepared to wait a little longer.

His brother Alfred, however, fared considerably worse. It is not clear if he set out at the same time as Edward, in a two-pronged attack, or rather later. He certainly sailed from further north, probably from Flanders, and took with him fewer men than the Count of Flanders recommended. This might have been through lack of money to pay them, for the men he took were from Boulogne not Normandy, and he seems to have had little Norman backing.

He must, however, have been aware of the dangers of his expedition for we are told he did not go ashore at the first place his ships touched in England, seeing that there were enemies there waiting to attack him. Instead he sailed along the coast until he felt he had outflanked them and landed probably somewhere near Dover. Then he started making his way towards his mother but was intercepted by Earl Godwin and his men.

There are a number of accounts of what happened next, all more or less agreeing on the basics, though differing in the amount of detail. Most say that Alfred and his men were taken to Guildford, fed and found lodgings for the night. Then, in the course of that night, while they were asleep, they were set upon and taken prisoner by Harald Harefoot and his men. At this point the writer of the *Encomium* found himself in great difficulties. Having previously said that Godwin was Queen Emma's staunchest ally, he now had to find a way to account for the fact that at Guildford he apparently handed over Alfred and his party to her bitterest enemy. He does this by saying that Godwin took Alfred under his protection and swore to be his man – and then never mentioning him again.

What had clearly happened was that, at some point before this, Godwin had changed sides. It must have become more and more apparent to him that Queen Emma's position was untenable without the active support of Harthacnut, and that through indifference or sheer force of circumstances that support was not going to be forthcoming. No doubt he discounted the abilities of Edward and Alfred to tip the balance, maybe even waited until Edward had been repulsed, and therefore moved to the side that was clearly going to be the overall winner. A charitable view might be that he wanted to ensure peace and a continuity of good government in England, while doing what he could for Emma and her sons. An uncharitable view would be that he intended to hold on to the wealth and power he had amassed while serving Cnut.

Either way, if the letter to the princes in Normandy was genuine it would have given him a valuable bargaining chip while negotiating his progress to the side of Harald. Even if Harald had not had designs on the princes earlier, he would certainly have jumped at the chance of putting at least one of them out of the way. Whether or not Godwin knew how that was to be achieved is another matter.

In the event Alfred and his men were literally caught napping, and while the writer of the *Encomium* declares that his pen trembles with horror as he writes and he wishes to spare the feelings of the queen, he then seems to take great delight in detailing how nine out of ten of the men were tortured and killed, while Alfred was taken to Ely and there blinded so savagely that he died soon after. It should be noted that blinding an opponent was at the time seen as a merciful way of putting him out of the game while avoiding the sin of outright murder, and the death of Alfred was likely to have been a bungled job. Nevertheless the horror of it was still being invoked against Godwin decades later, though he swore a sacred oath that he had not known of Harefoot's intentions.

Soon after this Harald Harefoot was declared king over all the country and crowned at Oxford as King Harald I. At the same time Emma either fled or was exiled, depending on which account is to be believed. Instead of going to Normandy she went to Flanders, to the court of Baldwin V, and there called again for Edward to visit her. When he did – probably meeting his mother face to face for the first time in nearly two decades – she demanded that he raise an expedition to overthrow Harald. Even then it was not made plain whether he would be claiming the throne for himself or for her clearly more favoured son, Harthacnut.

Even if Edward had felt inclined to do as she wished, he had no resources or contacts with which to raise the necessary forces. Normandy itself was about to be plunged into turmoil and its duke was a boy of ten. He had the fate of his brother fresh before him, and maybe even more importantly, the failure of his own attempt to return to England. It is apparent that he felt he owed his mother nothing, and though his reply was phrased more diplomatically, it was no doubt with a certain bitterness that he told her that the English had sworn no oaths to support him, and that he was therefore unable to help her. In the same vein he recommended that if she wanted help, she had better look to Harthacnut, who was at least the King of Denmark, rather than to himself – and with that he returned to Normandy.

Emma had to wait until 1039 in order to obtain the help Edward had advised. Then Harthacnut at last managed to come to terms with Magnus of Norway and so to end the conflict between them. Immediately he set out for Bruges, accompanied by a part of his fleet amounting to ten ships and their crews. It was clear he would need a great deal more to successfully invade England, but he seemed in no hurry to raise them. It has been suggested that he was aware that Harald was already ill and that he was simply biding his time. In fact the king died at Oxford on 17 March 1040.

A few weeks later Harthacnut, together with his mother, sailed for England with a show of force of sixty-two warships. The *Encomium* is probably overstating facts when it says they were gloriously received. Peacefully received was probably closer to the mark, but on 18 June Harthacnut was crowned king of England at Canterbury Cathedral. In an act of revenge that may have been partly intended to appease Emma, one of his first acts was to exhume the body of his half-brother from its burial place at Westminster and have it beheaded and flung into the nearby marsh. This was not, however, Harald's final resting place for we are told that the body was later recovered by his supporters and reburied at the church of St Clement Danes, the Danish church marking the boundary between Wessex and the Danelaw on the north bank of the Thames in London.

Harthacnut was in his early twenties when he came to England, for the first time since he was a small child. It is unlikely that he felt any particular love for the country of his birth, and in fact he seems to have used it as his Viking forefathers had used it, as a source of finance for the resources of men and materials he needed to maintain a grip on his two kingdoms. The *Encomium* tells us he ordered all his affairs in peace and tranquillity but this is certainly poetic licence, a striving for a happy ending for its story. Other sources, particularly the *Chronicle*, describe a ruthless operator who did nothing worthy of a king in the whole course of his reign. It records that he betrayed those he had sworn to protect and levied fierce taxes, and when the people of Worcester revolted and killed two of his housecarls sent to collect the taxes, he dispatched an army to destroy the place. In fact most of the inhabitants successfully escaped to an island in the River Severn, but the town was burnt to the ground and the surrounding area harried for a full five days.

In the midst of all this one good deed stands out. In 1041 Harthacnut sent for his half-brother Edward to come over from Normandy and live at his court. No doubt in the light of past history Edward was wary of accepting this invitation, but come he did, and some accounts state that he was even sworn in as co-ruler. The *Encomium* declares this was done out of pure brotherly love, though it seems unlikely the two had even met before. Others have suggested different reasons. Harthacnut may have wanted to return to Denmark while leaving England in safe hands. He might have been ill and, lacking a wife and heir, have sought to secure the succession, perhaps at the suggestion of the mother of them both. There is some support for the suggestion that he might have become so unpopular that he felt, again at the prompting of Emma, that bringing back the last remaining son of the former English king would help reconcile the English people to his reign.

Whatever the reason, it meant that when in June of the following year Harthacnut suddenly dropped dead while drinking at a wedding feast (probably of a stroke though poison cannot be entirely ruled out), Edward was at last in the right place at the right time to become the next king of England.

3

EDWARD AND THE ENGLISH
1042–1066

Edward was around forty years of age when he became king. From the time of his birth the chances of him achieving such a prize had varied from slim to almost non-existent, and there is very little evidence to show that he had ever actually sought it or taken any steps to bring it about. He simply outlived all his brothers and half-brothers, very few of whom had produced any heirs. Such heirs as did exist were out of the kingdom and Edward, therefore, became the obvious candidate. The *Chronicle* declares that it was his 'true natural right'.

He was apparently acclaimed as king, even before Harthacnut was buried, by 'all the people', though this may only mean the people of London, where he was at the time. It is interesting that all the versions of the *Chronicle* mention this popular acclamation, and none mention the claims that were variously put about later, that Edward was made king either by the efforts of Earl Godwin or of William of Normandy. It would probably be true to say that Edward would not have become king if strenuously opposed by Godwin (though Harald Harefoot had achieved that feat), and certainly it seems that the acclamation began in the south and spread northwards. There is nothing, however, to suggest Godwin had to actively canvass support for Edward. Nor is there evidence of any kind of intervention by William, who was, in any case, around fourteen years old at the time and struggling to hold on to authority in his own duchy.

Despite the best efforts of propagandists on different sides, therefore, it seems that at the time Edward was simply seen as the obvious successor to his half-brother, who may even have made this clear in the months following Edward's return to England. There is no record of any rival claim on the ground, and in fact the *Chronicle* moves straight on to relate that the weather was bad that year and there were crop failures and loss of cattle. The fact that the king's coronation was delayed until the following Easter, nearly ten months later, may also suggest a peaceful transition, with ample time taken to create an impressive ceremony. By contrast the coronation of Edward's father, Athelred, had been rushed through within weeks of the murder of his predecessor.

The coronation itself seems to have been modelled on that of King Edgar, with the king being anointed with holy oil and thus claimed as protector of the Church as well as the people. Both archbishops were present and it was Eadsige of Canterbury who crowned the king and invested him with the other regalia of ring, sword and rod. We are also told that he instructed him well and reminded him of his duties through the prayers offered up on this occasion. Ambassadors were present, representing among others the Holy Roman Emperor and the French king, and the ceremony would have ended with the assembled English nobles offering fealty and service to the new king.

Many have tried to assess the character and personality of the man who now occupied the throne of England, and most have concluded, from lack of evidence and otherwise, that he is an enigma. We can probably identify caution as one of his chief characteristics. It was no doubt caution that had prevented his entanglement in any of Robert of Normandy's hostilities, and caution that turned him back from Southampton in 1036 when his brother persisted in the journey that led to his death. Probably it is the same deeply ingrained caution that so effectively masks his deeper feelings from us. It is hard to imagine him blurting out a strong opinion or passionately committing to a cause. This is not to say he did not have strong opinions and causes close to his heart (and a famously hot temper too on occasion). He seemed, however, to be content to bide his time and advance in small steps towards his goal, while still being prepared to take decisive action when an opportunity arose. The closest parallel in circumstances is probably found with Charles II some six hundred years later. Like Edward he had spent a considerable number of years in exile and he was famously determined that he would never go 'on his travels' again. No doubt Edward had a similar determination.

In one respect his position was very different from that of Charles II. While that merry monarch had a ready-made group of supporters to back him on his return to England, Edward seems to have had no one he could call his own. The traditional view contained in stories put about later by mainly Norman writers was that he returned to England with a host of Norman nobles and supporters and even some Norman soldiers. This, however, does not stand up to close examination. There were certainly no soldiers, and the few others that accompanied him were at the level of priests and clerks. Those whose names we have seem to have been drawn from several places, with Brittany well represented, and by and large his entourage seems to have been a poor one.

In fact, if we look at the solid evidence of who was carrying out the king's business in the land, in both secular and Church matters, what is most striking is the sense of continuity. Bishops and archbishops, of course, remained in post from the previous reigns, indeed a few were originally appointed by Athelred, but the same names of earls, thegns and clerks continue to appear as witnesses to the king's charters for some time. This is not so surprising when we reflect that Edward had been in England for a little time before he became king and would probably have known all of them.

Of the earls, the most important were the three marking the ancient divisions of the land, Earl Godwin of Wessex, Earl Leofric of Mercia and Earl Siward of Northumbria. Pre-eminent at the time was Godwin, rising from nothing under Cnut and keeping his place in the upheavals that followed that king's death with all the sticking power of the fabled 'Vicar of Bray'. 'For whatsoever king shall reign', Godwin would be found at his right hand giving him counsel. Edward would be his fourth royal master, and while it would probably be overstating it to say he had put the king in place and virtually ruled the country for him, it is certainly true that his wealth and power reached a peak under this king.

In many ways, despite his troubled start in life, Edward was a lucky king. Had Godwin been the only power in the land, he could have found himself nothing but a figurehead. The presence of two other powerful earls, however, gave him at least a possibility of playing a hand in the game. Of the various factions at the time, Godwin represented most strongly the Scandinavian. Owing his fortune to a Danish king, with a Danish wife and four sons with Danish names, no doubt he saw the split that now followed between England and Denmark as a loss. That his preferred policy of support for that country was not always adopted by Edward may be an example of how the king was able to limit Godwin's power.

Of the other major earls, Leofric of Mercia, from an old English family, may be said to represent the English faction, and more specifically to look out for his own people of the Midland shires. His wife has come down to us as the famous Lady Godiva, but her ride through the streets of Coventry, allegedly to spare the people the harshness of Harthacnut's taxes, is entirely mythical. Siward of Northumbria was reputedly older than the other two. Although Norwegian in origin, he had married an English wife and his interests lay in the north. Any ambitions he held were towards Scotland rather than England, and in divisions over matters southern he tended to side with Leofric. The north/south divide in England is by no means a modern creation. It has been estimated that, at least later in the reign, Godwin and his sons held estates valued at almost three times those of the other earls and not far short of the king's own. Still the natural rivalry between these three and their heirs gave Edward an opportunity for manipulation that he seems to have used on several occasions to get his own way, while appearing simply to hold a balance between them.

The king's luck held with events in the wider world as well. The fact that no challengers appeared in England at the time of his accession did not mean that there were none who felt the crown might have come to them. Cnut's own line may have come to an end, but there were nephews and nieces who could put in a valid claim if the Danish succession had been continued rather than reverting to the English bloodline.

In particular Cnut's nephew Sweyn Estrithsson may have regarded himself as a general heir to what was left of his uncle's empire. Unusually he is known by his mother's name rather than his father's – Estrithsson, rather than Ulfsson – perhaps emphasising his close connection to Cnut through the king's sister, Estrith. Since Ulf's sister Gytha had married Godwin, Sweyn was also the nephew of that earl, giving another reason why Godwin favoured a continued connection with Denmark.

Sweyn, who was born in England, had been sent by Harthacnut to hold Denmark on his behalf and was therefore out of the country when Edward was proclaimed and crowned as king. Immediately after the death of Harthacnut Sweyn claimed Denmark for himself, a claim that was disputed by Magnus of Norway, and whatever protest he might have made was lost when Magnus began a prolonged attack on Denmark. Later Sweyn claimed that Edward had paid him not to challenge his right to the throne, and that he had been promised the crown after the king's death. It may be that Edward was rather free with such promises.

Another possible claimant was Thorkell's son, Harold, who was married to Cnut's niece. When he was murdered in 1043 his widow and sons came to England, but were expelled by Edward for reasons unknown.

By far the most serious threat, however, was seen as coming from Magnus of Norway. The pact he had made with Harthacnut in 1039 to end the hostilities between them had provided that Magnus should have Norway and Harthacnut Denmark, but that the survivor of the two should inherit the lands of the other. It is quite likely that Harthacnut meant to break this pact as soon as he was able and that, in any case, he only meant that the lands referred to should apply to Denmark. Magnus, however, laid claim to both kingdoms and it was only the dogged resistance of Sweyn Estrithsson in Denmark that prevented him launching an invasion of England.

A most surprising supporter of Magnus in England was Edward's mother, Emma of Normandy. She had always shown a marked preference for her second marriage over her first, and for Harthacnut over Edward, and possibly believed in the justice of the claim Magnus put forward. For whatever reason, it is recorded that Emma was offering encouragement and support to Magnus, and also that she intended to use the royal treasure at Winchester for his aid. Once again she seemed to have obtained control over this, and once again she was to have it firmly taken from her.

Immediately after his coronation Edward, accompanied by Godwin, Leofric and Siward, visited his mother and seized from her all her property, 'because she had held it too closely from him'. One account says it was the three earls who advised Edward to do this, and there is a suggestion that she had been assuming an authority which she did not possess and acting in the name of the king, as, perhaps, she had been permitted to do by Harthacnut. An example might be the recent appointment of Bishop Stigand to the see of Elmham. Stigand had been Cnut's own priest and was a close advisor to the queen. At this time he was dismissed from his bishopric, and he too was deprived of property. While this action may well have been a sharp rebuke to a woman grown too fond of wielding power, it is hard not to see in it also a sweet revenge on the part of Edward for all the slights and lack of motherly love that he might have felt sharply over a period of many years. It is worth noting that within a year both Emma and Stigand seem to have been restored to a measure of power, although the Queen now remained in semi-retirement at Winchester for the rest of her life.

The threat from Magnus was taken seriously enough for the English fleet of thirty-five ships to be mustered at Sandwich in

1044 with Edward himself in command. Again the following year a 'great ship force' was assembled in preparation for a possible invasion. Once again this came to nothing, with Magnus still engaged in trying to drive Sweyn Estrithsson out of Denmark, but when at the end of that year he succeeded, the danger of invasion rose again. The history of all concerned might now have turned out very differently but for the re-appearance in Scandinavia of one of the most formidable Viking warriors of the time, Harald Sigurdson.

Later to be known as 'Hardrada' or harsh ruler, Harald was the half-brother of Olaf Haraldsson, who had ruled Norway until thrown out by Cnut. He had left his homeland at the age of fifteen and, according to the sagas, had then filled another fifteen years with fighting and plundering as far afield as Kiev, Constantinople and North Africa. Now immensely wealthy and battle-hardened, he was returning to Norway when he met Sweyn Estrithsson in exile in Sweden. An alliance was agreed, and with the support of the Swedish king Anund, an army was raised to seize back Denmark from Magnus.

They had got no further than raiding along the coast, however, when Harald was secretly approached by messengers from Magnus. The Norwegian king had been advised by his counsellors that he should not fight Harald, who was, after all, his uncle, both being related to their well-loved and sainted King Olaf. Instead Harald was offered a deal. Magnus would share Norway with him as co-ruler if he would break his alliance with Sweyn.

The sagas, in fact, go a great deal further, with Magnus and Harald each agreeing to give the other half of all their moveable property. In this Magnus came off considerably the better. He declared that, after paying for his wars, the only gold he had left was contained in one finger ring, whereupon Harald gave him half of all the treasure he had amassed in his years of adventuring.

The alliance with Sweyn was duly broken. The saga tells us that, suspecting treachery, Sweyn tried to have Harald murdered while he slept, and in response Harald quietly sailed his ships away so that, when morning came, Sweyn found himself alone. Once again without an ally, Sweyn appealed to England to send him fifty ships with which to fight Magnus. Earl Godwin urged Edward to do so but this was opposed by Leofric and the king sided with the Mercian. The reputation of Magnus's fleet was formidable and it was likely that that of Sweyn and England together would have been outnumbered and outfought.

This decision of Edward's is often seen as a consequence of internal politics within England, with Godwin out of favour and the king exercising the opportunity to divide and rule. As a matter of foreign policy, however, it makes complete sense. Such a fleet would probably have represented the majority of England's naval forces at the time. If it was defeated and maybe devastated by Magnus, not only would that king achieve his goal of uniting Denmark and Norway under his rule, but England itself would be laid wide open to invasion. It was well known that Magnus had ambitions to re-create Cnut's empire of the north, and the risk that he would do so far outweighed any advantage to England of propping up Sweyn's rule in Denmark.

In the event, in 1047 Magnus swept into Denmark, Sweyn was once again forced into exile, and Edward's decision seemed to be proved the wiser. Once again a fleet was gathered and there were strong rumours Magnus was preparing an invasion force to attack England. Then, on 25 October of that year, Magnus suddenly died. Among the many different causes of death reported in various accounts, one claims that he drowned when falling overboard from one of his invasion vessels. Again it is tradition that claims he named Sweyn as his successor in Denmark and Harald Hardrada in Norway, but certainly each immediately laid claim to the country indicated, and the pressure on England was eased when, as recorded in the *Chronicle*, Harald sent envoys to make peace with Edward.

It is with his fleet and with foreign policies that we see Edward at his most decisive, possibly because this was seen by the controlling influences within the kingdom as less important. Since the time of Cnut there had been a permanent, professional naval force, sometimes referred to as the 'king's fleet'. These paid mercenaries were often Danish and they were financed by a tax called the 'heregeld'. In normal times around forty ships made up this core navy, though Harthacnut had increased the number to ninety-four, with a consequent heavy increase in the taxes to pay for them.

In times of emergency this would be added to by the so-called 'people's fleet' or 'provincial fleet', made up of ships and crews provided in the same way as soldiers were provided for the fighting militia. It appears that the earls had responsibility for this part of the naval force, since the *Chronicle* refers to the 'Mercian fleet' and the 'Wessex fleet'. Most years during Edward's reign, this fleet would be summoned for manoeuvres, usually based at Sandwich, and Godwin and his sons seem to have played a large part in command. Possibly since one of their major estates was at Bosham on the edge of Southampton Water, they were more used to the sea than some of the other earls. It is clear, however, that the king was almost always present on these occasions and was in overall charge of activities.

Some major changes were made to the fleet at this time. From the late 1040s onwards Edward began to pay off the ships of the king's fleet. At the beginning of 1049 only fourteen were recorded and by the end of that year nine had been paid off, with the remaining five disposed of the following year. A number of reasons have been suggested for this. On the one hand it is claimed that, since England felt under threat from Denmark, the loyalty of the Danish crews making up this force could not be relied on. On the other it may be that Edward now felt secure enough to dispense with the protection of his personal force, and also gained popularity by abolishing the hated heregeld tax that paid for them.

It seems odd that a king who so obviously enjoyed commanding naval forces should dispose of the most skilled and experienced part of them, and in fact its loss was to prove a severe problem after his death. On the other hand it may be that he now felt that the ships and crews that were provided from within the country itself were sufficient to ward off outside threats that in themselves had changed during the years of his reign. In particular at this time an agreement was made with certain strategic ports along the south coast – Sandwich, Dover, Fordwich, Romney and later Hythe and Hastings – that they could keep the profits arising from the courts they held in return for an undertaking to provide a certain number of ships and crews for the king's service when needed. This is recognised as the early origins of the Cinque Ports, with their privileges and responsibilities that were continued long after the death of King Edward.

The ships provided by these ports were in general smaller than those of the now disbanded king's fleet, and were probably intended more as a watch on the coastline and a mobile deterrent to small-scale raids rather than full invasion fleets. The threat of invasion had, in any case, retreated when Harald Hardrada had re-opened hostilities against Denmark that would occupy both countries for a number of years to come.

More relevant now was the general threat to the west from the Irish, Welsh and Norwegian raiders, and the hostility of Flanders, where Count Baldwin was ever ready to give shelter to Edward's enemies. In 1049 the fleet was used to 'close the seas' to Flanders at the request of the Holy Roman Emperor. This was in response to a rebellion in Lotharingia, in the borderlands between present-day France and Germany, involving Baldwin, his brother-in-law Henry, king of France, and that king's vassal William of Normandy. Unusually, in taking the Emperor's side in the rebellion, England lined up alongside Denmark and against the normally friendly Normandy.

In the same year a part of the fleet was also dispatched against an Irish Viking raid up the rivers Severn and Usk into Wales, but this became entangled with a matter of internal politics that had been becoming increasingly troubled for some time.

Whether or not Godwin had a hand in Edward's succession to the throne, he was still the most powerful and influential of the earls and was to become even more so as time went on.

Almost at once his eldest son, Swein, had been made an earl, with responsibility for the shires of Somerset, Berkshire, Oxfordshire, Gloucestershire and Herefordshire – a holding carved partly from that of Godwin and partly from Leofric's Mercia. Soon after, the second son, Harold, became Earl of East Anglia. Then, as if to put the seal on the family's influence, on 23 January 1045 Edward married Godwin's daughter Edith.

Although this has been seen as the ultimate bid for control by Godwin, in fact this was only the sort of marriage that was usual for English kings before the time of Cnut. Athelred's foreign bride caused far more of a stir. It has been pointed out that, at around twenty-two years of age, Edith was rather older than average for a first marriage, and possibly Godwin had been holding her back until he could secure this royal match, but even so she was some twenty years younger than her new husband.

Like Queen Emma before her, Edith in later years commissioned an account of her times, in particular detailing the life of her husband. This *Vita Edwardi* spends some time on the talents and virtues of Edith herself, describing her beauty, virtue, intelligence, modesty and extensive education. The only slightly jarring note comes when it tells of how she looked after her husband more like a mother or daughter than a wife, and that he tolerated this with good humour. One suspects it might be more resignation than humour, but then Edward may well have been used to doing as he was told.

No doubt Godwin now hoped – even expected – to become the grandfather of a future king but it was not to be. Years passed with no sign of a child and the queen's prestige, along with that of her father, is likely to have fallen as a consequence. In later years all manner of stories grew up to try and explain the king's childless state. At the time when there was a strong move to have him declared a saint, the favourite was that he had taken a vow to remain celibate and that therefore the marriage had never been consummated. In the eyes of churchmen this would be a most virtuous thing to do, though rather an odd attitude on the part of a king, but Stigand, later Archbishop of Canterbury, seemed rather unconvinced of the king's alleged extreme piety. A story that Edith on her deathbed declared she was still a virgin lends some little support, though this could have been deliberately misinterpreted and taken out of context since the accusation she was denying at the time was one of adultery.

Another version is that Edward was forced into the marriage by Earl Godwin and took his revenge on the earl and his family by deliberately shunning the queen. If this was so, there is little sign of it in contemporary accounts, where the marriage is generally depicted as perfectly normal. Indeed, prayers were later offered for the childless king with no suggestion that the state might be of his own choosing.

Soon after the king's marriage, the cosy solidarity of the Godwin family showed its first signs of cracking. Swein, the eldest son, seems to have been wholly in tune with the Scandinavian – even Viking – side of his character. At times, in fact, he claimed that Cnut was really his father, a claim denied with horror by his mother. In 1046 he allied himself with the Welsh prince Gruffydd ap Llewelyn to make a raid into south Wales. This would probably not have been seen as too startling. With lands on the borders, it was fairly common to play one Welsh prince off against another. What he did on the way home, however, was seen as outrageous. He ordered the abbess of Leominster to be brought to him, and in the words of the *Chronicle*, 'had her as long as he listed, and after that he let her go home'. Whether this was rape, seduction or possibly even romance is never made clear, but it resulted in Swein being outlawed by the king and his earldom being divided between his brother Harold and his cousin Beorn, the brother of Sweyn Estrithsson.

Swein Godwinson took himself off, first to Bruges where he was welcomed by Baldwin of Flanders, and then later to Denmark, though whether to fight for or against cousin Sweyn is not clear. According to one of the chronicles unspecified crimes then led to him being expelled from Denmark, although this may simply have been the result of the victory of Magnus there at this time. In 1049, when King Edward and his earls and his fleet were assembled at Sandwich, guarding the seas on behalf of the Holy Roman Emperor, he arrived back in England.

With a fleet or seven or eight ships he put into Bosham harbour and then travelled overland to ask the king's pardon for his offences. Apparently he was expecting cousin Beorn to back him up in this, and if he had been fighting for Sweyn in Denmark he might have had some reason for such optimism. In the event he was implacably opposed by Harold and, seeing this opposition, Beorn too backed down. The king gave him very short shrift, ordering him to return to his ships and leave the country within four days. It is possible Godwin himself was not present at this interview, but if he was he kept silent.

It was now that news of the Viking raid into Wales was received. Edward immediately sent two of his own ships along with forty-two belonging to the Wessex fleet to deal with this matter, under the command of Godwin and Beorn. The wind and weather were against them, however, and while they were sheltering in Pevensey Bay, Swein came again to talk with Beorn. Somehow he convinced him of his good faith and persuaded him to accompany him once more to the king to plead his cause.

No doubt they both believed Edward was still at Sandwich, though he may have sailed north to try and intercept another exile who was raiding the Essex coast about this time. Rather than ride overland, it seems that Swein suggested they return to Bosham and sail with the favourable wind to Sandwich. As soon as they reached the ships, however, Beorn was seized and bound and taken on board. What prompted this abrupt act of violence – whether Beorn changed his mind once again, or if there was a sudden quarrel between them – we really don't know, but instead of sailing to Sandwich Swein headed westward to Dartmouth, where Beorn was summarily murdered and buried on the shore. Most of Swein's ships then deserted him, and with the two that were left he sailed again to Flanders to the safety of Baldwin's court.

There followed a very Scandinavian procedure. After the body of Beorn was located, exhumed and reburied in some state at

Winchester, the *Chronicle* tells us Edward called together the whole army and put to them the outrageous behaviour of Swein. Thereupon he was publicly declared 'nithing', worse than an outlaw, a man totally disgraced and without honour.

Once again we have no word of Godwin's reaction to this, but no doubt he must have felt sorrow and not a little anger at the shame brought on the family by his eldest son. It has also been suggested that he worked away quietly behind the scenes, trying to persuade Edward to allow his son to return. If this is so, it may go some way towards explaining the bizarre anti-climax that occurred the following year.

Ealdred, Bishop of Worcester, was returning from a synod at Rome via Flanders when he met Swein, still languishing there and apparently genuinely repenting his many offences. The good bishop had known Swein for some time and, being convinced of his sincerity, brought him back to England and obtained for him the king's pardon. It seems that some but not all of his lands were returned to him, for in his absence Herefordshire had been given to the king's French nephew, Ralf of Mantes. This was to become a source of further trouble in the future.

How this return of the exile was received by the rest of the family we can only speculate. Certainly Harold had shown very little brotherly love the previous year, though he might now have been reconciled to losing the lands he had gained from Swein, being compensated for this with some of those previously held by Beorn. On the other hand he clearly felt some affection for his murdered cousin since the *Chronicle* states it was Harold that arranged for his reburial at Winchester. It is likely, therefore, that he felt Swein's repentance fell far short of what was needed to make up for his crime. The *Vita* commissioned by their sister Edith simply describes Swein as a monster.

There are those who view the relationship between Edward and Godwin as one of barely veiled dislike on the king's part, and a constant intolerable pressure to control on the part of Godwin. This may be overstating it, though it is clear Godwin never achieved the personal favour with Edward that he had had with

Cnut. Where gifts are made to Godwin and his sons there is always an undercurrent that these were satisfying expectations rather than being freely given, and certainly towards the end of the first decade of the king's reign, Godwin's stock had taken something of a battering. The continued childlessness of the queen did not help, nor the rebellion of Godwin's son, and there are many who see what happened in the next few years as a conscious attempt by the king to shake off an irksome encumbrance.

There are several equally plausible and probably complementary versions of the cause of Godwin's fall from grace, depending on which account is followed. According to some it was the fault of the Normans whom Edward was beginning to favour at court. By others it was Edward taking revenge for years of oppression by Godwin and his family, and in yet another the whole crisis was engineered by Edward, with the help of his brother-in-law Eustace of Boulogne, to get rid of the childless queen and enable Edward to marry again and get an heir.

The movement of the first pebble that led to the landslide was the death of Eadsige, Archbishop of Canterbury, on 29 October 1050. The monks of Christ Church Canterbury sought to replace him with one of themselves, Aethelric, who was related to Earl Godwin, and asked Godwin for his support in this. The appointment made by the king, however, was Robert of Jumièges, a longstanding friend of Edward's from his time in exile in Normandy, and whom he had already appointed Bishop of London. Although the royal appointment of archbishops would become hugely controversial in the future, there was nothing questionable about this at the time. Robert seemed eminently suitable for the role, and it would, in fact, have been far more unusual if the monks had got their way, particularly in such an important appointment. It did, however, look like another slight to Godwin and a favouring of 'foreigners', and it seems clear that there was little love lost between Robert and Godwin.

The appointment was made on 1 March 1051 and Robert went straightway to Rome to receive his pallium from the Pope as was customary. Pope Leo IX had himself only been in office a short while, but in that time he had begun a major reform of some of the unacceptable practices which had become current in the Church, in particular the payment of money in return for Church offices. Fired with zeal for reform, Robert returned and immediately opposed the appointment made in his absence of Abbot Spearhavoc of Abingdon to replace him as Bishop of London. Apparently money had been paid to Bishop Stigand in relation to this and Robert flatly refused to accept Spearhavoc as bishop. The Pope, he declared, had forbidden it.

Next he found that some estates belonging to Canterbury had been taken by Earl Godwin, and, possibly believing that this too had been done for corrupt reasons, demanded that they be returned. A refusal, and a failure to regain the lands through courts dominated by Godwin, led Robert to approach the king complaining of the earl's behaviour over this and other matters. This might have had little consequence had he not decided to rake out into the open once more the issue, already sworn away once by Godwin, of his involvement in the death of the king's brother some fifteen years before.

No doubt already alarmed by this turn of events, Godwin was to be pushed even further by matters unfolding within his own earldom at Dover. In the summer of 1051 the *Chronicle* records a visit to Edward by his brother-in-law Eustace, Count of Boulogne. What the reason for this was we don't know, although, as mentioned above, a conspiracy has been suggested. The record simply states that Eustace spoke to the king on some unspecified matter and then set out for home. The different accounts here do not tell exactly the same story, but in essence they agree that at Dover there was some trouble and a number of householders and followers of Eustace were killed. In general the blame for this is put on Eustace, and a suspicious detail in one account tells of the French contingent stopping to put on their armour before entering the town, an action only explicable if they were already anticipating trouble, or were themselves determined to cause it.

Eustace immediately returned to pour out his complaints to the king. He put the blame squarely on the people of Dover, though the *Chronicle* adds, 'but it was not so'. Edward's response was to tell Godwin to go and punish them for this outrage. Such a punishment usually involved sacking and burning the town and had been carried out occasionally in the past when the king's officers had been attacked in discharging their duties. It is not clear on this occasion if it was a cold, calculated application of the 'eye for an eye' principle, or a sudden loss of temper on the part of the king. It may even have been part of a pre-meditated plan to test Godwin. The earl was almost certainly reminded of the most recent example of such a punishment, when Harthacnut burned Worcester. In any event he refused to obey the order, and this point-blank rejection of the king's authority brought them abruptly to a point of no return.

Edward summoned a council to meet at Gloucester on 8 September to decide how to deal with the matter, and by this time Godwin must have clearly got the message that his position in the country, if not much else besides, was under severe threat. He now made a mistake that was to cost him dear.

On 1 September he appeared with his two eldest sons and a considerable number of men at Bevestone, some fifteen miles south of Gloucester, where the king was staying. This surprising show of force caught Edward by surprise. Although the earls Leofric and Siward were on their way to the council meeting they were not yet arrived, and in any case had only a small number of attendants with them. If Godwin had intended to threaten the king he had succeeded. If not he had stirred up more trouble than he could well deal with.

The accounts here become confused. A more northerly one ignores completely the happenings in Dover and decides that what followed was a straightforward showdown between the English earl and the 'foreigners' who had infiltrated the king's court. The giving of land in the area to Earl Ralf, the presence of Count Eustace at Edward's court, the advancement of Robert of Jumièges and particularly the building of a new-fangled Norman-style castle in Herefordshire were all part of the complaint. Earl Godwin and his sons, it said, had come to consult with the king as to how this menace could be dealt with, but the 'foreigners' got at the king first, poisoning him against the earl and declaring he was intending an armed rebellion against the king.

Godwin's show of force had badly misfired. Instead of moving to conciliate, Edward immediately called up more men and soon there was a standoff with earls Leofric, Siward and Ralf and their forces on one side backing the king, and Godwin and his sons with their men on the other. It was a critical moment and a single rash move could have sparked a civil war, though the *Chronicle* tells us that it was 'hateful' to Godwin and his men that they should stand against their lord the king. Fortunately cooler heads prevailed, a truce of peace and friendship was negotiated and it was arranged that all would meet again with a full session of the Witan in London on 21 September. It may be that it was at this time that hostages named as Godwin's son Wulfnoth and Swein's son Hakon were given to the king. These would somehow be found later at the court of Duke William in Normandy.

Edward now showed the strength and advantage of his position as king. As they travelled to London – Edward north of the Thames and Godwin south – he called out the full levy of troops required to give military service to him in times of emergency. This meant that even those thegns who would normally be under the orders of the great earls were now required to serve the king himself, and Godwin found his forces thinning considerably as many of the thegns of Wessex and East Anglia answered this call.

When he reached his manor of Southwark, across the river from the king in London, Edward renewed his demand that all thegns should transfer their loyalty to him. While Godwin and Harold complied with this, Swein did not and was immediately outlawed for his refusal. The weakness of his position was now clear to Godwin. With Stigand, Bishop of Winchester, acting as a go-between, he asked for a safe conduct guaranteed by hostages before he would to go to the council and prove his innocence of the claims made against him. The initial reply was that Godwin and Harold might come with no more than twelve men. A further request for safe conduct with hostages was turned down. One account gives the king's reply that Godwin might have his safe conduct when he could return unharmed the king's brother Alfred and all his men. In the end Godwin was given five days to leave the country with no hearing of his defence at all.

Without more ado Godwin fled to his manor of Bosham, joined by his wife and sons Swein, Tostig and Gyrth. Quickly gathering all the money and possessions they could, they took ship to Flanders, where Tostig either just had or was just about to marry Judith, daughter of Count Baldwin. Harold and another brother, Leofwine, meanwhile travelled to Bristol, where a ship was already awaiting Swein. On the orders of the king they were pursued by Bishop Ealdred of Worcester, but perhaps deliberately he failed to catch up with them before they had sailed, and after a stormy crossing they reached the shelter of the court of Diarmaid, King of Leinster and Dublin.

It is a central plank of Norman claims made on behalf of William of Normandy that Edward, having got rid of Godwin and his family, immediately filled their places with his Norman friends and promised the throne to William as his nominated successor. Certainly the removal of Godwin's influence was complete. Even the queen was sent to a nunnery and deprived of all her property. Whether this was with the help of, and in favour of, Norman friends is far less clear.

Robert of Jumièges was archbishop before the split with Godwin and he does not seem to have acted consistently on the side of the king. In fact his opposition to Spearhavoc was decidedly against the king's wishes, though when he now got his way in the removal of that bishop he was replaced as Bishop of London by Edward's own Norman Mass priest, William. There is also a suggestion that several sheriffs may have been replaced with Normans.

The 'foreigner' Ralf of Mantes seemed to benefit very little from his part in the drama. Odda of Deerhurst, an Anglo-Saxon relation of Edward's, was given Swein's earldom, while Harold's in East Anglia went to Aelfgar, the son of Leofric of Mercia. It seems that Edward kept Wessex for himself. The other 'foreigner' involved, Eustace of Boulogne, while technically a vassal of William of Normandy and later to be found fighting for him, was at the time keen to maintain the independence of his lands, and more likely to side with Baldwin of Flanders to maintain a balance between his two mightier neighbours. Nor does he seem to have received any particular benefit from his actions.

It is interesting to see how the same set of facts has been viewed so differently over the years. From one viewpoint Edward was the victim, rescued by his Norman friends from the overpowering arrogance of the mighty Earl Godwin. From another it is Godwin, the long-time servant of the Crown, who has been forced out unjustly by a crowd of foreigners. Certainly by the end of the year there was a strong measure of sympathy for the earl, at least in the more southerly parts of England, and a feeling that he and his family had been badly treated in being denied a fair hearing. Whether any of this got through to Flanders and Dublin is uncertain, but the next year Godwin was back at least to test the waters again.

By some accounts he had already sent a petition for mercy, backed by Baldwin of Flanders and Henry of France. When this was refused he assembled a fleet and came himself. In June 1052 the English fleet under earls Ralf and Odda was assembled at Sandwich, but Godwin slipped past and landed at Dungeness where he was welcomed by the people of his old earldom. Then, with land and sea forces turned out against him, he sailed to Pevensey and, with bad weather disrupting the pursuit, back to Flanders again. The foray was enough to show him that not everyone in England was against him.

The English fleet was recalled to London where there was some muddle about changing crews. Since the professional fleet had been paid off, those called to serve at sea normally owed only two months' service and it is likely that their time was up. In the meantime Godwin sailed again, taking by force from the Isle of Wight whatever was not offered willingly, while Harold and Leofwine, sailing from Dublin, did the same at Porlock on the Somerset/Devon border. Meeting at Portland, the two fleets united and proceeded along the south coast, receiving provisions and volunteers to boost their passage all the way.

By mid-September Godwin and his supporters had arrived at Southwark. Upriver Edward had fifty ships assembled but it is likely Godwin had more. Similarly, Edward had called out the militias again but they were slow in assembling, while Godwin had all his supporting forces at his back. Once again it was a stand-off and once again civil war was averted by the reluctance of the leaders of each side to fight each other.

A council meeting was called, probably at Edward's palace at Westminster since all the Londoners seemed to be backing Godwin. All the earls and chief men were assembled when Godwin and Harold, both fully armed, approached. By one account Edward met them at the entrance to the palace, whereupon Godwin, with a fine sense of the dramatic, threw away his weapons, knelt at the king's feet and begged for a chance to swear to his innocence of all wrongdoing. We are told that Edward returned his weapons, allowed them in and listened while Godwin once again swore he had had no part in the killing of Alfred, and had never intended rebellion against his king.

In the form of trial by oath-swearing, which was usual at the time, the oaths of the accused would normally be supported by others swearing to the truth of the story, the number varying with the seriousness of the matter. It should be remembered that at the time there was a strong belief that to swear falsely would damn one's soul to eternal torment – a prospect not to be taken lightly. The numbers of people, particularly people of some rank, who were prepared to swear an oath in support of the accused would, therefore, show how firmly the story was believed, or at least how many people were prepared to undertake some considerable risk on his behalf.

On this occasion it was clear that Godwin had overwhelming support, and in the end the Witan advised the king to accept that he and his sons were free of guilt and to give the kiss of peace. Clearly if Edward had won the first round, Earl Godwin had won the second and with it the entire campaign. He and his sons were restored to their lands, the queen returned to court and certain 'Frenchmen', Robert of Jumièges among them, who were blamed for causing all the trouble, were outlawed. In fact Robert had long since fled, along with Bishop William of London, though the latter returned the following year. Stigand replaced Robert as Archbishop of Canterbury but without giving up his Winchester diocese, which was to make him an object of censure later.

The return of Godwin was possibly made easier by the absence of the troublesome Swein. Perhaps as part of a penance imposed by Bishop Ealdred some years earlier when he brought him back from exile, Swein had set out to walk barefoot to Jerusalem, a task he achieved but did not survive. He died on the way home near Constantinople at about the same time as his father was triumphing in London. Nor did Godwin have long to enjoy his victory and renewed influence. On Easter Monday, 12 April 1053, while feasting at Winchester with the king and most of his family, he suffered a stroke and died a few days later. Some have viewed Godwin as a man greedily grasping for land and power, thrusting his children into positions of prominence and more like a king than the king himself. It should be remembered, however, that he served four monarchs over an extended period, and that it was in general a time of peace and stability. Though no doubt happily accepting all the good things that came his way, he may have viewed himself as offering counsel and service to his king and country, a role that seemed to have no attraction for the other major earls of the time.

His death at around the age of sixty undoubtedly left a vacuum, and though all his children had been brought up and educated to be of service to the king, Edward himself clearly made his own choices about how that vacuum was to be filled. Harold, now the eldest son, was appointed Earl of Wessex, but while it might have seemed obvious to replace him in East Anglia with his next brother Tostig, that earldom went instead to Aelfgar, the son of Leofric of Mercia, thus giving some balance in the south of England between the two leading families. Ralf of Mantes and Odda of Deerhurst continued in their roles along the Welsh Marches, where continuing raids by Gruffydd ap Llewelyn, now king of all Wales, were beginning to be troublesome.

At this time, in fact, with Harald Hardrada and Sweyn Estrithsson still fighting it out in Denmark, Flanders friendly through the marriage of Tostig and Judith, and the Norman and German lands well disposed towards England, the only problems to arise came from within the British Isles themselves. In 1054 Siward of Northumbria finally got permission to mount his campaign against the Scottish king, Macbeth. Supported by a squadron of the English fleet under Harold, a great victory was won, but at the cost of Siward's most obvious heirs, his son Osbeorn and nephew Siward. Siward's own death in the following March left only a young boy, his remaining son Waltheof, as heir. Even if he was to succeed to the earldom eventually, some other strong figure would be needed in the meantime, and Tostig Godwinson was chosen.

It seems clear that Aelfgar had also wanted Northumbria, no doubt thinking he had seniority and that Tostig could take his place in East Anglia. Such a move would, however, have divided the country too completely, with Mercia powerful in the Midlands and north, and Wessex in the south. This Edward was not prepared to allow, though the appointment of Tostig again increased the power of the Godwins. Maybe Aelfgar protested too much. Certainly it appears that at the same council meeting that approved Tostig he was declared an outlaw, in one account on the basis of admitted treachery, in another of hardly any crime, and in yet a third for no crime at all.

His earldom in East Anglia was given to Gyrth Godwinson, and Aelfgar fled, first to Ireland and then to Wales, where he seems to have been friendly with Gruffydd ap Llewelyn. Together they attacked Hereford, where they sacked and burnt the town in spite of an attempted defence by Ralf of Mantes, whose new-fangled Norman cavalry tactics were ridiculed in the *Chronicle*. Immediately Harold was sent with an army, but instead diplomacy ruled and peace was achieved with the reinstatement of Aelfgar in his East Anglian earldom.

Increasingly Harold was proving himself not only a master of army and navy, but also skilled in negotiating peaceful solutions. Stepping into his father's shoes, he showed again and again that he was a man on whom Edward could rely to put down these sudden flarings of rebellion with a minimum of harm. Reputedly he got on well with everyone. He has been described as the ablest of the Godwin brothers, and more and more it seemed the king was prepared to rely on him, not only in military matters – understandable enough in a man now entering his fifties – but also for good counsel and energy in managing affairs.

One affair which was becoming more urgent was the securing of an acceptable heir for the king. Though he seemed strong and healthy and would in fact live another decade, no one knew that at the time, and if any promise had been made to William of Normandy it does not seem to have been taken seriously. Certainly it never appeared in any *Chronicle* at the time. A search was now instigated for the heirs of Edmund Ironside, thought to have fled to Hungary after their father's death. Bishop Ealdred travelled to the court of the Holy Roman Emperor and is likely to have established there that the older boy, known as Edward the Exile, was alive and thriving in Hungary, although difficult relations between Germans and Hungarians prevented him from pursuing his quest further.

In fact, having grown up at the Hungarian court, Edward was well established there. He had married Agatha, who was at least a high-ranking lady related to the Holy Roman Emperor, and possibly the daughter of King Stephen of Hungary himself. They had three young children. Not surprisingly Edward took a little persuading to leave such a position and return to a homeland he could certainly not remember, and whose language, even, was unfamiliar to him. A further journey by Harold Godwinson in

1056, at least as far as Cologne if not further, may have helped to decide him, and in the spring of 1057 Edward, accompanied by wife and children, arrived in England.

Unfortunately for all concerned, he then died on 19 April without even meeting the king. One account goes so far as to suggest he was prevented from doing so. In the years since, some have accused Harold of murdering him, though there is no evidence of this and no suspicion at the time. What happened to Agatha at the time we don't know, but the children, Margaret, Edgar and Christina, were at once taken into the royal household to be reared and 'showered with love' as the *Vita* puts it, by Edward and Edith. Edgar, aged about five or six at the time, was henceforth known as the 'Atheling' or throne-worthy prince, and in effect adopted by Edward as his heir.

In the autumn of 1057 both Leofric of Mercia and Ralf of Mantes died, leading to a further shifting of power in the country. It may be that Leofric's age or state of health had been another reason for denying Aelfgar's ambitions in Northumbria. Edward would not have wanted two such mighty earldoms in the same hands and Aelfgar was the natural, indeed the only, realistic heir of his father. As he became Earl of Mercia, Gyrth Godwinson once again received East Anglia, while a younger brother, Leofwine, became earl of a new territory carved out of Wessex around the mouth of the Thames and comprising of Kent, Surrey, Middlesex, Essex and Hertfordshire. In giving up this area, Harold was compensated with the earldom of Ralf around the Welsh Marches, since Ralf's son and heir was only a child.

Once again the power of the Godwins was extended and some have blamed the influence of Harold, Tostig and Queen Edith for this. Realistically, however, unless making a huge policy shift, Edward may have had little alternative. If Leofric had had more sons and Godwin fewer, the balance may have been better kept, but with Odda of Deerhurst dead the year before, the king would have had to search far and wide for another family to promote, and that too may have been controversial. It is noticeable that he was either unwilling or unable to promote any 'foreigner' to such a post.

Soon after this Aelfgar once again found himself banished, possibly as a result of his close relationship with the Welsh king, Gruffydd, who about this time married Aelfgar's daughter Eadgyth. Once again he returned in force, this time with backing not only from Gruffydd but also with a mixed Irish and Norwegian fleet, headed ominously by Magnus, son of Harald Hardrada of Norway, who was possibly testing the out the openness of England to invasion. In the event diplomacy won the day as before, with Aelfgar returned to Mercia, though we don't quite know how this was achieved as the Chronicler declared that 'it is tedious to tell how all these matters went' and therefore omitted them.

In fact, over the next few years the *Chronicle* and other written contemporary evidence is very sparse. We know that Bishop Ealdred of Worcester was appointed Archbishop of York in 1060, and that the following year Tostig and his wife accompanied him on an eventful journey to Rome to receive his pallium from the Pope. We also know that in 1063 a campaign was launched against Gruffydd in Wales to put an end to Welsh raiding, which had become an increasing problem since the death of Aelfgar and the succession of his son Edwin the previous year.

Early in the year Harold had led an initial raid to Rhuddlan which just missed capturing the Welsh king. Then a two-pronged attack was made in May. While Tostig travelled overland from Chester, Harold went by sea, sailing from Bristol and ravaging the Welsh coast all the way to Anglesey, giving particular attention to that important island. The attack succeeded in forcing the submission of most of the Welsh nobles, and though Gruffydd himself escaped to Snowdonia, he was later killed by one of his own men, and his head sent to Harold as a symbol of the completeness of his victory. He was replaced in North Wales by two of his half-brothers who then swore allegiance to Edward as their lord and king, while in the south a number of local lords fought among themselves for power. The success of this campaign kept Welsh raiders from the English borderlands for some time to come.

This was possibly the last joint action of the brothers Harold and Tostig, who were described by the *Vita* as being like Atlas and Hermes, supporting the weight of the world on their backs and keeping heaven and earth in their place. Although nowhere specifically stated, this seems to imply that Edward was leaving more and more to his trusted lieutenants, and it has been used to declare that at this time the king had more or less retired. This may be overstating the case, since he seems to have remained vigorous to the end, but he certainly devoted more time to hunting and to 'good works', in particular the founding of his famous abbey at Westminster.

In 1065, however, events conspired to overturn the stability of the regime. Though he had been Earl of Northumbria for ten years, Tostig had never been popular. He was frequently absent, either with the king or elsewhere, his firmness – some said harshness – with wrongdoers was resented and it is claimed he took sides in local feuds and had murdered men of opposing factions who had been granted safe conducts. The Danelaw area had always had its own customs and had in general been taxed more lightly than other parts of the kingdom but Tostig attempted to align it more closely with the customs and taxes of Wessex. It may well be that this contributed to his downfall.

In October 1065 a number of thegns around York took over that city, killed all they could find of Tostig's officials, helped themselves to the treasury and declared the earl himself an outlaw. In his place they installed Morcar, son of Aelfgar. He in turn led them south to Northampton where they were met by his brother Edwin of Mercia, strongly supported by a force of Mercians and Welsh. Harold was sent by the king to meet them, and they demanded that he go and persuade Edward to appoint Morcar as their earl. In the meantime they killed, burned and ravaged a wide area around.

A council was called by Edward, meeting near Salisbury on 28 October. Here Tostig found very little support. Even Harold, who was by now convinced the Northumbrians would not compromise on their demands, spoke against his brother to such a degree that Tostig publicly accused him of plotting the whole thing. There is some evidence that Edward wanted to use force to put down the rebellion but this came to nothing and in the end he agreed to the rebels' demands. Morcar was confirmed as earl, and Tostig was exiled for refusing to accept the king's decision.

It has been suggested that Edward was already ill at this time. A picture is given of a feeble old man, weakening towards his end. This seems to be drawn with the benefit of hindsight since until this violent interruption he had been pursuing his normal autumn practice of hunting in the Savernake Forest. Nor did his ranting against the rebels at the council meeting suggest enfeeblement. From this time on, however, his health certainly declined.

The court that year spent Christmas at Westminster instead of the usual Gloucester, with an unusually large gathering of nobles and clergy from around the country. Edward's new abbey church – the West Minster, as opposed to St Paul's, the East Minster – was due to be consecrated immediately after Christmas and a great celebration was planned. In the event, however, the king fell seriously ill on 26 December and was unable to attend. On the night of 5/6 January 1066 Edward died, and the problems of his kingdom were left to be settled by another, stronger hand.

4

A DISPUTED THRONE
JANUARY 1066

The traditional image of Edward as a weak and aged man whose end was long anticipated seems to be fundamentally wrong. His death came as a surprise and even his last illness may have been very short. Some have suggested a stroke. What is clear is that it came at a very unfortunate time. After more than twenty years of peace and increasing prosperity England was once again a wealthy nation, a plum ripe for the picking. A strong succession from father to son would have discouraged all those adventurers eyeing up such a prize, but unfortunately that was the one thing Edward had not provided for his people. Instead, in January 1066 quite a crowd of people not only felt themselves entitled in some way to claim the throne of England, but were also ready and willing to back up that claim by force.

It should be remembered that the rules of succession were not then as firmly settled as they would later become. Nowhere were they set down in writing. Instead it is necessary to look at previous successions and draw out some common factors.

In the first place, except when interrupted by conquest as with Swein Forkbeard and his son Cnut, no king of Wessex – and by extension no king of a united England – had come to the throne unless he was a member of that 'royal' family that traced its ancestors back to the possibly mythical Cerdic. Sons, brothers, nephews, uncles had all been acceptable at different times, and there was certainly no rule about inheritance by the eldest son. Nevertheless, some 'royal' blood was a common factor.

Whether the line of Danish kings, Swein and his descendants, had rendered this obsolete is a matter for conjecture. Certainly Edward himself had qualified on the traditional basis, and the search for his nephew Edward the Exile implies an intention to return to it, but there were those in Scandinavia who could argue that the line had been broken forever by Swein, and the Confessor himself had obtained the throne on entirely different grounds.

The second common factor seems to be the acclaim of the leading nobles and clergy. Formally this was the role of the Witanagemot, the assembly of leading earls and thegns, archbishops, bishops and abbots, who together could sift the claims of rival candidates and elect the one they felt most able to lead the country. The nomination of a successor by the previous king would obviously carry weight here, but it was by no means a rubber-stamping exercise. On some occasions, no doubt, the choice was obvious. On others one can imagine the kind of behind-the-scenes bargaining going on that is found in the corridors of power to the present day.

Less formally, any reasonably representative assembly would do to acclaim a king, and even potential conquerors would seek this. Cnut, for example, was acclaimed by a gathering of noblemen and bishops at Southampton following the death of Athelred, though he would still have to fight to attain the crown. It seems odd to accuse the Vikings of democracy but there was a strong tradition of election among them. A leader was a leader because men had chosen him or chosen to follow him (hence the need for so much looting to keep them sweet) and the Saxon tradition was very much the same. Only later would this be replaced by a right of succession.

As a purely practical point, too, no one could hope to rule the country without the support of its more powerful factions. To do so would lead to the kind of civil war fought between Cnut and Edmund Ironside. Even Harald Harefoot needed the support of Godwin before he could be crowned.

Once chosen, the new king's authority was recognised by a formal coronation and consecration ceremony carried out by an archbishop, the highest ranking clergy in the country. Though Cnut's coronation was at St Paul's in London, these had traditionally been held at Winchester. Some claimed that it was the consecration which actually gave a king his authority, and certainly a consecrated king was seen as something more than just a man. He was now God's choice as the ruler of the kingdom.

In January 1066 the first of these factors would seem decisively to favour young Edgar the Atheling, great-grandson of King Athelred. The other direct descendants of Athelred had been Edward's nephews, Ralf and Walter, the sons of his sister Goda and her first husband Drogo. Of these, Ralf had died in 1057 leaving a young son and Walter had died childless in 1064, a prisoner of William of Normandy.

Edgar had been brought to England specifically to continue the old English line and had been brought up at court with that in mind, so it might be thought he was the obvious choice to succeed to the throne. There were, however, a number of factors that told against him, not the least of which was his age. In 1066 he was probably only around fourteen years old. In times of peace this would not have been insuperable. A regent could have been appointed and, with goodwill on all sides, his kingdom could have been held for him until his majority.

Unfortunately the times of peace were clearly drawing to an end. It was obvious to all, and particularly to Harold Godwinson, who had been so closely involved in all the king's business, that within a very short time the kingdom was going to come under threat from a variety of different sources. Not the least of these was likely to be his own brother, seeking to return as Godwin and Aelfgar had done before him, through force of arms.

It may be, too, that there were some reservations about the character of the young Atheling. He had certainly been granted none of the favours that had been showered on Ralf of Mantes. True he was over-young for an earldom and maybe this and large estates would have followed had the king lived a few more years, but at the time of Edward's death the Atheling seemed to have almost no property in the country at all. Nor did he have any following of his own to speak up for his claim to the throne. So in spite of the general assumption beforehand that Edward's heir was securely growing up at his court, Edgar seems to have been the least regarded of the possible claimants.

If the line of Cerdic was to be permanently broken, there was a two-fold threat from Scandinavia that would seek to reclaim England as part of the world it had certainly belonged to barely thirty years before. Sweyn Estrithsson was not only the nephew of Cnut but also a cousin of Harold Godwinson through Harold's mother, Gytha. On the death of Harthacnut he had claimed the throne of Denmark, but had spent almost the entire time since in fighting to retain it. Driven out by Magnus, he had returned after that king's death in 1047, only to be challenged immediately by Harald Hardrada of Norway. In defiance of the settlement of Magnus, Hardrada was determined he would have both lands and spent the next fifteen years raiding Denmark, though unable to bring about a decisive victory against Sweyn. In 1062 the naval battle of Nisa was intended to achieve this but was only partly successful. Sweyn himself escaped from the defeat along with enough of his men to enable him to continue resistance. By this time, however, the cost of the prolonged warfare had told heavily on both countries, and in 1064 they finally agreed to a lasting peace.

This left each of them free to turn their eyes elsewhere just at the time when the throne of England seemed to be falling vacant. The claim of Sweyn could be seen as quite legitimate if it was accepted as an extension of the dynasty of Swein Forkbeard. He had, indeed, suggested earlier that he had a better right to it than Edward. Now, however, it did not seem that he was ready to go to war again to achieve such a prize. Possibly he felt that to do so might be to leave his hard won kingdom of Denmark wide open to further attacks from Harald Hardrada.

The king of Norway apparently had no such qualms, though his claim to the throne was considerably weaker. Everything was based on the pact that Magnus had made with Harthacnut in 1039. According to Magnus this entitled him to all Harthacnut's lands when he died, and this covered England as well as Denmark. Then in 1048 came the agreement with Harald himself, which the latter claimed was on similar terms. Possessions would be shared in life and the survivor would take all. He had failed in his attempt to impose this view on Denmark but now England seemed to be open for the taking. The apparent heir was no more than a boy, and the all-powerful family that could possibly have held the kingdom against him was now divided among itself, with Tostig already actively canvassing support around the courts of Europe.

In addition, Harald had already tested out the situation in the country in 1058 when his son, Magnus, had headed the Norwegian fleet that had helped return Aelfgar to his earldom. Since Magnus was at most ten years old at the time his leadership would have been purely nominal, but the fleet must have been large enough to be taken seriously. Irish sources claim it was intended as an invasion fleet to enforce Harald's claim to England, though others suggest its intention was only to impose Norwegian dominance on Orkney, and the extended voyage down the Irish Sea was only for plunder. As far as the English *Chronicle* is concerned, whatever fighting was done was in cooperation with Aelfgar and Gruffydd and probably confined to the Welsh Marches at best. How this was ended – whether by a show of English force or by the age old method of buying off – we really don't know. The *Chronicle* found it too tedious to bother with. At least, though, reports would have been carried home to Harald Hardrada about the distribution of power in the land and the readiness of the English to defend their territory.

When we turn to the final overseas claimant of the English crown, the weakness of his case makes us at once begin to wonder why he thought he had a claim at all. The sole connection between William of Normandy and the throne of England was Queen

Emma, wife of both Athelred and Cnut, and since she was merely his great aunt the connection seems gossamer thin. On the other hand, since William appears not only determined to have the crown but adamant about his entitlement to it, clearly something must have happened to raise this expectation in him.

Here we need to be very careful. Although the background to this is fully stated in several near-contemporary accounts, these are all Norman accounts, produced a few years after the events and intended to glorify and justify William's actions. The first of these, the *Deeds of the Norman Dukes*, was written by a monk of Jumièges Abbey known as William of Jumièges. It is based on an earlier work revised and brought up to date by William, and completed around 1070. It is a simple, straightforward account with no added detail, by a chronicler with a good reputation for accuracy. As with the other contemporary writers, though, it is very difficult to strip from it the obvious bias and the benefit of hindsight.

Probably produced between 1071 and 1077, the second account is the *Deeds of William, Duke of the Normans and King of the English* by William of Poitiers. Poitiers came from a knightly family and himself undertook military training before entering the priesthood around 1049. The story he relates is substantially the same as that of William of Jumièges, though offering a great deal more detail, quite a lot of which can be proved to be incorrect. He was well placed to hear eyewitness reports of Duke William's campaigns, but his clear aim was to praise the duke who, to him at least, could do no wrong, and one critic has described his account as 'biased, unreliable and unrealistic'.

The third source of the Norman side of the story is perhaps a unique historical record. Although there is no documentary evidence as to exactly when or where the Bayeux Tapestry was made, the general consensus following numerous investigations is that it was produced in the last quarter of the eleventh century and was probably made in England. Its known connection with Bayeux is that it was displayed in the cathedral there each year in the weeks immediately preceding the anniversary of the cathedral's dedication. Bishop Odo of Bayeux, half-brother of Duke William, is frequently identified as the commissioner of the work, and it has been suggested that it could well have been presented to the cathedral on the occasion of its dedication on 14 July 1077.

Its form is that of a strip cartoon covering the events of 1066 and the years immediately before that date, and while the story it tells is broadly similar to the written accounts, it is considerably more enigmatic in the important details. It would be interesting to know exactly who designed it and who wrote the captions that accompany the pictures. In the absence of such information we can only guess whether the intention was to hint at an alternative English version of events, or to avoid telling a deliberate lie, or whether at the time the details were seen as too well known to need recording.

Taken together, the story told by these three accounts is that which has been repeated with more or less detail by all later writers on these events over many centuries. It claims that Duke William's interest in the throne of England began as far back as 1051 when Edward promised he would make him his heir. According to William of Poitiers an oath was then sworn by Archbishop Stigand and earls Godwin, Leofric and Siward that they would accept William as king of England in succession to Edward.

Then, shortly before his death, Edward sent Harold Godwinson to William in Normandy to confirm this promise, and again to swear an oath to help William achieve the crown. These promises and oaths are, therefore, the basis of the claim put forward by William, but since all are recorded after the event, and most with the avowed aim of justifying William's actions, they all need to be carefully examined and tested against other records at the time before accepting that what they declare is in fact the truth.

As regards the promise allegedly given in 1051, a number of arguments can be made both for and against it. William of Jumièges simply records that it was made, giving no suggestion at all as to why this should be so. William of Poitiers, however, advances as a reason the fact that Edward loved the Normans and wanted to surround himself with them in England, and specifically offered the crown in gratitude for all they had done for him before he became king of England.

The first point to make here is that, of course, the crown of England was not Edward's to give away. His nomination might have influence, but only if other considerations were also satisfied. There is also some evidence that he made a similar promise to Sweyn Estrithsson, and maybe even Magnus of Norway. Nor do the reasons given stand up to much scrutiny. True, Edward was sheltered and protected at the Norman court, but he seems to have had few other favours there. The story that he was made king of England with William's aid is pure myth, as is the one that he returned to England with a large retinue of Norman followers who were then shoe-horned into important roles in England. There has been a tendency to regard anyone with a French name as a Norman, whereas in fact the areas of Brittany and the Vexin, where many came from, were often at war with Normandy. The court of Eustace of Boulogne was for a time a place of refuge for William's enemies. The most notable 'foreigners' to be raised to prominence by Edward were his nephew Ralf, who received an earldom, his friend Robert of Jumièges, who became Archbishop of Canterbury, and two other Norman clerics, Ulf and William, who became respectively Bishop of Dorchester and Bishop of London. Though Robert, Ulf and William all fled after Godwin's return to power in 1052, William was soon welcomed back, and Earl Ralf remained at the king's side throughout, seeming perfectly acceptable to all factions.

Even supposing Edward felt gratitude to the Normans in general (and it has been pointed out that friendship between England and Normandy might have been useful in deterring Scandinavian interest in the country) it is difficult to see why he should have favoured Duke William particularly. A twelfth-century chronicler, probably quoting William of Poitiers, declares that he 'loved Duke William as a brother or child', but there seems little reason for him to do so. William would have been around fourteen years old when Edward came to England and there seems to have been little close contact in the ten years that had passed after that.

The timing of the promise also sits awkwardly with other events. It is generally accepted that 1051 was the relevant year, though this is not mentioned specifically in the accounts, but at what time of the year was it given? William of Jumièges says Edward sent Robert, Archbishop of Canterbury, to tell William of his nomination as heir, and we know that Robert travelled to Rome in the spring of 1051 to receive his pallium from the Pope. It has also been suggested that Edward announced his decision at a council meeting in March and that this was a cause of the trouble with Godwin that occurred later that year.

There are a few problems with this. First, it seems odd that, if such an important declaration was openly made, there is no mention of it in the *Chronicle*. Though different reasons for the split with Godwin are recorded in different versions, none gives the naming of a Norman heir as being involved. In fact the trouble only seems to begin in the summer of 1051, after Robert's return and at the time of the visit of Eustace.

Another problem comes with the added detail from William of Poitiers that the oath to accept William as heir was sworn by 'Archbishop' Stigand, along with the major earls. Stigand was not archbishop, however, until 1052 when Robert had fled the country. Similarly it has been claimed that it was after Edward had driven out the Godwin family that he was then able to name William as his chosen heir, in which case Godwin would not have been able to swear along with the others.

Something else that muddies the waters is a story that William himself visited England, probably in the autumn of 1051 after Godwin had departed, to receive personally the promise of the throne. This is contained in a later account by a monk known as John of Worcester, and may be based on a description of a visit by William in one of the northern versions of the *Chronicle*, though that gives no reason for his coming. A number of different reasons for such a visit have been suggested, including the very implausible one that William was paying a call on his old great-aunt Emma, who was to die the following year. Given the situation in Normandy, however, it is the visit itself that seems hugely unlikely. In the summer of 1051 a whole chain of enemies of William were beginning to line up against him, and his duchy was threatened on all sides. It is hard to imagine that at such a time he would have torn himself away, however briefly, to receive a promise of a possible future crown from a king who could well still produce an heir of his own.

Nevertheless, there are details attached to this story that make it possible that someone came from Normandy at this time, though even these cause further questions to be raised. It is said that William knelt before Edward and took an oath of fealty, swearing to be his man – something, incidentally, he had already sworn to the king of France. Then the promise was given and hostages were exchanged before William left to return to Normandy. This giving of hostages was a common practice at the time when agreements were made. They were intended to act as a guarantee of good faith on each side, and we have seen how Cnut treated hostages given to his father when an agreement was broken. In this case we can identify two hostages that were held by Duke William for some considerable time. These were Godwin's son Wulfnoth, and his grandson Haakon, specifically referred to by William of Poitiers.

Now, these cannot have been given before September 1051, which is the earliest date mentioned for Godwin giving hostages to Edward. It is also fairly certain that they were not in England the following summer when Godwin was restored to his former position. If they had been they would surely have been part of the settlement made at that time. At some point, therefore, they must have been transferred to the custody of Duke William, and it is at least possible that this occurred at the time of the 'visit' in the autumn of 1051.

The whole story of this visit, however, is unsatisfactory. It has been pointed out that it is not mentioned in either of the southern versions of the *Chronicle*, compiled at Canterbury and Abingdon, though if William had landed at the usual place on the south coast, he would surely have passed through Canterbury at least. If, on the other hand, he had sailed to Southampton to visit Edward at Winchester he might have gone unnoticed by these chroniclers, and John of Worcester might have had access to another version of the *Chronicle* which has since been lost.

The hostage story, too, is not entirely convincing. Though Wulfnoth and Haakon undoubtedly appear later as prisoners of William, it seems odd that Edward, who was after all bestowing a huge gift on the duke, should have to give hostages to guarantee it. Nor is there any later mention of the hostages supposedly given by William in exchange.

The unlikelihood of Edward choosing to name William as heir designate at that particular time has also been pointed out. True, it coincides neatly with the downfall of Godwin and his family, but it has also been suggested Edward intended to divorce his wife and marry again, and he was by no means too old to produce an heir of his own if he did so. If that was not his intention, he had at least one family member close at hand to take on that role. Ralf of Mantes, his nephew, was of the correct 'royal' bloodline, albeit through his mother, and had already been favoured with an earldom. Although 'foreign' by birth, he was likely to prove more acceptable to all factions in England than Duke William, whose connection was tenuous in the extreme.

An interesting alternative has been put forward which accounts for many of the known features of this story. We know that when Godwin reappeared in the Thames in 1052 backed by both a fleet and land forces, Robert of Jumièges, along with other 'hated' Normans, fled. There was apparently some kind of scuffle at one of the London gates as they went, which suggests that the Londoners at least might have wanted to detain them. It is possible that, in order to secure the safety of his good friend, Edward may have transferred to Robert the custody of the two Godwin hostages, and equally possible that on reaching Normandy they were given over to Duke William. It has also been suggested that it was at this time that Robert of Jumièges, with or without authority, told William that Edward wanted him to be his heir. It is notable that William of Jumièges, a monk at the same abbey, names Robert as the messenger, and he would have been well placed to know this detail.

Out of all these variations, there are only two things we can state with some certainty. The first is that from at the latest 1052, Duke William of Normandy believed he had been named as the heir to the English throne, though whether anyone else knew at the time of the alleged promise remains uncertain. In addition he had in his hands two members of the Godwin family who had been originally supplied to Edward as hostages, and who had somehow ended up in his custody. Beyond these two facts all else is down to interpretation of the scanty evidence, but the facts themselves were enough to establish that a very real challenge to any other successor was likely to come from Normandy.

If Edward did make such a promise, it seems to have been seriously undermined by the strenuous search in the following few years for another heir of Athelred. The locating of Edward the Exile and his return to England must surely have at least hinted to William that his succession was not assured, though at the time he was no doubt too busy with domestic struggles to make any protest. It has been suggested in any case that the search was more the policy of the Church and the Godwins than Edward's policy. If, however, the sudden death of the new heir is regarded as suspicious (for which there is no evidence) it should be noted that William would have had at least as much to lose by his existence as Harold Godwinson, who seems to have had no thoughts of a crown at all at that early date.

Moving on to the second part of the Norman story, we come to the visit of Harold himself to Normandy. Again, no precise date is given for this but certain events are mentioned which would help to pin it down if they were not contradictory. It was said to be around the time Duke William had conquered Maine, which would put it towards the beginning of 1064. Certainly there seems to be a gap in Harold's recorded deeds about this time which would allow for such a journey, and the *Vita* rather vaguely mentions him visiting foreign lands to meet their rulers and learn their policies. On the other hand, William of Poitiers declares the trip was triggered by Edward, who 'felt the hour of his death approaching', and later that 'Edward in his illness could not be expected to live much longer'. This certainly does not fit the spring of 1064, when Edward appears hale and hearty with his death nearly two years away. Towards the end of 1065, when Edward's health may well have been declining, it is certain that Harold made no such visit, and none is mentioned on any date in the *Chronicle*. In fact the Norman texts and the Bayeux Tapestry are the only evidence that Harold ever went to Normandy.

Should we accept that some visit did take place, and that 1064 is the most likely time for it, the purpose of the visit also needs to be examined. Both texts are clear that Harold was sent by Edward, specifically to confirm to William the promise of the throne made to him earlier. William of Poitiers adds that Harold was 'to confirm his promise by an oath' and (inaccurately) that his 'brother and his cousins had previously been offered as hostages in respect of the same succession'. He also says that Harold was particularly chosen for this because he could later use his authority to stop the people overturning what had been agreed, 'with their accustomed perfidy'.

It is at this point that the Bayeux Tapestry, at least in its surviving form, begins. King Edward with sceptre in hand is apparently giving some instructions to two figures, one of which is identified as Harold. Unfortunately, in the delightfully enigmatic stance that is maintained at all crucial points throughout its story, the Tapestry fails to tell us exactly what instructions are being given. In the absence of this important detail all manner of speculation has been made about the nature of Harold's journey.

A fairly plausible suggestion, put forward by the monk Eadmer of Canterbury early in the twelfth century, is that he might have been going to negotiate the release of his brother and nephew, who had now been held hostage for more than a dozen years. One interpreter has declared that, rather than sending him, Edward could well be warning him that this attempt is likely to be fruitless. Others have declared that Harold had no intention of visiting anywhere and his voyage was just a fishing trip that went wrong.

Wrong it certainly did go, whether the intention was to reach Normandy or not, for Harold ended up on the shores of Ponthieu at the mouth of the River Somme instead. Storm-driven, says William of Poitiers, though the Tapestry merely says that 'wind-filled sails' carried him there, and shows a calm sea. No doubt so brief a story cannot be expected to deal with the weather conditions at the time, but it does rather obscure the point of who it was that Harold was supposed to be visiting.

In the event he was taken captive by Guy (Wido in the Tapestry), Count of Ponthieu, who had recently been at loggerheads with Duke William but now was, nominally at least, his vassal. Whether William heard of Harold's captivity from Harold himself or from other sources is not clear. The Tapestry shows messengers going in both directions. When he did hear, however, he demanded Harold be handed over to him and Guy was quick to comply. What Harold's status was at this point is uncertain. In the Tapestry it looks more like an exchange of captivity than the happy release of a prisoner. William of Poitiers, however, insists he was given 'splendid hospitality' by William, who was delighted to receive such an illustrious guest, 'sent him by the nearest and dearest of his friends', a reference to Edward in England which seems well over the top.

After a brief pause for a scene involving a woman named as Aelfgifu and a cleric which no one has ever successfully explained, the Tapestry moves rapidly on to a military expedition against Brittany. Here Harold, accompanying Duke William and his men, seems to have distinguished himself, in particular by rescuing two soldiers from quicksand as they crossed the River Couesnon, an action thought worthy of being recorded for posterity in a detailed scene of the Tapestry. The written texts, however, put this expedition later. They go straight to the most important point in their justification of the future actions of Duke William – the oath.

All three accounts agree that at some point Harold swore an oath to William. What has been controversial ever since, however, is the where, when and why. William of Poitiers as usual gives the most detailed explanation. He places the scene at Bonneville, near Caen, though others have suggested Rouen, and the Tapestry, not surprisingly, says Bayeux. He says that beforehand Harold had performed 'ceremonial homage' to William, in other words had accepted William as his overlord, and had then asked for and received from the duke confirmation of all the estates and honours he held in England. This was then followed by the oath, sworn in the presence of 'the most truthful and honourable men', and using 'the sacred ritual recognised among Christian men'. He is anxious to emphasise that Harold took the oath 'of his own free will', and goes on to detail exactly what was sworn to. Harold would be Duke William's representative at the court of King Edward, he would use all his wealth and influence to ensure that the crown came to William on Edward's death, he would garrison Dover castle for William with the duke's own knights maintained at his own expense, and also he would garrison and maintain other castles throughout the land as specified by William, again at his own expense. Then, says William of Poitiers, since Harold was eager for new glory, the duke gave him arms, weapons and fine horses and they went off together to fight in Brittany before he sent him home laden with gifts and having greatly increased his honour.

This account raises a number of hugely important questions, not the least of which is why on earth Harold would do such things 'of his own free will'. Even if he had travelled to Normandy to confirm a promise made by Edward, there seems no reason why he should immediately humble himself before a mere duke. Their titles might be different but it is clear that, in Harold's eyes at least, he ranked on a par with William, who was, after all, a vassal of the French king. Harold was the most powerful man in England, even accorded by one enthusiastic account the title of 'sub regulus' or sub-king. It is hard to imagine him bowing the knee to anyone other than Edward himself 'of his own free will'. And to then be kindly given back his own titles and estates would rank as the gravest insult.

There is a scene in the Tapestry captioned 'Here William gave arms to Harold', and it has been claimed that this shows William knighting Harold, or at least bestowing arms on him as his vassal. This, though, comes after the expedition to Brittany, and a leading French authority declares that nothing in the scene suggests that this is the true interpretation. The helmet being placed on Harold's head, he says, is more likely to be simply a mark of honour, a reward for the part played by Harold in the campaign just completed. Nor do the attitudes of the figures suggest subservience. In fact, nowhere in the Tapestry is Harold shown kneeling to William, or even bowing before him as he does before King Edward, which might be expected if this was intended to show him accepting an inferior position.

When we come to look at the oath itself, as witnessed by those truthful and honourable men, the first thing that strikes is how unnecessarily elaborate it is. If all that is necessary is to confirm Edward's promise to William, why all this business about castles and garrisons?

Castles as such – to be garrisoned with knights and used to control an area of land – were a Norman invention. English fortifications tended to be defensive rather than offensive. The burghs founded by Alfred were walled towns, such as at Wareham in Dorset where the remains of the walls can still be seen. They were intended for the defence of the local population, not for their oppression. True, by this time there were a few Norman-style castles in England, but these were along the Welsh border, founded by Earl Ralf and his 'foreign' fellows. Dover may have had similar fortifications to Wareham, but no evidence has been found of a Norman-style castle dating from before 1066, and though William of Poitiers later talks of it being burnt and then repaired by the Norman army, it is likely that the motte and bailey then established was not based on an existing structure.

So why did Harold include in his oath 'of his own free will', details of castles that did not exist? One suggestion could be that it was to show up the very falseness of his position. He was using a 'sacred ritual' and is shown in the Tapestry to be swearing on no less than two sets of sacred relics. Some have suggested he was surprised or tricked into doing this, or that he didn't know what was in the boxes on which he laid his hands. This seems unlikely. The Tapestry shows a formal occasion with William seated on a throne and bearing a sword. With its usual reticence it says only that Harold took a sacred oath, without disclosing what that oath was about, but a well-placed stitch or two shows a very glum expression on the earl's face.

It seems more than likely that the appearance of free will is merely an illusion. Although ostensibly a guest, Harold could very easily turn into a prisoner, and William was not renowned for his gentle treatment of enemies. Only the year before, Edward's nephew Walter, brother of Earl Ralf, had died in suspicious circumstances while held captive by the duke. It seems likely that Harold was very well aware of his position and used his wits to find the best way out of it.

There is a possibly less than flattering description of Harold in the *Vita Edwardi*, which declares that he was a crafty man who could pass unscathed through all sorts of ambushes, treating them with 'watchful mockery'. It may well be that the oath he took was a good example of this. The nobles present at the oath-swearing in Normandy had probably very little knowledge of England and its fortifications and it is likely that they would take his words at face value. He clearly had no intention of keeping any part of the oath, and this additional swearing to an impossibility would be an obvious demonstration to any English person who was told of it that none of what he said was spoken freely and that it therefore had no power to bind him.

Another alternative, of course, is that Poitiers is simply inventing extravagant detail to increase the sense of Harold's wrong-doing when he failed to keep to this oath. There is certainly no evidence of Harold ever maintaining either castles or soldiers for the benefit of William.

The other point to make about this oath-swearing is that it was a very Norman ritual. This was the way Robert I had appointed William himself as his successor. It was the way William would pass on Normandy to his son Robert, and we find it again when Henry I of England wanted to pass on his throne to his daughter the Empress Matilda. Investiture during the life of the existing ruler was also a regular part of Norman and indeed French tradition – but it was not the English way. Thus we can account for both the certainty of William as to what he had received, and the fact that Harold himself would not attach any such weight to his actions. Similarly those Normans who wrote about this occasion would also be clear about its significance, even if they did not know exactly the words of the oath. Only the Tapestry with its possible English influence remains enigmatic, reflecting what Harold himself would have known: that the crown was not in Edward's gift and whatever occurred in Normandy, whether under duress or not, would have no bearing at all upon the choice made by the Witan after the king's death.

What he would also know now, however, even if he had not been sure of it before, was that William was quite determined he would be the next king of England. It may, in fact, have been this very knowledge that turned Harold's thoughts to the crown in the first place. The Norman accounts relate that he spent some considerable time at the duke's court in Normandy. He accompanied him on campaign, watched his methods and no doubt heard stories of his earlier exploits. As a seasoned campaigner, himself a little older than William, he would have been well placed to assess his strengths and weaknesses. It has been suggested that, with his own recent Welsh expedition in mind, he might have been less than impressed with William's brief and not entirely successful efforts, but he would have seen the potential there. He would have known that England now faced serious threats from the south as well as the north, and the thought that a fourteen-year-old youth might soon be expected to wear the crown would not have filled him with confidence.

The Tapestry jumps straight from Harold's homecoming to the death and burial of Edward, but of course there was more than a year between these events, and a momentous year at that. We don't know how far Harold shared his new knowledge with others. The *Vita* describes him as one who tended to share his plans, in contrast to Tostig who was the secretive one. The Tapestry also depicts him bowing rather apologetically before Edward on his return, but as usual gives no further clue as to why, or what might have been discussed at the meeting. If the mission had been one to redeem the hostages, it had been only partly successful. Haakon had been released but Wulfnoth remained in captivity. On the other hand if the aim had been to confirm Edward's promise to William, it is hard to see why Harold should be apologetic.

It seems reasonable to suppose that Harold would at least have informed Edward of what had happened, and probably of his fears for the future. If he had further shared this with his fellow earls it might give a reason for Tostig's outburst later in 1065, that Harold had engineered the Northumbrian revolt in order to remove a rival. Possibly Tostig did not support the solution that was being proposed to the succession problem. The exile of Tostig and subsequent promotion of Morcar changed the balance of power between the leading English families considerably, but there is no evidence that Harold's position changed. He was, after all, the one who had negotiated the settlement, and seems to have maintained good relations with all concerned – except his brother.

The gathering of Edward's court at Christmas 1065 would have been another opportunity for Harold to spread the word, especially as there may by then have been comments on the state of the king's health. Certainly Edward's very rapid decline after Christmas Day would have focussed minds on the pressing nature of the succession problem.

The Tapestry gives us a deathbed scene peopled by those who had parts to play in the rest of the story, but this is not so very different from that described in the *Vita*. Certainly there would have been quite a number of people there, witnessing the death and the important last words of the dying monarch. In the event, by the *Vita*'s account, some at least of the last words would have been extremely unsettling to the listeners.

According to this, after a time of delirium the king returned to consciousness and described a vision he had had. In this a prophecy was made that within a year and a day of his death England would be delivered over to its enemies who would scour the land with fire and sword, so that it would seem as though devils were let loose in their midst. This would be punishment for the people for their sinful way of life, and one can imagine how the feelings of the clerical writer of the *Vita* might be divided between horror at the prospect and glee that such sins would be properly punished. Archbishop Stigand is said to have dismissed this vision as mere delirious ravings, but whether delirious or not, it seems to be just the sort of thing that might occupy the mind of the king, knowing what he knew about the threats to his land, and, indeed, the horrors of the Viking wars of his youth.

There is no such dismissal of the other pronouncements of the king. Even the words are recorded by the *Vita* and they were sufficiently enigmatic and controversial for us to have some faith in their accuracy. After asking those present to pray for his soul, and paying tribute to the devoted service of his wife, he is said to have reached out to Harold and told him, 'I commend this woman and all the kingdom into your protection.'

There are those who declare that he was merely asking Harold to undertake some kind of regency role, but if that was the case it seems odd that he did not go a few words further and name the heir he was to be regent for. Similarly, allegations of duress seem misplaced. It is hard to see what threat could be effective against a man already on the threshold of death. Those present seem to have had no doubt as to the meaning. Clearly as his dying will Edward was nominating his successor, and the nomination seems to follow logically from the preoccupation of the king's mind as evidenced by his vision. With all this turmoil threatened in the near future, who else but Harold could expect to rally and lead all the English to the defence of their land?

We must remember that the *Vita* was commissioned by Queen Edith and intended to praise and justify the actions of her family. It is therefore just as likely to be biased as the writings of the Norman clerics. However, this nomination of Harold was apparently widely known. It is recorded in the *Chronicle* and indeed mentioned by the Norman writers themselves. It seems to have given rise to little surprise or comment in England and to have been immediately accepted; indeed there is no record of any of those assembled at Westminster speaking against it. Nor in the events that followed were there any substantial desertions or treacheries in favour of any of the other claimants. In modern parlance we might say that Harold was the 'unity candidate' for the crown.

So, despite having not a drop of royal blood in his veins, Harold clearly satisfied the other necessary criteria. Nominated by the dying king and accepted apparently unanimously by a full meeting of the Witan, he became king of England on 5 January 1066.

5

HAROLD: AN UNEASY PEACE JANUARY – SEPTEMBER 1066

'No man can make himself king, but the people have the choice to elect whom they like; but after he is consecrated he has authority over the people and they cannot shake off his yoke from their necks.' So said Aelfric, abbot of Eynsham, in his *Catholic Homilies* at the beginning of the eleventh century. It is a startling comment for its time – and after 1066 it would be another six centuries before the people again had any say in such matters – but it represented the English way of appointing a king. The question remains, how far did Harold 'make himself king'?

To his detractors – chiefly the Norman commentators, though later with some English writers seduced into supporting them – he was not 'born great' but strove with all his might to achieve greatness. Ruthlessly gobbling up land and power, and disposing of all rivals, Edgar Atheling and his own brother among them, he had always had his eye on the prize of the throne itself. They point to his 'hasty' coronation at Westminster Abbey, possibly on the day of his predecessor's funeral or at the latest the day after, as evidence of his tyrannical determination to have the crown on his head before news of Edward's death had even reached the majority of the country.

On the other hand his supporters declare that the coronation was simply a matter of convenience. Everyone of importance was already gathered at Westminster and had approved the choice of king, and to disperse them, only to call them back again at a time of year least suitable for travelling, would have been the greatest nuisance to all. Not only that but the situation in which they found themselves, with threats to the country from all sides, made it only a matter of common sense to have a king securely approved, consecrated and crowned at the earliest possible opportunity. In their eyes, in fact, Harold had his greatness thrust upon him. The *Chronicle of John of Worcester* gives the most straightforward account of the transmission of power. Harold, it says, was nominated by Edward as his successor (a proposition accepted by all), was chosen as king by the chief magnates of all England and was crowned with great ceremony by Ealdred, Archbishop of York.

We have, of course, only the vaguest idea of what he looked like. The earlier part of the Bayeux Tapestry depicts all the English with long hair and extravagant moustaches. Since this was clearly the fashion of the time, we might expect Harold to follow it. The *Vita* describes him as a handsome, graceful man, but then it would, being commissioned by his sister. Even his height is controversial. The *Vita* says he was taller than Tostig and other sources suggest something around six feet. In *King Harald's Saga*, however, Harald Hardrada describes him as 'but a little man'. Of course, Hardrada was reputed to be something of a giant so his view of the height of others might be skewed accordingly.

Harold also had a reputation as a womaniser, though whether this was really deserved or simply the clerical writers of the day being sniffy about his 'handfast' marriage to Edith 'Swan-neck', we don't know. Edith, who may also have been known as Edith the Fair and Edith the Rich, was a well-born lady of East Anglia who seems to have been in possession of extensive lands of her own. The liaison probably began when Harold was Earl of East Anglia in the 1040s, and was long-lasting, producing at least five children with a mixture of Scandinavian and English names. Why it was never made a Christian marriage we have no way of knowing, although those who see Harold as a schemer after the throne would point out that it left him free to make a more spectacular or advantageous marriage later if his plans bore fruit.

Given the life he led, we would expect Harold to be strong and active, though the scene in the Tapestry showing him pulling a man from the quicksand with one hand while carrying another on his back is likely to be an exaggeration. He is also described as more intelligent than his brother Tostig, more open in his dealings, more likely to accept criticism and more likely to discuss his plans with others before finally deciding on a course of action.

With all the contemporary sources biased one way or the other, however, we would do better to look at his actions and their consequences in trying to assess the character of the new king. He was clearly an able administrator. For more than a decade he took the burden of administration from the shoulders of the ageing king, and it seems to have been in general a time of peace and prosperity. As a soldier and commander of forces he also seems to have been more than competent, and equally at home on land and sea. Though his taking over of Earl Ralf's position on the Welsh Marches when that earl died has been seen as simply a land grab, it is more likely the sensible placing of a suitable military man in an area where conflict was a regular occurrence. Nor did he seem anxious to resort to violence unless that was truly necessary. Time and again we find him talking down a dangerous situation and finding a way to avoid conflict. The fact that Tostig is generally seen as more popular with the king and queen may suggest that Harold was lacking some of his brother's charm, but he must have made up for that with a cool head and a great talent for diplomacy.

It was no doubt a similar cool head and shrewd brain that had him travelling abroad to discover the characters and policies of the rulers of other European states, as stated in the *Vita*. Again, some would say this was in preparation for his own seizure of power, but such knowledge would be equally useful to the king he served. Even when he discovered a little too much at the court of William of Normandy, the same shrewdness got him safely home again to use that knowledge to good effect in England.

Good administration, military prowess, diplomacy and shrewd intelligence – these seem to be the characteristics that made Harold the clear choice of the leading magnates in January 1066, and to those must be added the attribute of long-term loyal service. Whatever the view of history, coloured with hindsight, the *Chronicle* at the time seems to have had no doubts on this score. At the end of a eulogy devoted to Edward it declares that that 'sage' committed the kingdom to Harold, who 'in all time obeyed faithfully his rightful lord by words and deeds, nor aught neglected which was needful to his sovereign king'.

What is indisputable about Harold in 1066 is that he was a very wealthy man, and to understand the source of this wealth it is necessary to examine briefly the system of administration and landholding that existed in England at the time.

England was, of course, an agricultural economy with probably nine-tenths of the population involved in working the land and producing food. The land itself was divided into administrative units, the shires, that had existed from time immemorial. The names of Dorset, Sussex, Norfolk and Berkshire would have been as familiar to King Alfred as they are to us today. Less well known are the sub-divisions into 'hundreds', the equivalent perhaps of our modern 'districts', though in some parts the names can still be found on old maps. MPs seeking to resign their seats in the House of Commons are still required to apply for 'Stewardship of the Chiltern Hundreds'.

Both shires and hundreds held courts where the king's justice was dispensed according to the codes of law laid down by Cnut or by local customs. Though lacking the finesse of our modern law courts, they were accessible to all, and may well have contained the germ of the idea of jury trial. There are records of groups of local people establishing the facts of the matter in dispute in such courts long before juries became a regular part of the judicial process.

The chief officer of the shire was the shire reeve (later sheriff), appointed by the king himself. As well as presiding over courts, his duties included the catching of criminals, the collection of taxes, the administration of royal estates in his area and mustering and commanding the shire levy, the militia of the day, when the king called this out for military service.

Hundreds were themselves groups of hides, the basic landholding unit giving rise to all manner of duties such as the payment of taxes and provision of services of various kinds. Originally a hide was the amount of land needed to support a peasant farmer and his family. As such its size might be expected to vary according to the nature of the land and the type of farming carried on in that locality. Hides of forty acres were typical in the fertile south, but there were large variations in other parts of the country. In Danelaw areas the equivalent was called a carucate or ploughland, and in Kent the sulung was roughly the same as two hides.

Over time the hides and their equivalents became standard units for the assessment of taxes, each shire or town being allocated a nominal number of hides for this purpose. For example, Worcestershire was deemed to contain 1,200 hides, while Bath was assessed at twenty. This highly sophisticated system allowed the raising of a 'geld' or land tax by the king to meet any special expenditure, and the repeated paying of the 'Danegeld' shows just how efficient this was, although the burden on those having to pay it must have been considerable.

The population, too, was clearly split into different ranks. Each freeman had his price or 'wergild', the amount of compensation payable for his death, and this varied according to his level in society. At the top were the earls, the king's chief officers in the country, each one responsible for a group of shires. By 1066 the four major earldoms were Wessex, Mercia, Northumbria and East Anglia, though from time to time others had been created such as that of Earl Ralf around Herefordshire, and the one established for Harold's brother Leofwine around the Thames estuary.

An earl was second only to the king himself in importance and had a wergild of 3,000 shillings. He was appointed by the king, and though there was an expectation that his eldest son might be appointed after him, at this stage the post was not yet hereditary. His role was political, administrative and military. He was the voice of the area in the Witan, was expected to keep the king's peace and administer justice through the shire courts, and to summon and lead the shire levies in times of conflict. In addition he would oversee the general administration of the area and the collection of taxes both for the king and for himself, the earl being entitled to the 'third penny' of certain kinds of revenue. This, together with the profits of certain estates that went with the earldom, was intended to pay for the administration and recompense the earl, in the same way as the king's own royal estates were intended to maintain the royal administration and the king himself. An earl was also expected to be a statesman and advisor and courtier to the king, though some took a larger share in this than others, as we have seen. In the absence of the earl the shire reeve would take over many of his day to day functions in his own shire, including deputising for him in the shire courts.

Ranking below the earls came the thegns. In earlier times these would have been the warrior companions of a king or warlord, and the rank never lost its association with service to a lord rewarded by a grant of land. Typically a thegn would have some specified duty in the household of the king or an earl, or even a greater thegn. He might be an advisor, an official or, in the case of younger thegns, a bodyguard. He should also hold at least five hides of land and have his own fortified dwelling house with a gatehouse and a bell, together with a church. In essence he had his own 'manor'. In fact, by the eleventh century the rank of thegn had become hereditary and could be split among brothers with estates split accordingly, so some manors were smaller, though the nobility of the thegn was not diminished. The wergild of a thegn was 1,200 shillings.

The lowest rank of free man was the ceorl, essentially an independent farmer with a wergild of 200 shillings, but even this rank was subdivided into different classes. We find details of these in a treatise on estate management, the *Rectitudines Singularum Personarum*, written shortly before 1066. At the top was the geneat, often translated as the tenant, a man of some standing in the community. He paid rent, probably in the form of produce, to his overlord, and could be called upon for certain services such as bodyguard or mounted messenger. The only agricultural work he was required to perform for his overlord was to assist in getting in the harvest.

Below him in status comes the kotsetla, usually translated as the cottager. In return for a minimum of five acres to cultivate himself, he was required to work on his overlord's land for varying amounts of time. Typically this would be one day a week all the year round, and three days a week at harvest time, when he would be expected to reap half an acre of corn in a day.

The lowest level of free man was the gebur or peasant, who held a 'yardland' or quarter hide that might vary between ten and thirty acres. He might be the son of a ceorl starting out in life, though many would rise no higher, and in addition to his land the overlord would provide him with some livestock such as a pair of oxen, a cow or half a dozen sheep, furniture for his house and implements for his farming. In exchange for these the gebur worked for his lord two days a week all the year round and three days a week at harvest and in the spring between February and Easter. He had to plough an acre a week between the end of harvest and St Martin's Day in November, and perform certain other services such as watching over the lord's sheep fold and fetching corn for sowing, in addition to paying rent partly in money and partly in produce.

Below the level of the ceorl there were, of course, the slaves or unfree men and women, who in England and elsewhere at the time performed all manner of work for their masters. There was always a danger that, in hard times, a ceorl who could not pay his rent or taxes might have to give up his freedom and himself drop into this layer of society. On the other hand, it was not unknown for a slave to be freed by his master and set up as a gebur.

In good times upward progress was equally possible. A ceorl paying taxes on at least five hides could be assessed as a thegn, and if this could be maintained by his son and grandson the status became hereditary. Similarly a merchant who crossed the sea three times in his own ship could also achieve this rank, while a thegn favoured by the king could rise as high as an earl, as evidenced by Harold's own father, Earl Godwin.

It will be clear from this that, although not named as such, something very like a feudal system existed in England before 1066, although it was considerably more flexible than that imposed after, and was much less focussed on the provision of military might. From the times of the earliest Viking attacks it had crept in as men voluntarily put themselves under the protection of lords stronger than themselves, and dangerous times, bad weather and outbreaks of cattle disease around the time of the millennium had accelerated this process. From its very origin, however, there was great emphasis on the lord's duty to protect 'his' people, rather than exploit them, one reason why Godwin was so reluctant to take action against the men of Dover following the incident with Eustace of Boulogne.

The wealth of Harold himself, therefore, was based on landholding, and the value of his estates immediately before his succession was second only to that of the king himself. These estates were predominately in the southern part of the country, mainly in areas where Harold had held his earldoms, and would have come from a number of different sources. First he would have inherited family lands, particularly in and around Sussex, the original homeland of the Godwin family. Second, he would have received the estates and profits attached to the earldoms he administered at various times, though these would have to be given up to the next earl when he moved on. Thirdly, he would have been given estates by the king. It was part of a king's duty to reward his followers with lands taken from the royal demesnes or from the confiscated estates of wrongdoers. In some cases, too, estates might be given to enable an earl to build up strength in a strategic location so as to be well placed to deal with any threat. An example of this might be a number of royal estates in Essex given to Harold at a time when an attack from Scandinavia was seen as likely. He is likely, too, to have benefitted from the estates of Edith Swan-neck, though the property of a wife, particularly a 'handfast' wife, did not at the time automatically belong to her husband. Finally, as one of the most important men in the kingdom, Harold would have been gifted estates or the profits from estates by those seeking his favour.

The upkeep of such a position would have been costly, too. He would be expected to spend freely, buying the best of everything including expensive textiles, gold and jewels, and maintaining extensive stables of horses and, his own particular favourite, falcons. We know he had books on falconry which later passed into the hands of a Norman nobleman, and he is usually distinguished in the early part of the Bayeux Tapestry by a falcon on his wrist. He would also be expected to provide lavishly for his own followers and give rich rewards for service.

So much for the new king; what now of the country he had acceded to? To a large extent it had recovered from the impoverishment of the early part of the century, caused by the repeated payments made to Viking raiders. It was also well on the way to thinking of itself as one nation united by king, language, laws and coinage. The latter was under the complete control of the Crown, with mints spread around the land needing royal approval. The moneyers bought their dies, from which to produce the silver pennies, direct from the king every half dozen years or so when the old currency was replaced by a new one. This was, in fact, a useful source of profit for the royal treasury.

Even the weather had improved since the appalling storms and cold winters recorded in the early part of the century. The climate was entering a warm period and agriculture was able to recover accordingly. King Edward, too, had done much to reduce the burden of taxation on the people, including the abolition of the heregeld or war tax that had paid for the largely Danish mercenary fleets maintained by his predecessors. The free men, at least, if not the unfree would have generally felt the benefit of this.

Once again England was a wealthy country, not just through her agriculture but through trade as far afield as Byzantium, Egypt and the Baltic countries, as well as with closer European neighbours. Exports included wool, cattle and leather, while jewellery made in Kent was highly prized. Gold, silver, ivory and precious textiles were imported and converted into art treasures that were the envy of other countries. Churches rebuilt and recovering from the ravages of earlier times were decked with precious reliquaries, gold crucifixes and precious tapestries, while exquisitely decorated books were once again appearing. English needlework was highly prized, perhaps one reason why the Bayeux Tapestry was manufactured in England rather than in Normandy.

All this was the result of more than twenty years of relative peace and prosperity, but it meant that once again England was a prize worth striving for, and the new king was well aware that he would have to fight to retain that peace and that prosperity to which he had contributed perhaps more than any other. Envious eyes were already turning towards England, and William of Poitiers, writing later of the treasures amassed there that were 'squandered shamefully in English luxury', was simply expressing the thoughts of many people who felt they would like to do some squandering of their own.

January, however, was not a month for fighting, and no doubt Harold would have realised that he had a little space at least to prepare for the challenges to come. In fact, the first few weeks passed smoothly enough. The same officials who had served Edward continued in their posts under Harold. No one was sacked, imprisoned or fled abroad. A new silver coinage was issued with the new king's head on it, neatly bearded and with a less extravagant moustache than that shown on the Tapestry. The news of the rise of Harold Godwinson to the highest position in the land was no doubt quickly spread around Europe, and later writers profess that William in Normandy, certain of his rights, made some form of protest. No record of it, however, appears in the *Chronicle*.

The only possible murmur of unease comes from Northumbria, though this is recorded in a later account of the life of Bishop Wulfstan. It is possible that the Northumbrians felt that, despite the settlement made the year before, Harold might now attempt to re-impose his brother on them as earl. Bishop Wulfstan accompanied the king on a tour of those northern lands soon after his coronation and reassurances were given that no changes were going to be made to what had been agreed.

Two things may have helped this reassurance, though we don't know the exact timing of either. At some point Waltheof, the young son of Siward, was made Earl of Huntingdon. This may have been a last act of Edward or an early act of Harold, but clearly he was confirmed in his earldom by the new king at the time of his northern tour, and this would no doubt have pleased those who had served his father for so many years.

It is also possible that this was the time that Harold entered into a Christian marriage with Eadgyth, the sister of Edwin and Morcar. Eadgyth had previously been married to Gruffydd ap Llewelyn and had been a widow since his death in August 1063. Some have suggested that Harold's marriage to her may have taken place soon after this, and others that there never was an actual marriage, only an agreement to marry. However, since the purpose of the marriage was clearly to unite the two most powerful English families and provide a legitimate heir for the new king (who already had a number of sons by Edith Swan-neck), it is most probable that it was arranged either at, or at some point soon after, the time Morcar became Earl of Northumbria, and took place very soon afterwards.

There is a striking resemblance between this marriage of Harold's and that of Cnut with Emma of Normandy some half a century before. In both cases there was a long-standing 'handfast' marriage which was not recognised by the Church and therefore did not bar the way to the second, essentially political, match. Nor was this 'handfast' wife specifically repudiated before or after the second marriage. The strong Scandinavian influence in Harold's upbringing would have influenced his outlook on such matters, though what the wives thought is not recorded. By tradition there was a strong bond of affection between Harold and Edith Swan-neck though she may well have recognised that he could always have intended a more regular dynastic marriage at some point. For Eadgyth this would be her second arranged marriage and her expectations of wedded bliss would probably have been considerably lower. There is no record of her ever being crowned as queen, but possibly there was no time for such a ceremony for events were beginning to move in such a way now as would require her husband's full attention for many months to come.

Harold returned from York to Westminster in time for Easter, which that year fell on 16 April, and then a week later something occurred which was recorded, along with a variety of omens, in all the chronicles of Europe. 'Then was, over all England, such a token seen in the heavens as no man ever before saw.' In fact it was the return of Halley's Comet, the 'long-haired star', on its regular seventy-six-year cycle of visits to earth. Very likely no man living had seen it before, although references to the comet are found earlier in the *Chronicle*. This must have been a particularly impressive show for it had all Europe agog for the seven nights that it blazed across the sky. It even features in the Bayeux Tapestry where a group is shown pointing at something that looks a little like a blazing space capsule, under the caption, 'They wonder at the star.'

Of course the Tapestry, with the benefit of hindsight, places the comet between the coronation of Harold and the preparations soon after begun by William of Normandy for his invasion. Its message is clear. The comet, widely believed to foretell some terrible disaster, is here foretelling the disaster that will befall Harold when William makes his challenge for the throne. As if to hammer home the point, immediately below the picture of the comet Harold is seen on his throne holding a lance, while in the margin below a group of ships is outlined but neither coloured nor crewed. Perhaps Harold himself is recognising the omen and foreseeing disaster as a result of an invasion. It is perhaps being over-subtle to see in the lack of colour and crews on the ships an indication that Harold does not know which of several possible invasions will be responsible for his downfall.

Whatever disaster, if any, Harold believed to be foretold by the comet, he did not intend to be caught unprepared. It is likely that in the course of his northern tour he reviewed the forces and fortifications available to defend that area. Edwin and Morcar were both young earls, untried in the field, and without undermining their authority he would have wanted to satisfy himself that they were sufficiently prepared to repel any attack on the long eastern coastline that would be the most likely target for any Scandinavian force. He would, of course, know of the reputation of Harald Hardrada and his claim that the English throne was rightly his, but he would not have been as intimately aware of his plans as he was of the plans of William of Normandy. It was, therefore, to the south coast that Harold himself would devote the greater part of his attention.

The initial warning that the invasion season had begun probably came with the appearance of Tostig, attacking the Isle of Wight in early May. Tostig had, by some accounts, spent a very busy winter scouring the courts of Europe for support to enable him to return to England. His immediate home when expelled the previous November had been in Flanders with his wife's brother, Count Baldwin, who had given him estates around Saint-Omer for his support. Tostig, though, was not prepared to accept so lowly a status.

In January he is said to have approached William of Normandy, who no doubt saw him as a useful propaganda tool, but William's plans were not Tostig's and he soon moved on. Next he tried Sweyn Estrithsson in Denmark. Sweyn was, of course, cousin to both Harold and Tostig and had his own claims on the throne of England. He was not prepared to risk all he had gained in

Denmark, however, even when Tostig urged him to act as his uncle Cnut had done and take an army to conquer England with Tostig's support. According to *King Harald's Saga*, admittedly composed from a Norwegian point of view, Sweyn declared that he was a lesser man than Cnut and would be contented with what he had. He, too, offered Tostig an earldom in Denmark but Tostig once again refused, saying he would instead seek a backer who was less of a coward than Sweyn. The saga says they parted, 'not just the best of friends'. One outcome of this, however, was that Sweyn sent a body of volunteers to fight on the side of King Harold, a sure sign that he had no intention of joining any northern challenge to his throne.

At some point, too, Tostig approached Harald Hardrada with a similar proposition, though it is not absolutely clear that he travelled to Norway himself. *King Harald's Saga* does in fact report a face-to-face meeting and a long, detailed conversation in which Tostig managed to persuade an initially reluctant Harald that the expedition would be worth his while. A large part of the persuasion consisted of Tostig promising Harald that most of England would support him if he mounted an invasion, because Tostig's brother was so unpopular there. It seems fairly clear that Harald had not enough contact with what was happening in England at this time to realise that this was patently untrue. In the end he agreed to gather ships and men for an invasion force and to meet Tostig by the Humber estuary later in the year.

In the meantime, perhaps, Tostig thought he would see what he could achieve on his own, or maybe just test the waters. Or it might be that, returning to Flanders and finding that ships and crews had been recruited on his behalf, the temptation was just too great. He would have remembered how he had stormed back into England with his father and brothers in 1052, and may have thought the same trick possible again. In this he was to be sadly disappointed.

His appearance on the Isle of Wight in May 1066 did not result in a mass of people rallying to him. True he obtained money and provisions there, but more because of the threat posed by some three dozen shiploads of fighters than for any love of his cause. Next he tried along the south coast as Godwin had done but with very little success. The men of Wessex were not prepared to support him and in revenge he attacked and burned his brother's estates as far east as Sandwich, where news of Harold's approach made him draw off to sea again.

He had picked up a few extra ships and men, though some accounts say by pressgang rather than volunteering, and now made his way up the east coast, raiding and plundering, possibly joined at this point by some reinforcements from Orkney. Certainly by the time he reached the mouth of the Humber his force amounted to sixty shiploads. Here, however, he was caught unawares by Earl Edwin and the local forces and soundly defeated. Most of his mercenaries now deserted him, taking with them the plunder they had amassed on the way, and Tostig was left with only twelve ships, retreating up the coast to Scotland where his good friend King Malcolm gave him shelter.

Harold was unlikely to have known that Tostig's raiding was simply one man trying his luck. Although early in the year, it could have been the start of all manner of things – a simple reconnaissance on behalf of William of Normandy, or maybe a diversion to draw Harold away from the true site of an invasion by either William or Harald Hardrada. What was clear, though, was that it was time to put in place the substantial defences that would be needed to either deter or defeat an attack coming from either of these two enemies. Consequently the *Chronicle* tells us that Harold now called out the greatest land force and ship force that any king had ever assembled.

The frequently offered theory that the English forces of the time were simply a bunch of peasants, untrained and poorly armed, is well wide of the mark. In fact the reputation of the English military was widely respected. One reason given in the sagas for Harald Hardrada's initial reluctance to get involved was the bravery of the English professional fighter that they called a 'thingsman', one of whom was felt to be better than two of his own men.

The 'thingsman' referred to was known in English as a housecarl and these formed the core of any English army. Although earlier kings would have had some form of warrior elite attached to their households, it was Cnut that introduced the 'huscarl' or housecarl as such, possibly drawing on the idea of the Jomsvikings with whom he had mingled in his youth. A housecarl would be a skilled professional fighter, one of an elite band that would live and train and fight together, bound by a code of honour that punished disloyalty with death. Unlike other forces they would be paid regular wages in peace time as well as in war, and this and the cost of their weapons and other equipment would initially have been financed by the heregeld or army tax. When Edward abolished that tax in 1051 he must have borne the cost himself for there was no reduction in the role and number of the housecarls. There is some evidence that the tax was in fact reintroduced in the later years of his reign.

The royal housecarl might be a mercenary or a person of the thegn class, with or without land of his own, but his obligations would be a personal bond between the king and himself. Bodyguard, standing army, garrison, even tax collector, he fulfilled a variety of roles and was highly valued. It has been estimated that in 1066 there were something like 3,000 royal housecarls, and by this time earls had housecarls of their own, similarly well trained and equipped. Together they would have formed the basis of a formidable army, but these were not the only forces on which the king could draw for the defence of his realm.

In a throwback to their German tribal origins, there was an obligation on all freemen in Anglo-Saxon England to bear arms when called upon by the king to defend their local area. This 'general fyrd' as it was called would have been the most numerous but also the weakest part of any army. Consisting mainly of local farming stock, it would have had the least training and the poorest weapons and equipment, and in addition could not be required to fight anywhere outside their own shire. Indeed the rules stated that they had to be allowed to go home at night. Like many of the ancient military arrangements found in England, the general fyrd was clearly seen as a defensive rather than an offensive body, and while no doubt they would fight fiercely for the protection of their own homes, they would only be of limited use to the king in more general conflicts.

Of far more importance would be the so-called 'select fyrd' or shire levy. This was a body of men that could only be called out by the king, though they were organised on a shire basis and would have been led by an earl, a bishop or a sheriff. The obligation to serve was based on landholding, and though we only have the fullest description of how this operated in Berkshire, it was unlikely to be significantly different elsewhere.

The system required that one man would be provided for the select fyrd for every five hides of land. This might mean that a thegn holding five hides would go himself, or if he held more land would select another or others to go with him. Those with less land would be grouped together to satisfy this duty, so that, perhaps, a village would send a man on behalf of all of them. The records seem to show that the same men would be sent regularly for a period of years, and they were largely but by no means exclusively of the thegn class. Ceorls, usually of the higher level, would also go to make up the shire levy, and no doubt it would be seen as an honour to do so.

The five-hide unit responsible for sending a man was also responsible for equipping him and providing him with four shillings per hide for his pay and support. This would cover the two-month period for which he could be required to serve anywhere in the kingdom and possibly beyond. The representatives from a shire would usually stay together while training and fighting so that they became an efficient unit, used to working together. King Alfred established a rota system so that only half the due number would serve at any one time. This was to enable necessary agricultural work to continue in their absence, and it is likely that this was continued except in times of real emergency. Nor would all the shire levies necessarily be called out at once but only when needed, perhaps from two or three areas at a time.

The shire levy would have been well equipped. Even a lesser thegn would be expected to provide at least one horse with its necessary saddlery and equipment, as well as his own basic weapons, while those of higher status would have more horses and better weapons. Even a ceorl would be properly equipped by those who sent him, and one can imagine the honour of the local area being at stake as village competed with village to provide the best possible representative for the king's army.

Together the housecarls and select fyrd would have given Harold a force potentially numbering many thousands. A maximum figure of 25,000 has been suggested, though changing circumstances make it difficult to be exact. There is no evidence that they would have been less well equipped than those they would eventually face on the battlefield, and given the wealth of the country, every reason to expect that the housecarls, earls and greater thegns at least would have had the finest weapons and best body armour available.

For these elite troops, armour would have consisted of a coat of mail made up of many thousands of metal rings linked together, hence the name of 'ringmail'. This, usually worn over a padded undergarment, covered them to the knee with wide sleeves reaching at least to the elbow. Earlier versions began at the neck with a laced-up slit down the chest for easy access, but later a mailed hood was incorporated into what became known as a hauberk, and it is this type of mail that is depicted for both sides on the Bayeux Tapestry. A slit front and back allowed the fighter to be mounted while the mail would still protect his upper legs. The weight of the hauberk would be considerable but it afforded a measure of protection from a sword slash while affording complete flexibility of movement. It could still be pierced by an arrow, though, and a blow from a battleaxe, while not piercing the rings, was likely to leave broken bones beneath.

Those without mail would have had some protection from a boiled leather jerkin, possibly reinforced by metal rings in places, and all but the very poorest of fighters would have worn a helmet.

These were made of iron, roughly conical in shape and fashioned either from one piece of metal or from four pieces riveted and bound by a metal ring. The better ones would have been padded with leather around the base to make them more comfortable to wear. Most would have had a metal nose-piece attached, and if the owner did not have a hooded hauberk there might be a metal or ringmail flap at the back to protect the neck.

Again, weapons would vary according to the wealth and status of the fighter. Spears were common to all, and with a variety of heads both broad and narrow, they were used for both throwing and stabbing. Earls and leading thegns would have had a number of these of both types, and lesser men probably only one of the latter.

Only the very rich had swords, a status symbol that has been likened to a top-of-the-range people carrier in modern motoring terms. That they were highly prized possessions is indicated by the fact that they were passed down from father to son, and the reputation of a previous owner would add to the value. An earl would have had several and a wealthy thegn probably one or two. They were broad bladed and double-edged, with a crossguard curving towards the blade to protect the hand and a heavy pommel at the end of the grip to provide the necessary balance. They would have been carried in a scabbard lined with sheep's wool, the lanolin in the fleece helping to prevent the blade from rusting. Those without swords would have had a 'long seax', the long, single-edged knife that curved to a sharp point. Many with swords, in fact, carried a seax as well.

The weapon most closely associated with housecarls is the broad-bladed battleaxe. First introduced by the Vikings and still common among Scandinavians and their descendants, this was a formidable weapon. Long-handled and wielded with strength and skill, the broad, curved blade could slice through wood, leather, flesh, bone and possibly some weaker forms of ringmail. Its disadvantage was that it was a two-handed weapon and therefore the wielder would not have the protection of a shield, though evidence suggests such fighters tended to operate with a partner armed with shield and sword, as well as relying on their own agility to keep from harm.

Smaller, lighter one-handed axes were used by other fighters when engaged in hand-to-hand combat, and these also formed one of a wide range of thrown missiles, from clubs to crude stone hammers, as well as the more sophisticated spears. Slings were commonly used for hunting and it is likely that the poorer but more skilled members of the select fyrd would have employed these in conflict. They may have been common among the general fyrd when these were called out to protect their homes.

More controversial is the issue of archers. It is frequently claimed that Harold had none, but it is inconceivable that a commander of his stature and expertise would have deprived himself of any useful weapon. It may be misleading that there is no mention of a bow among the war gear of earls and thegns, but at this time the archer had not achieved the status he would reach in future centuries, and even then the war bow was a weapon of the people rather than the great lords. The Danes in particular used the bow extensively in hunting and in war, and there would be a strong Scandinavian influence among the select fyrd drawn from the Danelaw regions. It is likely that, rather than using massed archers as a major offensive weapon, they would have been employed behind the main lines in something like a sniper role, picking off targets at short range. Further confusion is added by the fact that the word used for arrow in the language of the time is the same as that for a throwing spear, and it is among these 'missile men' that archers would be found.

As well as his land army, Harold could also call on the services of a navy, instituted centuries before by the far-sighted Alfred and maintained to a greater or lesser extent ever since. Though the strong mercenary core of ships and men had been paid off by Edward, he had nonetheless maintained a fleet and used it regularly, both in training manoeuvres in the Channel and in earnest against an enemy. Onslaughts on both Wales and Scotland had been supported by naval forces in the years before 1066, and Harold was probably more experienced in maritime matters than most of his predecessors.

The English ships, though based on the standard Viking longship of the time, were likely to have been modified for use in coastal waters. Alfred himself had ordered that they be made 'most serviceable', with thirty pairs of oars and a higher freeboard. There was a single deck with a central mast and one large square sail, and the ship was controlled by a steersman using a large steering oar pivoted on the starboard side. For fighting at sea a number of ships would be lashed together to provide a solid base for the soldiers, who would then fight in the same way as they would on land. During the winter the fleet would normally be beached at London, possibly in Viking-style 'ship-houses', but the country's major naval base was at Sandwich where it could command both the North Sea and the Channel. The Isle of Wight was also used extensively for harbouring and provisioning of ships.

There were a number of sources of ships and men for this navy. First the king himself would probably have owned some ships and could hire or commandeer others. More importantly, the embryonic 'Cinque Ports' along the south-east coast had to provide a number of ships and their crews for his service in exchange for their special privileges in other matters. In 1066, for example, Sandwich and Dover had each to provide twenty fully crewed ships for the king, while the numbers varied for other places. The length of service of these ships was, however, fairly short, though it is likely it could have been extended, perhaps by a rota system in times of emergency.

In addition to this there was a 'ship fyrd' relying on the same basic method as the select fyrd. In certain areas groups of three hundred hides would together be required to produce a ship and sixty fully equipped men for service at sea. They would not necessarily be sailors, for crews could be hired fairly easily, but their obligation would be to serve for the same two months as for the select fyrd. There is some evidence that, when the king called out the shire levy, he could specify whether service would be on land or at sea, and that different men could be sent accordingly. Some inland areas would also have alternatives if a ship fyrd was called, such as sending transport for provisions or money to hire specialist seamen.

These, then, were the forces on which Harold would call in 1066. It has been estimated that his great land force and ship force at its maximum could have been around three thousand housecarls, royal and otherwise, some twenty to twenty-five thousand from the select fyrd and maybe two hundred and fifty ships and their crews. He had now to deploy this force to the greatest effect to safeguard his realm from the multiple dangers that threatened it in the first months of his reign.

6

HAROLD: THE FIRST CHALLENGE
8–25 SEPTEMBER 1066

It has been well said that wars are won and lost on intelligence and certainly a good network of spies would have made Harold's job a great deal easier in 1066. We can be fairly sure he had some men in Normandy. William of Poitiers tells a story of one of them being captured and brought before the duke, who seemed happy enough to send him home to tell Harold of the preparations for invasion that he had been shown. According to this source, William of Normandy personally told the man to tell Harold he could keep his kingdom in peace if within a year William had not arrived to take it from him – but of course he did not specify when within that year he would be making his attempt to do so.

It is highly likely that William was better informed as to what was happening in England. There was close contact between certain abbeys on each side of the Channel, and in particular the Norman abbey of Fécamp had been given estates in Sussex. The ordinary course of business would involve regular coming and going between them, and even without any malicious intent a great deal could be discovered by simple gossip about what was happening in the area. Even better placed for gossip was King Edward's former chaplain, Osbern, a cousin of William of Normandy, who had been given the ecclesiastical estate at Bosham, right in the heart of Harold's own lands. Another relative of William, Robert Fitzwimarc, also had estates on the south coast.

It has been suggested that Harold could have improved his position by expelling these possible 'eyes' of his enemy, but he made no such move. Maybe he was himself profiting by the gossip. It has also been argued that they might provide a focal point for the invasion and therefore enable him to concentrate his defences. William might be more likely to invade at a place where he could expect to find a friendly welcome. He could not, however, concentrate his forces solely on these areas in case William, following the same line of reasoning, decided to strike elsewhere.

It seems less likely that Harold had spies at the court of Harald Hardrada in Norway. His contacts were mainly Danish and would be unwelcome in the land of their very recent enemy. He seems, however, to have regarded this as the lesser threat and left it to his northern earls to guard their part of the country. They had, after all, proved more than able to deal with the raids of Tostig and his followers. When, therefore, his forces were assembled at the beginning of May, they were deployed along the south coast, while Harold himself took his fleet to the Isle of Wight, ready to intercept any invasion force setting out from Normandy.

Much has been made of the logistical feat of Duke William in keeping his army together and fed for probably a little over a month, while waiting for favourable winds to sail to England. In fact Harold kept his on standby for something like four months. Sadly we have no details as to how this was achieved. Some three and a half centuries later Henry V had all the bakers and brewers in several counties working to feed his army of around twelve thousand men in the same general area, and no doubt a similar operation was needed in 1066, presumably paid for by the money the select fyrd had brought with them for their own subsistence. The chronicles simply record that they remained in the field all through the summer and into the autumn, from May to September. This was twice the normal length of service of the select fyrd, and though their service could be extended in a national emergency, it suggests that something like Alfred's rota system was being used. It also seems likely that some part at least of the general fyrd must have been involved, and again some form of rota must have been used or throughout this long time no hay would have been made, no sheep shorn and no livestock raised in all the country roundabout.

They waited, and they waited and no invasion came. By September food was running short and no doubt there was some desperation to get in the corn harvest. This was a time when all hands were needed in every village, and failure to harvest inevitably meant famine the following year. On 8 September, therefore, the army was finally stood down. The *Chronicle* records: 'Then were the men's provisions gone, and no man could any longer keep them there.' At the same time the fleet set out for its winter quarters in London, though not all reached this safe haven. Their losses are usually attributed to storms in the Channel, which would not be at all unusual at that time of year.

On the other side of the water the fleet assembled by William was also moving about this time and also suffering losses, again put down to bad weather. It has been suggested, however, that these two fleets, or at least some part of them, may possibly have encountered each other mid-Channel and fought some kind of action, and that their losses were at least in part as a result of this. William of Poitiers declares that Duke William tried to hide his losses and buried the dead secretly, though he too says the losses were due to storms.

Whether by storms or conflict, the remnants of the fleets limped home to their respective ports, the English to London and the Normans to St Valery at the mouth of the Somme. Either way this seemed to confirm what Harold had believed when he disbanded his forces. The fighting season was over. There would be no invasion in 1066.

We might regard Harold as an unlucky king – an inscription on a memorial calls him Harold the Unfortunate – although to those living at the time it was the hand of God that was against him. Just as he was beginning to see the threat of William's invasion receding in the south, another appeared in the north. It is very unlikely Harald Hardrada knew when the English king stood down his forces. He had simply been gathering his ships and men through the summer and, like William, waiting for a favourable wind. Indeed, if he had had his own spies in England he might not have been so quick to accept Tostig's promise that the English king was unpopular and the majority of the people would rise up to support a Norwegian invasion.

Our most detailed information about Hardrada's invasion comes from *King Harald's Saga,* part of the *Heimskringla* put together in Iceland by Snorri Sturluson in around 1230 from old poems and traditions relating to the kings of Norway. Though distinctly wobbly on the English background – it has Tostig as the elder brother and places him in England at the time of King Edward's death – it nevertheless gives a lot of circumstantial information about the campaign that could well have been provided by those Norwegians who were there.

According to the saga, what Hardrada lacked in concrete information he more than made up for in omens, which, if true, make it surprising he ever set off in the first place. No less than three dreams are reported all involving witch-wives, wolves and ravens, the scavengers of the battlefield, and all predicting woe for the king. Hardrada himself dreamt of his brother, the sainted Olaf, who told him that his own death was near and his corpse would feed the crows, 'the witch-wife's steed'. It is not surprising, then, to find that before he left Trondheim he had his son Magnus proclaimed king of Norway to rule in his absence.

Another son, Olaf, sailed with him, along with two daughters and their mother, his queen Ellisif (Elizabeth), the daughter of Jaroslav of Kiev, whom he had won on his travels. They landed first at Shetland and then Orkney, where the queen and her daughters remained. Here he collected more ships and men, together with two earls of Orkney, Paul and Erlend, before setting off again southwards down the east coast of Scotland. It is probable Tostig joined him somewhere here with whatever forces he had managed to assemble, though the saga places the meeting later, when Hardrada first landed in Northumbria.

Estimates of the size of the fleet vary – three hundred ships according to the *Chronicle*, five hundred according to John of Worcester – and allowance must be made for natural exaggeration by both winners and losers. The figure of three hundred is regarded as more likely, however, and taking a minimum of forty men in each, this gives a rough estimate of at least twelve thousand available as a fighting force for Hardrada. Unusually, we are told he also took some horses, having experience of transporting these animals during his time in the east.

The first place to feel the impact was Cleveland where, burnt and plundered, they must have thought the bad old days had returned with a vengeance. Scarborough put up some resistance. The saga describes how Hardrada had a mighty fire kindled on the cliff overlooking the town, and when all was blazing pitched the whole lot down upon the houses below, 'so that one house caught fire after the other' until the town surrendered. There was much plunder to be had here, but this force was after more than plunder and they quickly moved on down the coast.

By now news of the invasion was spreading. At Holderness by the mouth of the Humber, Hardrada and Tostig were met for the first time by some organised opposition, possibly the general fyrd stiffened by some of the select fyrd. There was a skirmish and the victory went to the invaders, who sailed on into the Humber and then up the Ouse towards York. With all this taking place in the first weeks of September, it is suggested that the earliest King Harold in London could have had the news of the sacking of Scarborough was the sixteenth of that month, and only then if a fast relay of horses had carried messengers at speed along the old Roman road.

In the meantime the northern earls, Edwin and Morcar, were summoning their own forces. There is some evidence that they had a fleet of ships at Tadcaster on the River Wharfe, and these were sent down river to the junction with the Ouse to try and intercept the invaders. Whether this was a serious challenge or simply a delaying tactic to give the earls longer to assemble the fyrd, we don't know. In the event they were clearly outnumbered and easily driven back by Hardrada, whose multitude of ships must have filled the river for miles.

The one effect of this brief contact was to persuade Hardrada that proceeding further up the Ouse might be dangerous. The English fleet had retreated up the Wharfe, but if they were to return, possibly in greater numbers, they could cut the Norwegians off from the sea. Consequently he turned back a little way and established a camp on the northern bank of the Ouse at Riccall, some ten miles south of York. Ships were beached and a body of men left on guard, while Hardrada and Tostig and the remainder of the men set out for the city itself. On 20 September, less than a mile from the centre of York, they found earls Edwin and Morcar blocking the way at a place called Fulford, and the scene was set for the first battle of 1066.

Overshadowed as it was by what followed, Fulford tends to be the forgotten battle and many of the details are controversial. In some accounts it is a brief, fierce clash, barely more than a skirmish, while in others it is a grinding battle lasting most of the day. Even the site is disputed although different accounts describe it clearly and the local inhabitants seem to have no doubts. Large parts of it are still visible though unmarked, but are about to disappear for ever under a housing estate.

Another point of debate is the size of the armies engaged. The saga describes the English as 'an immense army' while others have put the total number involved at less than a thousand. The largest estimate gives Hardrada something like six thousand men and Edwin and Morcar rather less, but again we must bear in mind the tendency to exaggerate numbers involved in any battle.

What is not in dispute is the difference in experience in the respective commanders of these armies. Edwin and Morcar were young men. Edwin was probably in his early twenties and had been Earl of Mercia only a few years. Morcar, his brother, was a couple of years younger and had received his earldom less than a year before. Neither had ever fought a battle or been involved in anything other than minor skirmishing. By contrast Harald Hardrada had been successfully leading armies in the east before they were born. Though probably in his late fifties by now, rather elderly for a warrior, there is never a suggestion that he had lost any of his skill and shrewdness in commanding a battlefield.

It has been said that the English earls need not have fought Hardrada at all, that they could have withdrawn inside the fortified city of York and waited for the king to bring a bigger army to their aid. This seems very neat with the benefit of hindsight but the picture at the time would not have been so clear-cut. York is a very long way from London, and though news of the invasion had been sent, there would be no way of knowing how long it would take for aid to reach them. Nor could they be absolutely sure that King Harold was not by now engaged in struggles of his own with a southern invasion from Normandy. There would be a strong disinclination to allow the Norwegians free rein to ravage the country round about (where no doubt the important work of getting in the harvest was still in full swing) and there may have been doubts about the strength of the fortifications around the city itself. And anyway, their king had told them to defend the northern part of his kingdom and that was what they intended to do. It would not at the time have seemed too rash a decision to tackle this threat head-on as soon as possible, while perhaps the invaders had not yet got their full strength assembled.

At Fulford there was a bend in the Ouse and the land rose gently away from the river to where the main road led, and still leads, into York itself. The ridge carrying the road was a few hundred yards wide and beyond this was marshy ground, increasingly boggy in the direction of what is today known as East Moor and West Moor. Across this ground a brook known today as Germany Beck flows and this is likely to be the ditch mentioned in all accounts of the battle.

The two armies drew up facing each other across the width of the ridge, with one flank on the river and the other on the marshy land. If, as is usually suggested, the English had the choice of the battlefield, they may well have felt that this position gave them the greatest protection from any outflanking manoeuvre. Hardrada placed his strongest forces next to the river on his left, where he himself commanded under his famous banner, the 'Land-Waster'. The weaker end of his line, probably containing English and Scots and some from Flanders, was to the right commanded by Tostig. Facing them, Edwin had his men nearer the river, while perhaps deliberately Morcar's forces faced those of his predecessor in the earldom across the beck towards the right of their line.

The standard method of fighting at the time for both English and Scandinavians was the shield wall, a predominately infantry battle. Close-packed formations of shields had been used as far back as Greek and Roman times for both offensive and defensive purposes, and something similar is still seen today with the shields of riot police. By eleventh-century England, however, it was deployed a little more flexibly. The common image of poorly trained yokels packed shoulder to shoulder behind round Saxon shields does little justice to the skilled infantry of the times.

By 1066 the round shield had largely given way to the kite-shaped shield, as depicted for both sides on the Bayeux Tapestry. The obvious advantage of this was to give some protection to the legs of the warriors standing in the front row of battle. Shields were typically made of lime wood, covered in leather and often rimmed with metal. A solid metal boss in the centre covering the handgrip could be used as a weapon in its own right, even if the shield itself was to be broken. Kite shields tended to be lighter and more easily manoeuvred than the earlier round shields, and the lower edge could be braced against the ground, giving added strength to a defensive formation.

When used in this way, interlocked shields bristling with lances and swords could make a very effective wall against an oncoming enemy, while for offensive purposes it could advance together as a pushing, stabbing weapon, or spread out a little, allowing freer access to the enemy for axemen, archers and javelin throwers. Its basic weakness was that it relied heavily on the morale of those making up the formation. Sudden panic, the death of a king or commander or a perceived weakness in part of the wall could result in its splintering into separate parts, all vulnerable to the attack of a more determined enemy.

The fullest account of the battle at Fulford is given in *King Harald's Saga*, which, though mistaken in details, is probably accurate as to the general course of events. It makes clear that, although it was the English that attacked first, the tactics were likely to have been dictated by Hardrada throughout. The positioning of Tostig opposite Morcar if accidental was very fortunate, and if deliberate very shrewd. This, together with the fact that the invasion forces here were clearly weaker, made it the obvious place for an inexperienced earl to attack.

Morcar duly did just that, following a bout of missile throwing with a steady advance and pushing back the weaker lines ahead of him. The saga records that Morcar obviously expected the Norwegian force to break and flee but they did no such thing. Instead he found himself attacked on the flank by the greater part of Hardrada's men, surrounded and cut off from his brother, and forced back into the ditch and the marsh beyond. There was such a great slaughter that these watery traps became filled with corpses, 'so thickly strewed ... they paved a way across the fen'.

On the right flank Edwin was faring no better. There is a suggestion that at the beginning of the battle not all of Hardrada's men had arrived, and that it was reinforcements that put to flight the forces of the Earl of Mercia. Whoever it was, their victory was complete, with those who could fleeing north up the river bank, and many others drowning in the waters of the Ouse. It was said that in fact more men were drowned than killed in battle that day, but the result was the same. At the end of the day it was the Norwegians that had the mastery of the battlefield.

One of the mistakes of the saga is to wax lyrical about the death of Morcar, who along with his brother in fact survived. Many others didn't. Once again there are disputes about the number of casualties – as high as 15 per cent by one account – but the *Chronicle* suggests they came from both sides, with the English inflicting considerable harm before they were in their turn routed. There is little doubt, though, that the defeat was a severe setback and greatly weakened the ranks of the English army. Certainly there seemed no question of a renewal of fighting.

Unusually, Hardrada did not immediately follow up his victory by attacking and burning the city so near at hand. Possibly Tostig wanted it intact, or it may have been seen as a useful winter base for an army. Nor, it seems, did he come with his full army when he did arrive. Harald and Tostig, we are told, came to York 'with as much people as seemed meet to them', and the city was immediately surrendered. On Sunday 24 September a 'thing' or council was held outside the walls where Hardrada stated his terms before all the people. He wanted provisions for his army and hostages from all the great families around, well known of course to Tostig. He proposed that in return for his peace and friendship, all the northern lords should support him in his campaign to claim the entire country. A further meeting was then arranged for the next day when provisions and hostages were to be delivered to him at a place some eight miles to the east of York, at Stamford Bridge.

Who named this meeting place and why, we don't know. The account in the saga is contradictory, first suggesting that Harald had moved his army there immediately after Fulford, and then saying he 'returned down to his ships' at Riccall after the Sunday meeting, and set off from there the next day. If the choice was Harald's it seems surprising. Although Stamford Bridge is on the River Derwent there is no suggestion Harald had any ships there. In fact it is clear his fleet remained at Riccall throughout, some ten miles away overland. Again, the saga describes him dividing his army on the Monday morning, with a third, including his son Olaf and the two earls from Orkney, remaining at Riccall, while two-thirds accompanied him to Stamford Bridge. Clearly, then, if the army had ever been at Stamford Bridge it had returned to base before this. One possible explanation for this manoeuvre might be if it was foraging for food in that direction, having exhausted the resources around Riccall.

If Harald chose Stamford Bridge it argues a confidence in his position bordering on recklessness. Otherwise it has been suggested that it was nominated as a suitably central place to which provisions and hostages could be brought and handed over, though it is hard to see what advantages it could have over York, just a few miles away. There is, however, just a small possibility that the meeting place was suggested by an Englishman who was aware that something else was happening in the country nearby.

It is a mistake to say that the defeat at Fulford caused King Harold to come north to rescue his beleaguered earls. In fact he must have left London long before any news of such a defeat could possibly have reached him. Once again there is a dispute about exactly when he left, the earliest date being 16 September and the latest the 20th. What is definitely recorded is that he reached Tadcaster, some ten miles south-west of York, on 24 September. This is a prodigious amount of ground to cover in a few days and means that the king and his followers must all have been mounted, and probably all had spare horses to share the rigours of the journey. He would have had with him his own housecarls and possibly those of his brothers, leading thegns and perhaps some of the select fyrd just stood down from the south coast, though it is unlikely he would leave that coast entirely unprotected. For the rest he must have called out the select fyrd for the third time that year as he travelled north. There is evidence for people from as far afield as Worcester and Essex joining his force so it is likely that the Midland and Eastern shires made up the bulk of this army.

Somewhere on the journey he would have heard of Fulford and also, probably, of the disposal of the Norwegian fleet at Riccall. The most direct road would have taken him straight past there and he clearly avoided it. At Tadcaster he would have had the full details of the rout at Fulford, probably from some who were there who had fled in that direction. He must also have learned of the current situation in York, how Tostig and Hardrada had withdrawn, leaving the city open and unguarded, and of the meeting arranged for Stamford Bridge the next day. It argues for his confidence in the local population that he believed they would rally to him again, despite their recent defeat and the still present and very real danger of the enemy forces. There was a strong Scandinavian presence in York but in general it was Danish rather than Norwegian and there was little love lost between them at the time. These were the people Harold had visited and won over earlier in the year, and though the saga talks of people flocking to Hardrada as Tostig had foretold, there is little evidence of any popular support for his invasion. Instead the *Chronicle* tells of 'Harold, our king' coming north to defend his people.

By some accounts having assembled and reviewed his forces at Tadcaster, Harold passed straight on to York, arriving after sunset and spending the night in the city. Others suggest he remained at Tadcaster and only entered York early the next morning. The detail recorded that all the gates of York were closed and closely guarded to prevent any word of the presence of the English army reaching the invaders perhaps argues for the former being more likely. Either way his men would have had at least a few hours to rest and recover after their long journey.

The loyalty of the English, or the precautions taken by Harold, proved supremely effective for it is clear that Hardrada set out the next morning with not the least idea that his enemy was close at hand. Not only was he separating himself from his fleet and from a third of his army, but, the weather being unseasonably hot, he and his men left behind most of their armour. They had ten miles to travel and no doubt the thought of doing this in padded garments and ring mail was unattractive, but to make this journey across hostile territory to such a meeting with only helmets, shields, spears and swords seems inexplicable in a commander with the experience of Hardrada. Perhaps once again he was relying on Tostig's word that the local population were in favour of his invasion.

Arriving at Stamford Bridge, he seems equally lax. On a hot day it is likely that he and his men would have waited near the river where they could cool themselves, but he seems to have set no lookouts around the place nor used any scouts to keep a watch round about. The 'Stone-Ford', a ridge of rock under the river bed, had been a crossing point on the Derwent from before Roman times. Four Roman roads crossed at the river, and a bridge soon gave the place its name, though in 1066 the wooden bridge was probably a little up-river from the current crossing. The land there is gently undulating, rising a little on each side of the river. It is the sort of place where it would have been a good idea to keep a lookout but apparently Hardrada had none.

The saga says their first sign of an oncoming force was a cloud of dust 'as from horses' feet' coming over the ridge of what is now Gate Helmsley Common, less than a mile away. Under this they saw the sun glinting on shields and armour. A discussion followed about who this host could be, whether friends or relations of Tostig's coming to join them, or some hostile army. It must have seemed improbable that, having soundly defeated the local forces only a few days before, another such could already have been assembled against them. There seemed even at this point no idea that King Harold himself could have been in the neighbourhood, but as the host drew nearer and their numbers appeared greater, it became clear that this was no friendly deputation, 'and their shining arms were to the sight like glittering ice'. Tostig suggested they should retreat with all speed to their ships since they were poorly prepared for a battle. Instead Hardrada decided to stand his ground, though he sent three of his fastest riders back to Riccall to call up reinforcements.

The bulk of the Norwegian force must have been already on the eastern side of the river, possibly receiving some of the provisions promised at this meeting place. Certainly they were all there by the time King Harold's army reached the western side, and there would have been little time for some thousands of men to cross on what was apparently the only narrow wooden bridge.

There are different accounts of what followed, both of them plausible as delaying tactics while Hardrada's forces got themselves prepared for some sort of defensive action, and both involving a certain amount of self-sacrifice on the side of the invaders. It is possible that both or neither actually took place.

The saga records that twenty horsemen rode out from the English ranks to parley with the Norwegians. One demanded to know if Tostig was there, whereupon Tostig himself stepped forward to reply that he was. A message was then delivered that King Harold would offer him the whole of Northumbria to rule for himself if he would submit to him rather than fighting. Tostig answered that this was rather different from Harold's attitude the year before, and that many lives would have been saved if he'd made this offer at that time. What, he then demanded, would the king offer to Tostig's ally, Hardrada, if he accepted these terms. Seven feet of English soil came the answer, 'or as much more as he may be taller than other men'. Then go and prepare for battle, declared Tostig, for it must not be said he would desert his ally in such a way. They would die together with honour or win all England by a victory. The horsemen then returned to their lines.

There was, however, a sting in the tail in the saga's account. Hardrada, who may not have followed the conversation very well in English, asked Tostig who the man was who had delivered the message so boldly. 'That was King Harold Godwinson,' came the reply. Whereupon Hardrada declared that if he'd known that earlier, the man would never have returned alive to his army. Here Tostig makes his second noble statement. I knew you would have killed him if I'd named him, he says, 'and I would rather he should be my murderer than I his'.

Stirring stuff and just the sort of thing the saga-makers loved. Whether Harold ever made such an offer seems unlikely. It would mean abandoning the two young earls who had just fought so hard for him a few days before. There was likely to have been some sort of parley, however, and Harold may have taken the opportunity to have a good look at his opponent, Hardrada, whose reputation he must have known well. Their assessment of each other, as recorded in the saga, is not particularly flattering. Hardrada described Harold as a 'little man', while in another passage where the Norwegian's horse is said to have stumbled and thrown him, King Harold asked, 'who is that stout man that fell from his horse', though he does add that he was a great man and of stately appearance.

The delaying tactic described in the *Chronicle* is of a rather more traditional turn. In a piece that was apparently added after the rest of the account it tells of one lone Norwegian warrior defending the wooden bridge against all comers. History is full of such heroics, from Horatius at the bridge in Roman times to the early part of the Battle of Maldon where the Vikings were held at bay until given permission to cross and fight on equal terms with Britnoth and his men.

This particular unnamed young man would not be so lucky. Hardrada was not likely to give permission to cross, and if he did it would not be an equal fight since most of the Vikings' war gear was ten miles away in their ships at Riccall. Any delay, however, would make it more likely that reinforcements from that direction might reach them in time, so if such a lone action was possible it would certainly have been attempted.

Presumably armed only with shield, helmet and battleaxe, this one warrior seems to have made quite a stand. When frontal attack failed he was shot at by an archer, and when that failed he was assailed from the river itself. While his attention was diverted by further frontal attacks a boat was launched to pass under the bridge, whereupon he was stabbed from below through gaps in the planking.

Again, while plausible enough, there are some problems with this tale. The *Chronicle* says the warrior was stabbed 'under the coat of mail' and we know the Norwegians had left all such armour behind. Then again it seems unlikely that if Harold had archers with him they could not have disposed of him fairly efficiently, or indeed if he had fallen and the bridge was such a crucial factor in Hardrada's plans, another or others could not have taken his place. Once again we are left to conclude that there was probably some delaying action fought at the bridge though whether it was on the heroic terms described is another matter.

In the meantime Hardrada had had ample opportunity to draw up his forces for action in the best way possible. He had moved up the rise away from the river to flatter land commanding the slight slope. He seems to have been anticipating cavalry action on the part of the English, possibly misled by the fact that a large part of Harold's force would have arrived on horseback. The saga refers to the English as 'an immense army of both cavalry and infantry', but actually fighting on horseback was not the English way and there was no real reason why they would do so on this occasion.

Caught by surprise and unprepared in the extreme, Hardrada's tactics had initially at least to be purely defensive, and once again it is the saga that provides details. Mindful of the dangers of mounted troops, he drew up his forces in a circular formation, thinly but evenly spread all round. Interlocked shields and spears braced against the ground formed a solid barrier and deterrence against cavalry attack. Within this ring were archers and other missile men, together with Hardrada and Tostig themselves and their own personal retinues ready to rush to strengthen the shield wall wherever this might be most needed.

By the time all this was arranged and the enemy was upon them it was probably early afternoon, the hottest part of a hot day. Again the saga describes the mounted English riding against the defensive wall and being easily repulsed and made to circle more warily around it. This may indeed have been an initial impulse to test the resolve of the defenders, but it would surely have been quickly apparent that something more decisive would be needed. The fighting at this point is described as 'light and loose'.

However, the shield wall was broken. It seems likely that this would have resulted from a determined assault by the heavily armed and armoured infantry of Harold's army against men lacking all body armour. The saga, on the other hand, insists that it was a deliberate act on the part of the Norwegians, who, finding the English mounted attacks to be weak and ineffective, thought they could charge them and put them to flight. If that is so it was a big mistake.

As soon as the wall was fragmented the English attacked in force, and in fierce hand-to-hand fighting their opponents were cut down in great numbers. Seeing this, Hardrada and his men rushed forward to reinforce the faltering line, the mighty warrior himself charging into the thickest of the fray in a beserker rage, carving his way through the opposing force with great two-handed blows from his battleaxe. The saga claims this charge came close to putting the English to flight but it carried Hardrada clear of his own men. Taking the opportunity that offered, an English archer took aim and an arrow in the windpipe put an end to the greatest Viking warrior of his age, while those around him were cut down without mercy. Only the famous battle banner was carried back to safety within a wall that reformed as each side briefly disengaged. It marked the end of the first phase of the battle.

'The army stands in hushed dismay,' wrote Thiodolf the skald. 'Stilled is the clamour of the fray.' Certainly there was a pause while both sides took stock. For a little it seemed as if the fighting might be over. King Harold apparently offered peace and mercy to Tostig and the surviving northmen, but instead his brother took up the banner of Hardrada, the Norwegians roared their defiance and the battle began again.

This second phase seems to have involved some of the fiercest fighting. Hand to hand with sword, spear and battleaxe, no quarter was asked or given on either side, but the losses of the invading army were greater than the English, and among them was Tostig. It has been suggested that he was killed by Harold himself but in the height of battle it might be hard to say who struck the fatal blow. The body, much mutilated, was later recovered and given honourable burial in York.

By now it was late afternoon, and just when King Harold might have felt victory was in his grasp, a new force arrived. The men dispatched to Riccall so long before had delivered their message and the response had been immediate. Eystein Orri, one of Hardrada's commanders and the man who was to marry his daughter Maria, had instantly set out, armed and armoured, with a large force of men to the relief of his beleaguered leader. Covering ten miles in the hot sun, and finding another river crossing at Kexby, they now came smashing into Harold's weary army in what has come to be known as Orri's Storm.

The saga says they were exhausted and hardly fit to fight when they arrived, but once the fury of battle came upon them they fought as long as they could stand upright, defending the Land-Waster banner that was now in Orri's possession. For a while it seemed as though they might carry the field, and certainly the English losses were heavy at this time, but eventually their exertions caught up with them. We are told they threw off their ring mail, which might seem a reckless action, but possibly the choice was between death in battle and death by heat exhaustion, and they preferred to die like Vikings around their fallen king.

By evening all the chief men among the invaders were dead, and those others who could were fleeing the battlefield in the direction of their ships. Even now they were not safe as the English pursued and slaughtered them all the way to Riccall, and very few were those who came back from Stamford Bridge that day. The field was Harold's, a mighty victory that had almost annihilated the prime forces of Norway.

Hardrada's son Olaf was quick to sue for peace, and it is a sign of the completeness of Harold's triumph and of his lack of vindictiveness that he not only agreed to this but allowed the survivors to sail away back to Norway. Some three hundred shiploads had come to this country. We are told that only twenty-four vessels were needed for the return journey.

Harold himself and probably most of his exhausted army returned to York and at last were able to rest a little and recover. As well as a mighty victory he had won great treasure and booty that Hardrada had brought with him or looted on the way to York.

On the negative side, however, he had lost numbers of fighters that he could ill afford, and the administration of Northumbria was in a certain amount of disarray. He might have felt, though, that for a little while at least he could have a chance to relax a little and take stock. Surely now he had survived all that this turbulent year could throw at him.

Then a few days later, on 1 October, he received the news that he least wanted to hear. The wind had changed at last and William of Normandy had landed on the south coast of England.

7

WILLIAM THE BASTARD
1028–1066

William the Bastard they called him, though probably not to his face. A strictly accurate description but not necessarily a term of endearment. In fact there were probably not many who really loved William of Normandy – his wife, probably, and his inner circle of trusted friends. Even his children seemed to have mixed feelings. Cold, grim and cruel are the adjectives most often found by his name, while William of Poitiers describes him as inspiring 'great love and terror', two emotions not usually discovered together. The source of this grim cruelty can probably be traced to a turbulent childhood involving little security and much casual violence.

His father's actions in life and death did him no favours. Illegitimacy itself was probably not too big a handicap. In an age when even bishops and archbishops kept wives and concubines, there were many who began life as he did and prospered. In Scandinavian society, from which the Normans were descended, it was no bar to even the highest positions. Whole lines of Norwegian kings are described as illegitimate sons. Times were changing, though, and certainly in Frenchified Normandy a legitimate heir would rank before an illegitimate one.

The real problems bequeathed to William, however, arose out of the way the previous duke began and ended his reign. The near anarchy of the early years had left deep scars and long-felt divisions between the noble families of the duchy. Feuds begun then had the potential to break out again whenever the firm hand of authority was lifted. Then again the abrupt departure and early death of the duke did little to pave the way for a smooth transition of power, particularly as the designated heir was at the time a boy of seven or eight years of age. It was, in fact, only the relative calm of the few years before that time, and the arrangements made for the guardianship of the boy, that gave William any chance at all of holding on to his new position.

Probably the key to his survival was the oath taken by the Norman magnates before the departure of Duke Robert. They had sworn fealty to the boy as heir of his father and an oath was an oath, however reluctantly given. There is also a suggestion that either at that time or soon after William was presented to the French king Henry, overlord of Normandy, and in his turn swore fealty to him in return for being acknowledged as his father's heir. This chain of fealty was to give him the little security he had in the years ahead.

Initially the prospects seemed good. Duke Robert had surrounded the boy with a strong group of guardians, major powers in the land and all with solid connections to the ducal family. Archbishop Robert of Rouen, the boy's great-uncle, had been for some years the chief supporter and advisor of the duke. Count Alan of Brittany and Gilbert of Brionne were both grandsons of Duke Richard I, and the powerful Osbern the Steward was himself connected to that duke through his father, who was the duke's brother-in-law. With these in place and the boy officially acknowledged as the new duke, it seemed that the administration might be expected to carry on in peace.

We know little of the childhood of William up to this point. The probability is that he spent his early years with his mother Herleve. He certainly showed a strong attachment to her and to her family later. Now he is likely to have had his own household under the stewardship of Osbern, and he had a tutor, Turold, to instruct him in all the things a duke would be expected to know, a little Latin and a great deal about the various arts of war. Three other boys shared his lessons, William Fitzosbern, Roger de Montgomery and Roger Beaumont, forming a bond of loyalty and trust that would endure through life.

The fact that William's accession to the title had apparently been accepted calmly did not mean there were none who might have felt themselves more entitled to such honours than a mere bastard. The archbishop himself, as uncle of the last duke, might have put in a strong claim but didn't. Even stronger was the case of Nicholas, son of Duke Richard III, who on his father's death had been sent to a monastery instead of inheriting the title. He, though, seemed happy to remain there and would in fact become abbot in due course and hold that office for over fifty years. Two other half-brothers of Duke Robert, Mauger and William, could also have felt seniority to a bastard child but clearly at the time lacked the backing they would need for a successful coup.

The first crack in the edifice of calm administration came with the death of Archbishop Robert in March 1037. In his place Mauger was appointed archbishop, and around the same time his brother William became Count of Arques, a title bestowed specifically to ensure his loyalty to the new duke. In fact from this time on, there began an unseemly and lethal power struggle to obtain control of the child that soon descended into near anarchy.

In October 1040 Count Alan of Brittany was killed at a siege. Early the following year, Gilbert of Brionne was murdered on the orders of Ralph de Gacé, a younger son of Archbishop Robert who was beginning to push his way into power. Shortly after this Turold was also killed, and, most audacious of all, according to William of Jumièges, Osbern the Steward had his throat cut while sleeping in the same room as the young duke himself.

Thereafter things went from bad to worse. Killings had to be avenged by more killings. Old feuds were re-opened, and Normandy reaped the whirlwind of the divisions of the past and the lax control that had allowed men to build and garrison fortresses as their own powerbases. These were not in general the great stone castles that would later appear, though some, such as the tower built by William of Arques, were stone-built. However, even a crude wooden structure on an artificial mound surrounded by a palisade could serve as a stronghold for terrorising the neighbourhood and launching attacks against one's enemies.

As Norman nobles murdered and fought each other and struggled to obtain control of the ducal administration, an attempt was made in 1042 to bring in what was known as the 'Truce of God'. This rather peculiar device, if accepted, would restrict private wars to certain days of the week and ban them altogether during the Christian seasons of Advent, Lent, Easter and Pentecost. Unfortunately those bishops that might have accepted and enforced such a 'truce' were themselves too involved in the families struggling for power and the attempt came to nothing.

At this time it is clear that the fight was to control the young duke rather than replace him. Orderic Vitalis, a not quite contemporary chronicler, recounts tales of William having to flee his bed in the middle of the night, accompanied by his mother's brother Walter, to seek shelter with some poor cottager, but there is little doubt that if they had wanted to kill him they could easily have done so. Osbern, after all, was murdered while sleeping alongside the boy. In the early 1040s, however, it seems that William was declared to be of age. Though he would only have been around fifteen years old, he was described by William of Poitiers as 'more adult in his understanding of honourable matters and in his bodily strength than in his age', and it may have been felt that this additional vesting of authority in him might have helped to put an end to the surrounding anarchy.

In fact it made little difference on the ground, although the introduction of the duke's own friends into charter witness lists probably indicates there was some small movement away from the power of those who had until now controlled him, and towards a more personal choice of supporter. Archbishop Mauger, William of Arques and Ralph de Gacé, who had been prominent until now, possibly felt the ground shift a little under their feet. The coming of age, however, meant that controlling the duke was now no longer the game, and it was not long before the first challenge was made to the authority of William himself.

Guy of Burgundy was the second son of Adeliza, wife of Count Renaud of Burgundy and sister of Duke Robert. As such he had no real claim to replace William as duke other than the fact that he was legitimate and William was not. In 1046, however, he launched such a claim, and was supported by a considerable number of minor nobles of Lower (western) Normandy and other lords and magnates of the area between Caen and Falaise. This coup began with an attempt to capture and murder William while he was staying at Valognes in the Cotentin peninsula, in the heart of his enemies' country. William escaped, and there followed a legendary sixteen-hour ride throughout the night, first to Ryes, near Bayeux, then to Falaise. Finally, seeing no other help available, the young duke continued on to Poissy, to the court of his overlord Henry of France, to throw himself on his mercy and request the help due from a sovereign to his vassal in such times of need.

Henry had already intervened from time to time when it suited him during the troubled years, sometimes supporting the boy he had acknowledged as duke, sometimes nibbling at the border to take a castle or two for himself. The relationship between Normandy and France had been rocky in the past, and it has been suggested that it might have been in his interests to let the duchy tear itself apart and then step in to pick up the pieces. There were, however, arguments against this. In the first place the major trade routes from France to the sea lay through Normandy, so anarchy there disrupted French trade and damaged its own interests. In addition, as overlord of William, Henry would be expected to act to protect him. This was part of the bargain involved in swearing fealty. In the same way an attack on a vassal was indirectly an attack on the sovereign himself and could not be allowed to pass without accepting a huge loss of prestige. Consequently Henry gathered his army and marched into Normandy to support its duke and put down the rebellion.

Battle was joined at Val-es-Dunes, an open plain south of Caen, close to the crossing point on the River Orne at Thury-Harcourt. Despite the assertions of William of Poitiers that Duke William practically won the battle single-handed, it was in fact a muddling affair, largely fought by separate groups of cavalry. The turning point came when one of the rebels, Ralph Tesson, abruptly changed sides, attacking his former comrades from the rear so that they were sandwiched between two hostile forces and fled. Many were killed. Many were drowned attempting to re-cross the Orne, while Guy of Burgundy, though wounded, managed to escape and retreat to his castle at Brionne. Though no doubt William had fought valiantly at his first violent encounter, he had brought few troops to the fray and the greater part of the credit for the victory belonged to King Henry.

Nevertheless it formed a turning point. From now on William would be acting to consolidate his authority rather than simply to cling on to it. When a little later Guy surrendered and asked for mercy, William felt strong enough to grant it and allow him to retire peacefully to Burgundy. Ralph Tesson was rewarded with the hand of William's niece Matilda.

The following year the Truce of God was finally proclaimed in Normandy. Thereafter, on pain of excommunication, private wars were banned from Wednesday evening to Monday morning and in the holy seasons. Since its provisions specifically exempted the duke and his overlord from such restrictions the effect was to give these two, and particularly the duke, a monopoly on violence in the duchy for a large part of the time, and implicitly to accept that he could legitimately employ violence in what was felt to be the public interest.

Consolidating power meant effectively building William's own inner circle of trusted advisers and supporters, while pulling down, often literally, the powerbases of those who had built themselves up in the earlier years. Among those who rose were his half-brothers Odo and Robert, the sons of Herleve and her husband Herluin of Conteville. In 1049 Odo became Bishop of

Bayeux at the tender age of, at the most, nineteen. Robert became Count of Mortain. The friends of his youth, William Fitzosbern and Roger de Montgomery, also came to prominence, working in harmony despite the fact that the father of one was responsible for the murder of the father of the other. William Fitzosbern was to become in his turn the duke's steward.

By 1049 William the Bastard was secure enough in his dukedom to make a formal request to Baldwin of Flanders to marry his daughter Matilda. All manner of legends have become tangled about this proposition, some of them embedded in early accounts and repeated in many biographies, however unlikely they may sound in the circumstances. They suggest that William first laid eyes on Matilda at the court of Henry I of France, which is certainly possible since Henry was her uncle. The story then goes that, when the duke asked for her hand, Matilda replied that she was far too high-born to consider marrying a bastard. Whereupon William is said to have stormed all the way from Normandy to Flanders, confronted her in the street, dragged her from her horse by her hair braids and possibly beaten her, before storming all the way back again. This charming courtship apparently changed the mind of the young lady, who now declared she would marry no one *but* William.

The truth is possibly a little more prosaic. It was certainly an audacious proposal on William's part. As the illegitimate ruler of a strife-ridden duchy he was putting himself forward as the equal of Baldwin, who, though only titled count, ruled over a settled and prosperous land that was a rising power in the area. He was also proposing to marry the niece of a king, and his overlord to boot. All this would make the antics described in the legends unlikely in the extreme. In fact it is doubtful whether Matilda herself had any choice in the matter.

What is more surprising is that Baldwin agreed to the match. At the time, however, he had got his fingers burned in the rebellion of the Lotharingians against the Holy Roman Emperor. Baldwin and Henry of France had backed the rebels and suffered a severe setback early in 1049. Baldwin was therefore looking for allies, particularly allies that might be acceptable to the French king, and William seemed to fit the bill.

Then, when the marriage seemed all set to go ahead the Pope stepped in to forbid it. No clear reason was given. It was declared to be against canon law and most have interpreted this as meaning the couple were within the prohibited degrees of relationship. Detailed examination of the pedigrees of each has, however, not turned up any such problem. True, William's aunt became the second wife of Matilda's grandfather, Baldwin IV, but Matilda's father, Baldwin V, was the product of his first marriage.

It is much more likely that the objection was purely political. The Pope at the time, Leo IX, was a German, elected only in February 1049 with the aid of the (German) Holy Roman Emperor. The Lotharingian rebellion had made France and Flanders the enemies of the Emperor, and with rumblings of that rebellion still continuing, he would certainly not want them to gain a new ally. There is no evidence that he put pressure on the Pope to forbid the marriage, but no doubt Leo himself was well aware of what would be pleasing to his benefactor.

William has come down to us as a devout and pious man, a true son of the Church, founding monasteries with the best of them. Some have suggested this was just a smokescreen, the shrewd tactics of a ruthless man seeking to clothe his actions with an appearance of morality. Certainly the decision of the Pope in the matter of his marriage seemed to cause him no qualms at all. At best the match was delayed a little, but it took place at the latest in 1053 and possibly as early as 1050, when Matilda's name first appeared as a witness on a Norman charter.

By 1053 the Pope had troubles of his own, being effectively a prisoner of those Normans who had established estates in southern Italy. There is evidence that his prohibition of the marriage was withdrawn informally at this time, though some have suggested this happened even earlier as the result of persistent persuasion on the part of various Norman clergy. William's championing of the

Pope's reforming programme may also have helped. In 1059 the prohibition was formally lifted, but a number of popes had passed under the bridge by then and the new incumbent, Nicholas II, was a Frenchman from Burgundy and considerably more sympathetic to Normans. A penance was apparently demanded for the original disobedience of the couple. This took the form of the founding of two abbeys in Caen, William's preferred capital, and they stand to this day – the Abbaye des Hommes or St Stephen's Abbey, and the Abbaye des Dames or Holy Trinity Abbey.

Whatever black marks may be listed against William, it is universally agreed that he was totally faithful to Matilda. It is possible there was real affection between the tall, grim warrior and his small, attractive wife. Certainly there was a strong bond of trust. They had ten children together, and most unusually for the time he seems to have regarded her as a partner rather than an inferior necessity. It is notable that when he was away from his duchy it was generally Matilda who acted as regent in his place.

By the year 1050 William was well on the way to consolidating his grip on his duchy but that didn't mean his challenges were over. He had the friendship of Henry of France and had secured that of Flanders through his marriage. To the south, though, there was a man of thrusting and ruthless ambition. Geoffrey Martel – Geoffrey the Hammer – had apparently chosen his nickname for himself on the basis that he intended to hammer lesser men into submission. He had inherited Anjou in 1040, and even before that time had been at war with one or other of his neighbours to the south and east in order to gain territory. In 1047 he turned northward and began attacks on Maine, which lay between Anjou and Normandy. When he captured the Bishop of Le Mans, capital of that county, neither action by the French king nor excommunication by the Pope discouraged him, and when Count Hugh of Maine died in March 1051 Martel moved in. He held on to the heir, a child of four or five years, but expelled the count's widow, who made her way to Normandy and asked William for assistance. When, shortly after, Martel advanced again, taking the fortresses of Alençon and Domfront, the former in Normandy itself, the duke struck back.

The situation was complicated by the fact that the Bellême family were lords of both these fortresses, owing loyalty for one to Normandy and the other to Maine, while the French king Henry was overlord of all. The Bellêmes gave their support to Martel in the autumn of 1051, and William, with the approval of King Henry, laid siege to their major stronghold of Domfront. This was a testing time for the duke, still in his twenties. Any sign of weakness now might do irreparable harm to his position in Normandy, still threatened from within as well as without.

With the siege of Domfront dragging on, and Martel apparently content to let him waste his time and resources there, William made a sudden dart at Alençon. Marching through the night he almost succeeded in taking the place by surprise, but just in time the defenders retreated inside the fortress, abandoning the town to the attacking force. To lay two sieges at once would surely have been beyond the duke but those inside the fortress must have believed that was the plan. They were also so confident in their ability to withstand such a siege that they made the mistake of taunting William about his origins. Hanging leather hides over the walls, they cried, 'Hides! Hides for the tanner!' The provocation brought an immediate retaliation. Taking thirty-two of the leading citizens of Alençon, William paraded them before the fortress and had the hands and feet of each hacked off in full view of the defenders. Even for the times this was a shocking atrocity, and with the threat of more such acts to come the garrison surrendered at once.

In fact, William achieved more than this. With his reputation for ruthless cruelty now marching ahead of him, when he returned to Domfront, that too was surrendered to him on condition that he would show them mercy and not inflict such atrocities there. It now became clear that, young though he was, William of Normandy was not a man to trifle with. It is, incidentally, at the very time of these sieges that William is supposed to have visited England to receive from Edward the promise of his kingdom.

1. Corfe Castle, Dorset. Here Edward the Martyr was murdered, bringing Edward's father Athelred to the throne of England. (Author's collection)

2. Remains of Saxon walls at Wareham. English burghs had been fortified by such walls since the time of Alfred to provide a place of safety for the local population in time of attack. (Author's collection)

3. The Old Hall, Gainsborough. This much later building occupies the site of Swein Forkbeard's camp. It was near here that he died in a fall from his horse. (Author's collection)

4. Poole Harbour approaches. Cnut's forces swept through these waterways on the south coast when they invaded England in 1015. (Author's collection)

5. The tomb of Athelred in Old St Paul's Cathedral was destroyed in the Great Fire of 1666. This memorial now commemorates his last resting place. (Author's collection)

6. This land at Deerhurst in Gloucestershire was an island in the River Severn when Edmund and Cnut met here to conclude a peace treaty effectively dividing the country between them. (Author's collection)

7. The remains of the Norman building of Shaftesbury Abbey. Cnut died here in the Saxon abbey in November 1035. The modern altar is a memorial to Edward the Martyr, whose remains were buried here. (Author's collection)

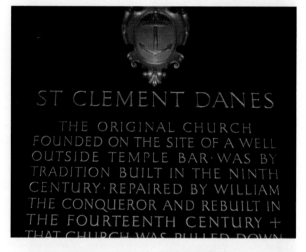

8. The Danish church in London, St Clement Danes, is reputed to be the last resting place of Harold Harefoot, Harold I of England. (Author's collection)

ST CLEMENT DANES

THE ORIGINAL CHURCH FOUNDED ON THE SITE OF A WELL OUTSIDE TEMPLE BAR·WAS BY TRADITION BUILT IN THE NINTH CENTURY·REPAIRED BY WILLIAM THE CONQUEROR AND REBUILT IN THE FOURTEENTH CENTURY +
THAT CHURCH WAS PULLED DOWN

9. This statue of Edward the Confessor sits atop a column outside his beloved Westminster Abbey. No doubt it is missed by millions of tourists each year. (Author's collection)

10. Bosham Creek. The Godwin family had a manor here. In 1051 it was from here that they fled abroad, and from here also that, according to the Bayeux Tapestry, Harold embarked on his fateful journey to Normandy. The church, though enlarged by the Normans, was here at the time and would have been familiar to Harold. (Author's collection)

11. This south bank of the Thames by Southwark was Godwin's land, facing the king in London opposite. Here his ships drew up in 1052 to threaten Edward, before the king accepted the inevitable and re-instated the earl and his family. (Author's collection)

12. In the Bayeux Tapestry Harold is shown taking leave of Edward. It tells us nothing, however, about where he was going and why. (By special permission of the City of Bayeux)

13. Here the Tapestry tells us 'Harold swears an oath'. Once again it gives no clue as to what he swore or the circumstances surrounding the occasion. Perhaps the fact that William is shown seated with a sword in his hand is intended to give the lie to claims that Harold swore the oath of his own free will. (By special permission of the City of Bayeux)

14. Again an English influence might be seen in Harold's apologetic approach to Edward on his return. If the oath he swore was according to Edward's instructions he would have no need to be apologetic. (By special permission of the City of Bayeux)

15. Edward on his deathbed (top) touches hands with Harold, delivering his kingdom into Harold's protection. At the foot of the bed the soon-to-be widow is shown weeping. (By special permission of the City of Bayeux)

16. The 'long-haired star' is seen in the sky. Is it an omen? Harold seems to see invasion ships approaching, but they have no colours or crew to indicate where they may be coming from. (By special permission of the City of Bayeux)

17. From this high cliff above Scarborough Harald Hardrada threw down fire onto the wooden town when he sacked the place in 1066. (Author's collection)

18. Hardrada's fleet was drawn up here on the banks of the River Ouse at Riccall while he fought battles at Fulford and Stamford Bridge. (Author's collection)

19. The eastern end of the battlefield at Fulford is still marshy today. The line of trees marks the course of Germany Beck. (Author's collection)

20. Cut off from the rest of the English army, Earl Edwin's forces were driven back by Hardrada to the River Ouse here at Fulford. Many of them drowned. (Author's collection)

21. In 1066 the crossing of the River Derwent here at Stamford Bridge was a wooden bridge a little higher upriver. According to the Saga it was stoutly defended for some time by a single Norwegian soldier. (Author's collection)

22. On this battlefield at Stamford Bridge Harald Hardrada, 'the Last of the Vikings', met his death along with Tostig Godwinson, while the Anglo-Norwegian army was almost obliterated. (Author's collection)

23. Pevensey Castle, an old Roman fort, was the first base in England to be held and fortified by William of Normandy. (Author's collection)

24. This field, known as Kingsmead, is believed to be the place where King Harold and his army spent the night before the Battle of Hastings. The land at the far side drops away to what may be the 'Malfosse' referred to in accounts of the battle. (Author's collection)

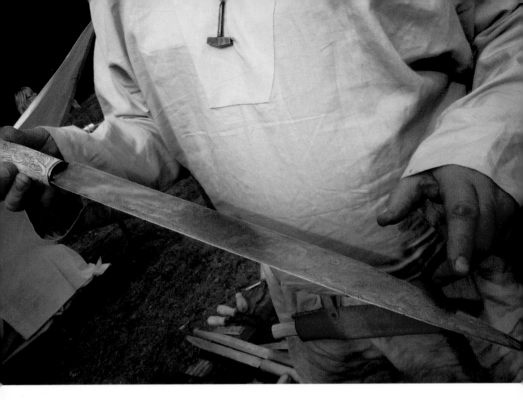

25. The long seax. Most of the select fyrd would have been armed with this weapon used for stabbing and slashing. (Author's collection)

26. Lances used for throwing or stabbing came with many different types of head. (Author's collection)

27. The Bayeux Tapestry shows a typical battle scene from Hastings with the Norman cavalry charging a solid shield wall of the English army. Only one English archer is depicted in the tapestry, as against many Norman archers, suggesting that Harold may have had far fewer of these missile men. (By special permission of the City of Bayeux)

28. The death of Harold seems to cover two alternative versions of this as contained in the different accounts. Most take the figure on the left to be Harold, but the caption covers both. (By special permission of the City of Bayeux)

29. Local legend says the Norman dead from Hastings are buried under this mound on the main road at Telham, East Sussex, though it is several miles from any of the suggested battlefields. (Author's collection)

30. Bosham Church interior. It has been suggested that Harold might be buried at the foot of the altar steps in this, his home church. (Author's collection)

31. One of William's first acts as king was to begin the construction of the Tower of London as a place of refuge within the city. (Author's collection)

32. Clifford's Tower, York, is a fine example of the motte-and-bailey castle. Though the outer bailey is long gone, the motte with its later stone fortification remains. Similar castles can be seen all over the country. (Author's collection)

33. It was here on St Giles Hill, Winchester, that Earl Waltheof was beheaded in May 1076. By one account the severed head completed its prayer before expiring. (Author's collection)

34. This wall painting depicting St Martin dividing his cloak with a beggar is a fine example of English art from about the time of the Norman Conquest. The style of the pictures, on the wall of St Martin's Church, Wareham, is very similar to that in the Bayeux Tapestry. (Author's collection)

35. The outline of Old Winchester Cathedral alongside the later Norman structure demonstrates that English churches were not the small, mean, wooden buildings the Normans claimed they were. Westminster Abbey was also completed before the invasion, showing the adoption of new European architecture that would probably have continued even without the conquest. (Author's collection)

36. Selby Abbey in Yorkshire was founded and endowed by William the Conqueror in 1079. Though much altered later, the round arches and thick, decorated pillars are typical of the early Norman style of architecture. (Author's collection)

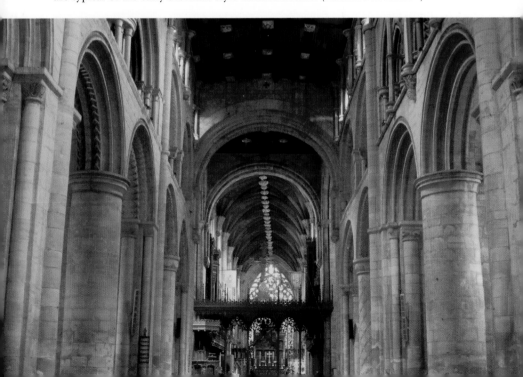

37. The effigy of Robert Curthose, son of the Conqueror, decorates his tomb in Gloucester Cathedral. An enemy of his father at the time of William's death, he was later imprisoned in Cardiff Castle until his death by his younger brother Henry. (Author's collection)

38. This medieval screen depicts fanciful images of (from the left) William the Conqueror and his sons, William Rufus and Henry, the next two kings of England. (Author's collection)

39. The slope below Crowhurst village is another suggested site for the Battle of Hastings, with Rackwell Wood on the left identified as the possible place for the last stand of the English fleeing the battle. (Author's collection)

40. 'Battle Roundabout' in Battle may mark the eastern end of Harold's line of battle. The only artefacts so far dated to 1066 have been found near here. (Author's collection)

41. Caldbec Hill, looking towards Battle Abbey on the skyline. This hill is one of the alternative sites for the battle, though tradition says it was fought on the ridge where the abbey now stands. (Author's collection)

He had at least secured the border area for Normandy, a situation made even more favourable when his close friend and supporter, Roger de Montgomery, married an heiress of the Bellême family. Thereafter they too became solid supporters of the duke. This seems to have been a clear tactic. Time and again marriages were used to weave a web of support, linking his followers together, tying them into his own family, so that all their interests would lie in the same direction as his. It was, however, from within the family that the next challenge would come.

It is likely that William, Count of Arques, had always resented the fact that a bastard nephew should have become Duke of Normandy ahead of himself. He had, however, bided his time and built up his strength in Upper (eastern) Normandy until he felt ready to act. Late in 1051 he and his men withdrew abruptly from the siege of Domfront and returned to the new stone fortress he had built himself at Arques, where he renounced his duty to the duke and seemed set to carve himself out his own duchy in Upper Normandy.

In this he had the support not only of his brother Mauger, Archbishop of Rouen, but also, surprisingly, of Henry of France. In the course of 1052, for reasons that are not entirely clear, Henry seems to have turned against William of Normandy. There was a tradition of challenge between Normandy and France and possibly he felt William was becoming too strong in his duchy and would be a potential threat. Perhaps he too found William's methods a little too ruthless. In the same year there was a reconciliation between Henry and Geoffrey Martel, still in possession of Maine, and this new alliance seems to have had the purpose of undermining or even replacing William of Normandy.

When the Count of Arques finally declared his open rebellion, then, in 1053, William was facing a possible encirclement, and had his enemies acted in a more co-ordinated manner they might have succeeded in their aim. The intention was that Henry would attack in Upper Normandy along with Count Enguerrand of Ponthieu, brother-in-law of William of Arques, while Martel would push up from the south. Had the duke been sitting in siege outside Arques, he would have felt the full impact of all these forces.

In fact William had laid his siege and then left it in the hands of his supporter Walter Giffard, while drawing off to watch for the approach of those coming to relieve it. Henry and Enguerrand found their way to Arques blocked, and while now and later William showed the greatest reluctance to fight his overlord, a part of their forces led by Enguerrand was ambushed on 25 October at St Aubin-sur-Scie and cut to pieces. Enguerrand himself was slain, Henry withdrew and Martel had never got moving at all.

Later that year the castle at Arques was starved into submission, Count William was exiled and fled to Boulogne to the court of Count Eustace, and the duke also contrived the removal of his brother Archbishop Mauger. According to the twelfth-century chronicler Wace, who came from Jersey, Mauger was banished to the Channel Islands where he took up the study of occult science, went mad and drowned.

Henry of France, however, had not finished with his attacks on Normandy. The following year a two-pronged assault was made. To the south Henry, along with Geoffrey Martel and others, invaded through Évreux and advanced along the River Seine. At the same time another force led by the king's brother Odo and Guy of Ponthieu, brother of the recently deceased Enguerrand, attacked the north-east of the duchy near Aumale. Both forces seemed to be given up to ill-disciplined rape and pillage, and perhaps thought William would not have the resources to resist such a widespread attack.

In fact the duke's call to arms was answered from all quarters of his duchy so that he too could divide his forces, shadowing the invaders and looking for an opportunity to strike. This fell to the northerly force when the French invaders under Odo and Guy entered the town of Mortemer. Wace, writing around a hundred years later, gives us a colourful though possibly overdramatic description of what followed. By his account the French spent the day pillaging the country round about and the night carousing and debauching in the town. The Norman forces then surrounded the place, blocked all the exits and set fire to the buildings. When the French poured out fierce hand-to-hand fighting ensued, lasting from dawn until three in the afternoon and with the French force utterly defeated. Those not killed were taken prisoner and only a few managed to escape either fate, among them the king's brother Odo.

When the news was brought to Duke William he was so delighted that, again according to Wace, he had a messenger go by night to climb a tree near to the French camp across the Seine and bellow repeatedly that they should rouse themselves and flee, and go to Mortemer in the north to bury all their dead comrades. This apparently so unnerved Henry that he withdrew at once, taking Martel with him, but the damage to his prestige was such that he immediately began plotting revenge.

In the meantime he was forced to conclude peace with William in order to free the numbers of noble prisoners being held in Normandy. Guy of Ponthieu, for example, spent two years in a dungeon in Bayeux before being allowed to return home. As part of this peace there seems to have been an understanding that if William were to attack Geoffrey Martel in Maine, Henry would turn a blind eye. By 1057, however, Martel and the French king were again to be found in a new alliance against William.

In August of that year another invasion was launched by these two and once again William seems to have been reluctant to attack the king head on. Instead, as the invaders headed northwards from Maine to the area around Bayeux and Caen, laying waste the country thereabouts, he seems to have been content to gather his forces around Falaise and merely shadow them. The sacking of his beloved Caen, however, may have stung him into action.

Advancing to engage the enemy, he caught up with them at Varaville as they were crossing the River Dives on the way to Upper Normandy, and here had an enormous slice of luck. By some accounts the French were using a ford, by others it was a bridge which collapsed. Either way, part of the army including Henry and Martel had crossed the river, while a large part became separated and stranded on the western bank. It was this latter part that was now attacked and utterly devastated by William and the Norman forces, and once again Henry and his allies withdrew. He was never to come again.

It is probably to this time, the late 1050s, that we can date William's expansionist policies. He was now clearly and securely in charge of his duchy. He had surrounded himself with young ambitious men, now fathers of young families as he was himself. They had received lands and honours and expected more for themselves and their children. It was the old Viking problem and would be answered in more or less the old Viking way.

William began putting pressure on the French king over the land of the Vexin that lay between their territories. At the same time he took up the cause of the young heir to Maine, Herbert, son of Hugh IV, who had escaped to Normandy in 1056. Herbert's sister Margaret became engaged to marry William's son Robert, while Herbert himself was to marry one of William's daughters. While both of these schemes were simmering nicely, William had another stroke of luck. In 1060 both of his former enemies died.

On 4 August Henry died while in the process of negotiating another peace treaty with Normandy. He left an eight-year-old son, Philip, whose appointed guardian was Baldwin of Flanders, William's father-in-law. Two months later Geoffrey Martel breathed his last. Though he had been married four times he had produced no children, and the new Count of Anjou was his nephew, Geoffrey the Bearded, who was immediately challenged by his brother Fulk. The resulting civil war would mean that neither would be any trouble to William for the foreseeable future.

William's theoretical support for the young Count Herbert of Maine was ended by the boy's convenient death in March 1062. Now he declared that Herbert had promised him the succession if he died childless and set about claiming this inheritance. The fact that this story has a familiar ring to English ears does not necessarily mean that it was untrue. In fact the promise seems far more likely. Herbert had, after all, grown up at William's court over the preceding six years and been closely associated with him up to the time of his death.

The promise was not made, however, with the consent of those in Maine who favoured the existing links with Anjou. The countship was instead offered to Walter of the Vexin, the uncle of Herbert, and the brother of Ralph of Mantes who had held an English earldom. Not taking 'no' for an answer, William invaded Maine, wreaking devastation in the countryside and aiming, in the words of William of Poitiers, 'to sow fear' in the hearts of the populace. Walter appealed for help to the new Count of Anjou but none was given, and by the end of 1063 Le Mans had been surrendered and Walter and his wife were prisoners of the Duke of Normandy. Both were to die soon after and an allegation was later made that they were poisoned.

By 1064, then, William was the pre-eminent man in the entire region, more powerful than the king of France, forged and hardened by struggle and endurance. 'I was schooled in war since childhood,' he is said to have declared, and it is clear his schooling was not all theoretical. Having learnt well the lessons of insecurity, he had made sure to surround himself with men who owed their positions to him, tightly bound together by ties of family that have been likened to the mafia. The most powerful men in the duchy were his half-brothers, Odo, Bishop of Bayeux and Robert, Count of Mortain. His close friends William Fitzosbern and Roger de Montgomery held similar positions of power, while cousins and second cousins and other relations filled all the main offices, both secular and religious.

He had also thoroughly shaken up the administration of the duchy. A class of 'viscounts' held positions similar to that of sheriffs in England. Appointed and removable by the duke, they administered his justice, collected his taxes and dues and provided military service when required. The coinage was also controlled by the duke, and increasingly he was encouraging a money economy rather than payment in kind. This meant that he always had money available to buy men and resources when needed, a flexibility that was to be of great benefit to him in his continuing policy of expansion.

It is against this policy that the 'visit' of Harold Godwinson in 1064 must be seen. Once again fortune seemed to be smiling on William. For a period of months he had his potential rival in his power, no doubt each of them aware of the realities of the situation beneath the surface civilities. By the time Harold returned home William may well have been convinced that he had only to wait to have the rich plum of England drop into his lap. It must have been all the more galling, then, when he discovered in January 1066 that it would not.

Wace gives us a vivid picture of the duke receiving the news. He was in his park at Rouen ready for the hunt, his bow already strung, when a messenger arrived, took him aside and told him Harold had been crowned as king. The hunt was abandoned. William returned alone to his hall and sat brooding on the end of a bench, knotting and unknotting his garments, while no one dared approach him.

It is easy to imagine what he was brooding about. Though Wace says he had spoken to no one, apparently the news was already being shouted around the town. William had taken pains that Harold's oath should be witnessed, and abandoning his claim now would involve a huge loss of face. It could not be done without showing a weakness that he had never shown before. And yet, could he mount an effective challenge? Had Normandy the resources to invade and conquer a wealthy and well-defended land like England? By the time his brooding was interrupted by his friend William Fitzosbern it is likely that he had already determined not only that it would be done, but also probably how it could be done.

The first step, and the least likely to succeed, was diplomatic. An envoy was sent to Harold in England, reminding him of his oath and requiring him to step down in favour of William. The reply was the same as Harold would give on all future occasions. The kingdom of England was not Edward's to give. He, Harold, had been correctly appointed and consecrated according to English law and was and would remain king of England.

Next William met with his inner circle of friends and supporters, men like Odo of Bayeux, Robert of Mortain, his cousins the Counts of Eu and Évreux, and friends William Fitzosbern, Roger de Montgomery, Walter Giffard and Roger Beaumont. All agreed to give him their full backing, but they pointed out that an enterprise like the invasion of England was a gamble that would involve all the resources of the duchy and therefore should obtain the backing of all the nobles before it went ahead.

A further meeting was held attended by the wider nobility and here William found the going much harder. Despite the tempting carrot of all the lands, riches and honours to be had in England, the magnates persisted in dwelling on all the risks involved. They would have to challenge the military might of England. They would have to cross the sea and they had no navy. They had not the resources to raise the force needed for such an expedition. Nor did William's assumption that they would all back him go down well.

After a while he withdrew to allow them to discuss and reflect among themselves. William Fitzosbern remained, however, possibly as part of a pre-arranged plan. Knowing he was close to the duke, the nobles seem to have poured out their fears to him, particularly their fear of crossing the Channel and the worry that service overseas might come to be seen as a normal part of their obligations. They asked him to speak for them, which he agreed to do, but when the duke returned Fitzosbern immediately declared that all the nobles were fully behind him, and furthermore would double the service they owed, so that if one was obliged to provide ten knights he would now provide twenty.

Not surprisingly this was followed by uproar. Wace tells us that 'the noise was great and the clamour loud. No one could hear another speak; no-one could either listen to reason or render it for himself.' The meeting was adjourned and afterwards each magnate in turn had a separate interview with the duke. There, face to face and without the backing of their equals, none had the nerve to refuse what Fitzosbern had promised, and just to make sure, William 'had it all recorded at once' by a clerk, noting down the details for each one. By the time they had finished each now found he was signed up to provide not only men but ships too for the expedition to England.

William was aware, though, that the resources of Normandy itself might be insufficient to overcome a tenacious enemy. He needed a way to attract others to fight for him, and one way to do this was to make it appear that the cause was not just personal to him but wide enough to involve others across Europe. According to a widely accepted tradition, backed by an account in William of Poitiers' chronicle, he achieved this by obtaining the backing of the Pope himself.

In the second half of the eleventh century great changes were underway in the Church. A reform movement was sweeping through, inspired by the influential abbey at Cluny in France. Old lax practices were condemned and a new morality promoted, particularly for the clergy whose recent example even at the highest level had fallen a long way short of the teachings of the early Church. One of the major figures connected to this movement was Hildebrand, a man of lowly origin who rose with Pope Leo IX to become a papal legate and a main force in papal administration. Influenced by Cluny, Hildebrand had his own agenda for reform. Beginning with the reform of monasteries and the morals of the clergy, his ultimate aim was to bring all of Christendom under the authority of one infallible pope who would be bound by no laws but his own.

Hildebrand was influential in the election of a number of popes after Leo, particularly Pope Nicholas II who reigned from 1051 to 1061, and Pope Alexander who followed him. Each pursued his reform movement, and each favoured rulers who seemed most enthusiastic in supporting it. Included among that number was William of Normandy. Whether as a smokescreen or otherwise, William had been active in promoting monastic reform, founding or reviving a considerable number of monasteries particularly in

Upper Normandy. The foundations of Fécamp, Jumièges and Le Bec were models of good practice, and from them came leading theologians such as Lanfranc and Anselm, the former being a particular friend of the duke.

When in 1066, then, William sent a delegation to Pope Alexander led by Gilbert of Lisieux, he could be confident of getting a favourable hearing. Although there are no surviving records of the meeting, we can be fairly sure of the basis of the Norman case. First William would have stressed Harold's perjury, the story told in detail in the Bayeux Tapestry. Clearly a man prepared to break an oath sworn on holy relics was no fit ruler for a Christian country. Then, playing specifically to Hildebrand's agenda, William undertook to bring about reform of the English Church, using his past record in Normandy to support his case.

In fact the English Church seemed no more in need of reform than any other in Europe at the time, and there is little evidence that previous popes had found it wanting. Despite being depicted by William as something alien and separatist, it had had a close relationship with Rome for centuries past. English bishops and archbishops regularly made the journey to Rome to receive their palliums, and papal legates had visited England as recently as 1062 without finding much amiss. There were some specific problems, particularly those caused by the earlier devastation of Viking raids. Bishops holding two sees at once was often the result of an impoverished northern diocese being supported by a more prosperous southern one. These were already in the process of being reformed, while the English monastic tradition had already undergone its own revival under Dunstan nearly a century earlier.

The case of Archbishop Stigand was certainly irregular but it seems clear the English were well aware of his uncanonical position with many of the functions that would usually have been carried out by an Archbishop of Canterbury being carried out by the Archbishop of York instead. In any case it is hard to see that his position was much worse than that of William's great-uncle Robert, Archbishop of Rouen, who had a wife and a number of children, one of whom was William's supporter the Count of Évreux. Indeed the political appointment of William's own half-brother Odo as Bishop of Bayeux at the tender age of nineteen, or some would say considerably less, does not seem to put the Norman Church on any particular high moral ground.

The state of the English Church, then, was a red herring, used as bait to catch a pope. In fact the whole of William's case was equally shaky. Though he declared himself ready to be judged by any law, English, Norman or papal, it is clear that English law defeats him at once, and neither Norman nor papal law had any relevance to the appointment of an English king. This cut no ice in Rome, however, where without even asking to hear Harold's side of the story Pope Alexander seemed happy to give his full backing to William's enterprise, and even by some accounts to give him a banner to carry with him on his expedition.

Some have doubted this story of papal blessing, and indeed it sits oddly with earlier pronouncements of this pope that 'God does not approve the shedding of blood'. It is pointed out that no mention is made of it in William of Jumièges' account. Nor is any papal banner featured as such in the Bayeux Tapestry, where it might have been expected to have pride of place. However a later letter from Hildebrand to William seems to leave little room for doubt. In it, while rebuking William for failing to deliver on his promise, he reminds him 'how diligently I laboured for your advancement to royal rank', suggesting that Hildebrand at least was fully behind him, and more than likely to have obtained the pope's blessing on his behalf.

Such a blessing was, of course, a major propaganda coup. William was not now fighting for personal advancement but in a kind of holy war sanctioned by the Pope. As a result not only would substantial numbers of men from outside the duchy come to fight for him, but it also meant that other European rulers would not line up to fight against him. It is interesting, though, that strict neutrality was the best he managed to achieve from the leaders of his neighbouring lands. Baldwin of Flanders, Philip of France and the new young Holy Roman Emperor all declared they would not oppose him, but none offered to back him either. It is possible that some or all of them were waiting to see him fail before stepping in and dividing his duchy of Normandy between them.

There was no shortage of recruits for his army however. Normandy was and had always been a military society. High-born young men were trained to arms from the cradle upwards, and in particular were trained in the essentially Norman practice of fighting on horseback. Knights as such did not yet exist; nor did the method of fighting with a couched lance so that man and horse together became one unstoppable weapon. Norman cavalry at this time were basically mounted missile men, riding to close quarters to throw spears and javelins with the added advantage of height above the shield wall. They would, however, have trained long and hard together, and learnt to manoeuvre together on a battlefield in squadrons of ten.

Eldest sons trained in this way would be heirs to magnates who would also have the pick of the rest as retainers. Younger sons might achieve lands and honours for themselves, particularly by hiring themselves out as mercenaries in all the many armed disputes across Europe. It is an interesting point that English thegns might be farmers or merchants when not needed as fighters, whereas the Norman equivalent were warriors and nothing else, all other occupations being regarded as inferior.

Mounted fighters needed good horses, and generations of selective breeding had produced in Normandy horses that were bigger and stronger than the native ponies elsewhere. One reason why the English had not taken to cavalry fighting is probably that their available mounts were not up to it. Small and sturdy, they could do sterling work in delivering an army to a battlefield, as they had in taking Harold north to York in a matter of days, but they were not large or fierce enough for the battle itself.

The one thing that Harold had and William did not was a navy. The sea-going instincts of their Viking forbears seem to have been quickly lost when the Normans turned decisively towards

France and away from Scandinavia. A Channel crossing brought such fear to William's magnates because then they would be most vulnerable to a sharp attack from Harold's well-maintained and well-trained naval force. Nevertheless the Channel had to be crossed and therefore ships were needed. A considerable part of the Bayeux Tapestry is in fact devoted to showing how these ships were acquired.

How many ships, and indeed how many men, made up William's expeditionary force has been argued over repeatedly by academics. Calculations as to how many trees must be felled, how many shipwrights employed, what weight of food and drink would be needed by men and horses and where this might come from, have all been used to arrive at greater or lesser figures. The contemporary records help very little. William of Jumièges declares there were three thousand ships. The so-called 'Ship List', a twelfth-century document claiming to be a copy of the numbers promised by William's magnates, adds up to 812, while Wace says his father was there at the time and told him he counted 696 vessels of all types. These are huge numbers for a fleet of the time. Even Harald Hardrada brought only three hundred, but he was not bringing the essential horses that William's soldiers would need. Allowing an absolute minimum of two horses per knight these would have taken up a great deal of space.

A figure of around seven hundred ships is most commonly accepted, and despite illustrations in the Tapestry it is most unlikely that these would all have been built from scratch. The pictures show the whole process of boatbuilding, from cutting down trees to the finished product, and it is recorded that shipwrights were called in from all around. However, green unseasoned timber would not have been used unless all other supplies had been completely exhausted, and the time factor seems to argue against, even if manpower itself was not a problem. In fact a considerable number of ships were likely to have been bought, hired or requisitioned in order to make up anything like the size of fleet needed.

Similar wide variants affect the numbers of men involved. William of Poitiers suggests between fifty and sixty thousand, while others go as high as a hundred and fifty thousand. These are wild exaggerations. Such numbers could neither be gathered nor maintained at the time. More acceptable estimates range between seven and ten thousand fighting men, with maybe another few thousand supporting non-combatants.

According to a document of 1070 the men fell into one of four groups: those armed by William, that is, his own retained troops; those who armed themselves, the leading magnates; those owing military service for their lands; and those fighting for pay. Among the latter were mercenaries from as far afield as Germany, Hungary, Aragon and Italy, as well as those from France, Flanders, Maine, Aquitaine and Brittany. One estimate suggests they made up nearly half of the entire army.

By early summer 1066 all these were coming together at the mouth of the River Dives where the fleet was assembling. On 18 June William, together with his wife Matilda, attended the consecration of Holy Trinity Abbey in Caen which she had founded and it was arranged that in his absence she would act as regent in Normandy, with the support of Roger Beaumont among others. With a similar eye to the future, William had his eldest son Robert accepted by all as his rightful heir.

At the beginning of August all was prepared. Men, horses, ships and supplies were gathered in the Dives estuary and William joined them, ready to launch his great invasion. One month later they were still there.

8

THE BATTLE OF HASTINGS
OCTOBER 1066

We can be fairly sure of the movements of William and his army in the summer of 1066. They are detailed and corroborated in a number of different accounts. Why he did what he did, however, has caused considerable debate.

From the beginning of August to the second week in September the army, fleet and all their necessary support were camped around Dives-sur-Mer at the mouth of the River Dives. Then, sometime around 12 September the whole expedition moved eastwards to St Valéry at the mouth of the Somme, where it remained for a further two weeks before embarking for England.

The generally accepted reason for all this hanging around is the weather, which, if true, would mean that the summer of 1066 must have been a thoroughly miserable one. William needed a good southerly wind and probably a spell of settled clear weather to get all his armada to the other side of the Channel. Although the Bayeux Tapestry shows oarports on many of his ships, it is likely that oars would only have been used for manoeuvring in and out of harbour. Certainly when they are shown at sea all are under sail, the only oar visible being that of the steersman.

Some have argued that the wind could not have been contrary for that length of time, but a summer blighted by a succession of Atlantic lows would not be unique by any means. A shifting of the jet stream winds could easily have brought a cool, wet August with winds stubbornly stuck in a westerly direction, veering and backing south-west, north-west, everything but south. This might also explain why, at the beginning of September, Harold's members of the fyrd were still needed to help get in the harvest, a matter of some urgency by that time.

The alternative suggestion is that, after assembling his forces, William was prepared to sit and out-wait Harold there on standby on the other side of the Channel. There is a close relationship between the dates when each moved that might suggest this. Harold had stood down his army and sent the fleet away home on 8 September and a few days later William moved his forces. On 20 September at the latest Harold set off for the north and a week later William crossed the Channel. We know that William had many sources of information available to him in England and it is tempting to see the time lapse as the time taken for his spies to inform him of what was happening. This, then, could be seen as an example of William's supreme generalship, frustrating and outwitting his opponent before the action had even started.

There are, however, a number of arguments against this view. In the first place an army of around ten thousand men is going to take a considerable amount of feeding in the course of a month, not to mention their horses and support staff. Calculations have been attempted as to the quantities of grain, wine, firewood and tents needed for the men, and the fodder, straw and even horseshoe nails needed for the horses, and the huge numbers that must have been involved in transporting all this and removing the waste. The implication is that this could not have been done, to which the only answer is that it was done, but whether it was a burden that would be willingly undertaken for the sake of a potential advantage over an opponent is a different matter.

The evidence is that the duke paid for all this personally. William of Poitiers tells us that no plundering of the countryside was allowed. The flocks pastured undisturbed and the grain was neither trampled nor stolen while awaiting the harvest. It is an interesting point to wonder from how far afield William brought in his supplies for his troops, since the harvest in Normandy must have been similarly delayed by the weather, and if the local grain was bought up as soon as it was harvested, the local population must have had a thin time the following winter.

Food was not the only problem. Many of William's troops were mercenaries, there only for the pay and the plunder. Keeping them happy for a month must have been another drain on the ducal funds. Again William of Poitiers tells us William 'made generous provision both for his own knights and those from other parts', and here he clearly felt the benefit of his policy of receiving taxes and dues in money wherever possible. He was, however, investing heavily in the success of this expedition, with more expenditure every day going out, and as yet no definite prospect of any return.

With this vast logistical operation to keep going, and a threat of desertions from the mercenary part of his force, it is of course possible that William was playing a waiting game. On the other hand it seems more likely that he was as frustrated as the chroniclers suggest, watching the wind, hiding his anxiety, and watching too as day by day the treasury gradually emptied. He had, incidentally, a reputation for avarice which also seems to argue against paying out money unnecessarily.

The movement of the fleet in mid-September is another event open to debate. It has been suggested that this was a planned move, that the crossing to England was shorter there, that William was advised a south wind would be more likely, and that, in any case, he would have exhausted the provisions around Dives-sur-Mer by this time and been forced to move elsewhere. St Valery at the mouth of the Somme has been depicted as a kind of forward base, a launch pad for a strike against England. It has even been suggested that the warhorses made their way there overland, which would certainly suggest considerable forward planning.

Once again, however, there are problems with this interpretation. St Valery was not in Normandy itself but in the neighbouring territory of Ponthieu, though this was by now more or less subjected to Normandy. Its ruler, Count Guy of Ponthieu, had fairly recently spent two years as William's prisoner following the disaster at Mortemer, and even more recently had been the captor of Harold Godwinson, obliged by threats or bribes to hand him over into William's custody. At best he would probably have been a very reluctant host to William's massed forces. At worst he could have been a disruptive troublemaker.

Nor was the coast around St Valery as straightforward as might be expected of a place from which an invasion was to be launched. It is noted that there was a local right to hold for ransom ships and men that foundered on those shores, suggesting that such was a likely occurrence. Indeed, St Valery had a reputation for shipwrecks and possibly a little light wrecking, and in all probability that was how Harold arrived there in the first place.

William of Poitiers tells us that the fleet set sail from Dives where it had awaited a south wind, 'but now by a west wind it was driven thence towards the harbour at St Valery'. Though he does not say so in so many words, there is a strong implication that St Valery was not the intended destination but the result of an unexpected wind change. Even more telling is his addition a few lines later that William was not daunted by the 'contrary wind, nor by the loss of ships, or even by the craven flight of many who broke faith with him', and that 'he caused those who had perished in the storm to be secretly buried'.

This does not suggest a planned transfer to a forward camp – far from it. It sounds far more like a near disaster and a struggle to retain control of an unravelling situation. That he did regain control, and indeed keep the great majority of his forces together for another two weeks before launching his bid, says a lot for William's reputation and skills of man-management, but praising the move as a strategic victory seems a step too far.

A more likely interpretation, then, is that having spent a month at Dives with supplies diminishing and some at least of his forces becoming increasingly restless, William gambled on a brief window of good weather. With or without knowledge of Harold's movements he embarked his forces and got out to sea, only to find the wind change and drive him rapidly eastwards along a dangerous lee shore. Had the wind swung to the north-west now the whole invasion might have been over and history changed forever. Instead, running ahead of a westerly or south-westerly gale, the majority of the fleet scrambled into the safety of the Somme estuary and landed at St Valery. Those calculating winds and tides at the time suggest they would have arrived well ahead of high water with an increased risk of shipwreck, duly noted by the chroniclers.

Now the pressure would really have been on William of Normandy. He claimed that his cause was just. He even had the Pope's backing to show that God was on his side, but God had so far done very little to prove it. If he felt any doubts, however, he hid them well. By 'varied exhortation he put courage into the fearful and confidence into those who were cast down', and since God was neglecting him he 'made pious and fervent supplication' that the wind might change in his favour. In a bizarre ceremony he even had the body of Saint Valery bought out from its shrine in the church and paraded before the whole army. This apparently was to demonstrate their 'Christian humility'.

And then at last the weather changed. On 27 or just possibly 28 September the wind blew from the south, the sky cleared and the sea became calm. Now, after days of idleness, the rush was on to get ready to sail with the high tide, calculated to occur at around 3 p.m. Our earliest source of information about the invasion itself is a poem, the *Carmen de Hastingae Proelio (Song of the Battle of Hastings)* composed in 1067. This talks of men flocking to their places in the ships like doves seeking their loft, but loading other things would have taken longer. There were some thousands of horses to be embarked, and despite various attempts at reconstruction we are still not really sure how this was done. According to the *Carmen* they were simply forced to clamber aboard. Similarly the Tapestry depicts the loading of supplies, bundles of swords and spears, mail hauberks being carried on poles and great casks of wine.

As each ship was loaded it would have put out to sea and there anchored awaiting the rest of the fleet. Among them was William's own ship which, according to a note added at the end of the 'Ship List', was called the *Mora* and had been supplied by his wife. This is described as bearing a small gilded figure of a boy blowing a horn and pointing forward towards England, and such a figure is visible on one of the ships in the Tapestry.

By the time all the ships were assembled it was already getting dark. An order was given that they should remain at anchor for a time so as not to arrive at the English coast before daylight the next morning. The signal to proceed would be the lighting of a lantern at the masthead of the duke's ship, whereupon they should all hoist sails and follow him.

Crossing the Channel in the dark with a flotilla of that size seems almost to be inviting disaster but once again William's luck held. Only two mishaps were reported. When daylight came the duke's ship had outsailed the others and he found himself alone on the sea. Calmly, we are told, he sat down and ate a hearty breakfast and by the time he had finished the rest of the fleet had come up to join him. The other incident had a less happy result. A few vessels became separated from the others and, arriving at Romsey, had their crews immediately massacred by the local population. Possibly the crews concerned were support staff rather than the prime Norman soldiery.

For the rest of the fleet, however, Pevensey was the target, a Pevensey rather different from the landlocked town of today. Drainage of the surrounding area begun in the Middle Ages has left a broad pastureland between town and sea, but in 1066 it more resembled the salt marshes of Essex, lagoon interspersed with grassy islands at high tide and dry land and mud flats at the ebb. The town itself stood on a peninsula of higher land thrusting into the lagoon from the west. The Romans had built a fort there and its name, Anderida, had been passed by the Saxons to the forested land behind known as Andredsweald. It is likely the place had been heavily guarded a month before but now the Normans appear to have landed unopposed. Possibly William himself landed at a wharf in the town but his hundreds of ships must have been spread far and wide along the coast.

Whether or not William was surprised to be unopposed we don't know. Some have suggested he knew exactly what was going on in England, even to the landing of **Hardrada** in the north. The idea that the two invasions were coordinated seems farfetched, however. It is hard to imagine William agreeing to share the land with the Norwegians or relishing the prospect of fighting them for it.

Nor do his immediate actions suggest overconfidence. Like any good invader, his first thought **was to secure** a bridgehead and on this occasion the Roman fortress was ideally placed. It was too large to be completely defensible and therefore the Normans set-to to erect within its strong walls a pre-fabricated Norman-style wooden castle. Before evening, so Wace tells us, they had completed this and filled it with their stores, before they all sat down to eat and drink their fill.

While the castle-building was going on the first reconnaissance parties were already abroad, seeking out the lie of the land and any possible resistance. Starting as they meant to go on, others seized provisions from the local population. The Tapestry gives a picture of mailed and armed men riding out and others in the everyday dress of servants bringing back a sheep, a pig and an ox, while another looks through a ring of what might possibly be sausage.

The reconnaissance would have shown, however, that Pevensey was not ideal for their purposes. For a start there was only one way off the narrow peninsula, which would make it easy to bottle up the entire invasion force. Then again at certain states of the tide the ships would be stranded on the mud far from the sea, making an emergency re-embarkation impossible. Just along the coast, however, at Hastings there was a safer anchorage for the fleet, with nearby the remains of another ancient fortress. Here again the coastline in 1066 was very different from today. Hastings itself lay on a bulge of land between two estuaries, and in fact the westerly one at Bulverhythe has been suggested as a likely shelter for the bulk of the fleet. Access inland was also better at Hastings and it was to Hastings, then, that the main camp was transferred within a day or two of the landing, with another castle rapidly erected and garrisoned.

The various accounts differ as to the day on which William landed, some saying Michaelmas Eve and some Michaelmas Day, 28 or 29 September. Almost at once local messengers would have been dispatched to notify Harold in the north, but it seems impossible, even by the fastest relay, that he could have received the news before 1 October. Though some suggest he had already set out to return to London, it seems more likely that the king was still in York at the time. This was a scant five days after the furious battle against Hardrada and Tostig at Stamford Bridge and only ten days from the rout at Fulford. There would have been wounded to attend to, bodies to be buried, including that of his brother, and the affairs of the earldom to put in order. We hear nothing of Edwin and Morcar at this time, but since Harold left his own man, Maerleswein, to oversee local administration when he left, it is possible they had been wounded and were not yet fully recovered.

As soon as he received news of William's landing he set out for London. Who was with him we don't really know. As the professional core of the army the housecarls must have been in the forefront of the fighting at Stamford Bridge and were sure to have suffered losses. The men of the fyrd would also have been reduced by death or wounds, and some others must have been left behind to secure the northern lands. On the way south, then, Harold would have been calling out the southern fyrd for probably the fourth time that year, and significantly we have records of men coming from places particularly in East Anglia and the southern counties which were not mentioned in connection with the previous call. This seems to show the sophistication of the English military machine in that it was able to answer four such calls and still provide a substantial army each time.

According to various accounts Edwin and Morcar followed Harold to London rather than accompanying him, which again may suggest they needed time to recover from their previous efforts, and probably to get their forces in order again after the mauling they had received at Fulford. Harold's brothers Gyrth and Leofwine joined him, however, with their own housecarls and other forces, so that when he reached London, probably around 7 October, he would already have assembled the core of a considerable fighting force, with no doubt more arriving every day. Now he had to decide on the best way of tackling this new invader.

Soon after the time Harold was first hearing of William's arrival, William himself was receiving news of Harold. This came from local inhabitant, Robert Fitzwimarc, Norman by birth, in some way related to Duke William and described by William of Poitiers as a rich man. He sent a messenger to the duke telling him of Harold's great victory in the north and warning him that the king was even now hurrying south with a great army. His advice to William was that he should avoid danger, refrain from battles and stay behind his fortifications.

It has generally been assumed that this Robert Fitzwimarc was solidly on the side of the invaders, but in fact he was advising William to do exactly what Harold wanted him to do. Harold had seen at first hand how William had conducted his campaign in Brittany, how mobile his forces were and how he would throw them rapidly forward to harry large areas of countryside, seizing and burning towns and setting up castles as a base for further operations. The last thing he wanted was for the duke to apply the same tactics to England. At present he was sitting on the coast with the thick forest of Andredsweald between himself and the interior. If he could be bottled up there and starved into submission, it would suit Harold very well.

Again, some of the words William of Poitiers attributes to Robert Fitzwimarc do not suggest he was a fully committed supporter. He tells William, 'You are accounted a wise man,' and warns that against Harold's 'innumerable troops, all well-equipped for war ... your own warriors will prove of no more account than a pack of curs.' William in his turn thanks him for his advice though saying it would have been better 'not to have mingled insults with his message,' and says he will in fact seek a battle as soon as possible. Actually he did exactly what Fitzwimarc suggested, clinging to the coast and never moving away from his line of quick retreat.

Poitiers then takes the opportunity to rehearse all the arguments on both sides by reporting an exchange of messengers between William and Harold. Here we have William's side, the full story of Edward's promise, the oaths of the leading earls, the exchange of hostages and Harold's own oath on holy relics in Normandy. Harold's justification, however, is limited to the deathbed nomination by Edward, suggesting Poitiers was unaware of, or chose not to explain, the part played by the witan in the selection of an English king. Here too we have an offer by William to fight Harold in single combat, in effect the Norman method of trial by combat. Harold's response, after apparently blanching with fear, was that there would be a battle and God would decide between them.

It is very likely that there was some diplomatic exchange between the two camps while Harold was in London considering his options. It is, however, most unlikely that it consisted of the details given by William of Poitiers.

Harold probably spent a few days in London, resting and collecting more men before setting out once more to cover the sixty miles south to the Sussex coast. Why he moved so quickly against William is a matter that called for comment in most of the chronicles of the time and has been debated ever since, particularly since a number of the accounts suggest that he set out before his full army was assembled.

One of the reasons put forward is that the estates that were now being ravaged by William and his foragers in the Hastings area were Harold's own estates, and that he was anxious to act quickly to spare his own people. It has been suggested that this was a deliberate ploy on William's part to provoke a confrontation at the earliest moment, before the English forces were fully ready. Certainly in the Bayeux Tapestry the scene where 'William is told of Harold' is immediately followed by, 'Here a house is burned,' and a picture of a woman leading a child from a rather smart, blazing, two-storey house.

The suggestion of William of Poitiers is that Harold intended a surprise attack on William in the same way that he had surprised Harald Hardrada such a short time before. Unless the Norman chroniclers are correct, however, in attributing Harold's actions to pride and overconfidence, he would surely have recognised that the two situations were quite different. Hardrada had had less than a full army, no armour and little chance of retreat or reinforcement, whereas William had all his forces and arms and, furthermore, had not fought another battle a few days before. The thought of a swift, sharp blow to make William retreat and sail away must have been attractive, but it would surely have been dismissed as unlikely.

Others have suggested that Harold might have been misled as to the duke's campaigning effectiveness by the less than wholly successful expedition he had witnessed in Brittany, or even that he might have been wounded, ill or depressed, and acting out of character in seeking to get the matter settled as soon as possible.

There is another possible explanation for his actions and that is that he was not actually seeking a battle at all. This might explain why he left London with less than his full force, and why arrangements were made for further reinforcing troops to assemble at the 'hoary apple tree', a landmark on Caldbec Hill some seven miles from Hastings and on one of the main exits from the forested area of the Andredsweald.

It was William that needed the battle. The longer he remained at Hastings the weaker his position would be. Quite soon the land about would be exhausted of provisions, and unless he could be resupplied by sea he would simply be starved into submission. There is evidence that Harold sent out a fleet from London to cut off any such supply line, and if he could position his forces so as to bottle up the invaders in the immediate vicinity of Hastings, he would be well placed to defeat the invasion with the minimum harm to the rest of the country.

It would have taken him around three days to march south from London and the evidence is that he arrived near Caldbec Hill late on 13 October. Certainly he might have been aiming to surprise William, not with an attack but with an occupation of the neck of the Hastings peninsula, roughly three miles across, between the estuaries at present-day Catsfield on one side and Sedlescombe on the other. William, however, was not taken by surprise. The suggestion is that either scouts or possibly a foraging party had spotted Harold's approach and rushed back to Hastings to inform the duke.

Seeing an approaching force is one thing. Knowing what it is intending to do is another. William clearly anticipated a night attack, called back his foragers and had his men armed and ready. William of Jumièges says he had them on standby all night, while William of Poitiers, emphasising the piety of the Normans, details how the bishops and clergy among them spent the night fighting the enemy with prayers. The story that the English spent the night drinking and singing comes almost a century later from Wace and seems to be pure fantasy. 'All night they ate and drank and never lay down on their beds,' he says. 'They might be seen carousing, gambolling, and dancing and singing.' For men who had marched three days this seems very unlikely. No doubt after a weary journey from London they all slept soundly at the place on Caldbec Hill now called Kingsmead.

A similar fantasy, and from the same source, is the story that Harold and his brother Gyrth rode out together early the next morning to reconnoitre the enemy host, and that, seeing the size of the force ranged against them, Harold immediately wanted to return to London. Gyrth then called him a base coward and they even came to blows about it before returning to camp. This seems to reference another claim by Wace that Gyrth suggested he lead the army against William instead of Harold because Harold's perjury might prejudice their chances of victory. The latter tale, though unlikely, has been accepted by some as a possibility, but as for Harold's cowardice, since Wace emphasises the two were alone at the time, it is hard to see where he would have heard the tale. Nor does any other chronicler suggest such a possibility.

In the end it seems likely that William and Harold managed to surprise each other. It would have been very clear to the duke that he needed to act quickly if he was to gain any possible advantage. At some time in the early hours of the morning, therefore, he left the shelter of his camp at Hastings and set out for an encounter with Harold. By daybreak, however, the king had his own forces on the move, just in time to see William's host approaching over Telham hill on the road from Hastings. There is a delightful scene in the Tapestry where soldiers from each side spot each other through a screen of trees and this is very likely what actually happened. The two groups would have been only about a mile apart at this point, far too late to avoid an encounter or choose a different meeting place. They would have to make the best of where they were.

It is possible that, with his local knowledge, Harold had intended to make his stand in this area anyway. The road from London to Hastings descended Caldbec Hill, then followed an undulating ridge in a south-easterly direction. A few hundred yards further on, a cross ridge stood up above land that fell away steeply on three sides to broken marshy land below. It was a good site for a shield wall and a very poor one for the deployment of cavalry. It also allowed for the arrival of reinforcements from the rear which Harold was expecting at any time, while the thick forest provided flanking protection. At the time the place seems to have had no name. We know it as Battle.

With neither achieving the kind of surprise they had aimed at, the two armies were forced to deploy in full sight of each other, the English on the ridge blocking the road to London, and the Normans in the valley below. Whatever formation Harold had used to attack at Stamford Bridge, this was to be a purely defensive action and the traditional shield wall the obvious tactic. Consequently all were dismounted with the horses sent to the rear.

A great deal of fuss has been made about whether or not Harold had archers at Hastings. Some have even suggested archers as such were unknown to the English, a rather odd claim when it is widely agreed that Hardrada was killed by an arrow a matter of weeks before. The fact that only one is depicted on the Tapestry, as against two dozen or so on the Norman side, may suggest that there were not many archers. The explanation offered for this might be confirmed by the reduced size of the archer in comparison to the accompanying men of the shield wall shown beside him. It was customary to depict the lower classes as smaller than their betters, and if in general archers were drawn from the ceorl class of the select fyrd it might well be that they had no horses to enable them to keep up with the pace of Harold's rapid journey south. There could well have been some archers drawn from the local area, but probably not as many as might usually be found among the men of the shield wall.

Another misconception is that Harold was at a disadvantage in not having 'modern' cavalry like William's. As has been pointed out the terrain was not at all suitable for cavalry attack, and in fact until the very end William's cavalry was as ineffective against the shield wall as Harold's had been at Stamford Bridge. Nor would cavalry have had much of a role in the kind of defensive action Harold was planning.

The forces available to Harold would have been a mixture of battle-hardened professional housecarls, generally well-trained and armed select fyrdmen and probably a turnout of the local fyrd as well. There are reports of men with no armour hurling stones fastened to sticks and it is most unlikely any of the select fyrd would have been so poorly turned out.

The losses of housecarls at Stamford Bridge would have been keenly felt, leaving them probably spread thinner than usual, at least as far as their role of stiffening lesser troops was concerned. Spreading out along the cross ridge, the king would have set up his golden banner of the Fighting Man in the centre surrounded by housecarls, with the select fyrd on each side to a distance of probably some three hundred yards, and likely fronted for some way at least by more housecarls. Despite the later claims that half the army was not there, other accounts describe them as closely packed, so close that the dead and wounded were unable to fall, so the suggestion that they were heavily outnumbered does not seem valid. Similarly the Norman accounts of such numbers on the English side as to cause rivers to dry up and forests to fall as they passed can be discounted as the usual exaggeration. In fact, given the unusual length of the battle and the bitterness of the struggle, it is likely that the numbers were roughly even on each side, with a possible slight advantage to the English.

William of Poitiers gives us a clear description of how William, down in the valley, organised his men. In the vanguard came the archers. Behind them were the heavily armed and armoured infantry, and to the rear the cavalry with William himself at their centre, from which position he could command the whole army. We are also told that the Normans among them filled the centre with the Breton mercenaries on their left commanded by Alan of Brittany, and the French, Flemish and others on the right under the command of Eustace of Boulogne, who had apparently decided to hitch his wagon to William's rising star.

Looking at the site today, standing below the abbey where re-constructions take place, it is easy to underestimate the actual slope of the battlefield. However, on the day Harold's men would have been lining the very top of the hill where the abbey remains now stand and there is a marked difference in steepness at that point.

No doubt it took some time to get everyone in place. William of Jumièges records that the battle began at the third hour of the day, that is at 9 a.m. A bizarre little flourish is added by Poitiers who declares that, just as it is for the prosecution to begin a case in court, so it was William, the claimant's, forces that opened hostilities.

The first attack was by the archers, advancing up the slope to discharge their weapons. Fired at that angle, though, they would have had little effect, either sticking in shields or passing overhead. In return the English hurled down on them javelins, axes and miscellaneous other missiles so that the archers were forced to retreat. The heavy infantry tried next but they could make no headway against the packed shield wall, and to save the situation William had to send in his cavalry. Many of these rode close up the hill to hurl their javelins, the usual form of attack and that depicted on the Tapestry. Others went even closer, using their swords to hack at the men in the shield wall. William of Poitiers acknowledges that at this stage the advantage was all on the English side, as they 'successfully repulsed those who were engaging them at close quarters,' while 'their weapons found easy passage through the shields and armour of their enemies'.

It was rare for medieval battles to last much over an hour. By that time some weakening of one side or the other usually proved decisive and at Hastings, too, there was just such a weakening. 'Panic-stricken by the violence of the assault,' says Poitiers, the infantry and Breton knights on the left wing fell back, causing their panic to spread along the line so that 'the whole army of the duke was in danger of retreat'. The alarm was fuelled by a sudden rumour that William was slain and in a moment the retreat could have become headlong flight.

It is here that people tend to point up the differences in the generalship of William and Harold, heaping praise on one and deriding the other. One swift charge by the English forces, they say, would have swept the Normans from the field and won the day. Maybe on another day that is exactly what Harold would have done, but we must remember that this army was not the army he had fought with in the north. He was undoubtedly missing numbers of housecarls who could have made all the difference, and we don't know how far he was having to rely on the less well-trained select fyrd who may possibly have been second-, third-, or even fourth-choice fighters from regions that had already answered at least two calls that year. What would have been absolutely clear is that, if once they abandoned their commanding position on the hill, they would never get it back.

In fact one part of the English force did make some sort of charge. Those on the right of the king, seeing the men before them turn and run, broke from the shield wall and pursued them. What we don't know is whether this was a deliberate attack on the orders of the king or simply an example of ill-discipline.

What happened next perhaps vindicates Harold's decision to stay on the hill. According to Poitiers, Duke William, who may possibly have been briefly unhorsed, stopped the headlong flight by spurring in front of those fleeing, and by a mixture of haranguing them and laying about him with his lance, managed to rally them to turn and fall upon their pursuers. The Tapestry shows him lifting his helmet to prove he was not slain, and gives Eustace of Boulogne the credit for shouting the news to the men, while Poitiers, always ready to put a stirring speech in his mouth, has William declaring, 'You are throwing away victory and lasting glory, rushing into ruin and incurring abiding disgrace.' Furthermore, he adds, running away will not save them, 'since by flight none of you can escape destruction'. There is a story that in fact William had destroyed at least some of their boats in order to make his men fight harder, though that seems a little extreme for the normally cautious duke.

Now, as the Normans rallied, it was their pursuers that paid the price and cut off from the protection of the shield wall, they proved easy targets. There is support for the suggestion that it may have been a deliberate charge by the English in the fact that the Tapestry appears to depict Harold's brothers, Gyrth and Leofwine, meeting their deaths at this point while cut off from their fellows. They would certainly be the likeliest to lead such a charge but other accounts say their bodies were later found close to that of Harold, where his battle standards were also set at the top of the hill.

After this potentially disastrous moment for both sides, there seems to have been something of a lull while each regrouped. Despite Poitiers declaring that the English had suffered great losses, he gloomily records that there did not seem to be any the less of them, and Harold's decision to remain on the hill meant he was still able to confound the attacks that William now launched at him.

It was the cavalry now that repeatedly attempted to breach the shield wall and was repeatedly thrown back. Poitiers describes this as 'a battle of a new type: one side vigorously attacking; the other resisting as if rooted to the ground'. He also relates a tactic that has been hotly debated ever since, the so-called 'feigned retreat'. He claims that, remembering how the earlier flight of the left wing had enticed substantial numbers down from the hill to their deaths, William now twice employed the same device with equal success. The cavalry pretended to flee, were pursued and wheeled round to cut down their pursuers.

Some declare that this simply could not have happened, that such a precise manoeuvre would have been beyond the skills of the cavalry of the time. It would certainly require a high degree of training and there was always the danger it would panic the rest of the army. On the other hand, these Norman proto-knights spent a great deal of time training and were used to acting together in regular units. And if, as seems to be the case, the heavy infantry and archers were less engaged at the time, there would be less chance of panic spreading. There were precedents for such manoeuvres. Examples have been quoted from the Huns, the Visigoths and the horsemen of Byzantium, the latter of which were certainly studied by William of Normandy. The *Carmen*, too, backs up this claim, although it declares that the first retreat was also feigned, which given the other evidence of the circumstances at the time seems unlikely.

We have to concede, therefore, that such a manoeuvre as the feigned retreat was at least possible and may have been employed by William on one or more occasion in the course of this long battle. It was not, however, to be a decisive factor. Though Poitiers declares that several thousand English fell for this trick and were duly massacred to the last man, still he says the remainder of the army remained rooted to the top of the hill and could not be dislodged.

As the day wore on, both sides must have suffered great losses. While the shield wall held, though, Harold was likely to win the day. With further reinforcements due, and maybe some already arriving through the day, he could afford to be patient. William could not.

As evening approached he massed all his forces, archers, infantry and cavalry, for one final assault, throwing everything he had at the line of stubborn resistance on the hill. It is likely that by now the losses on the English side had forced Harold to draw in his wings a little, so that this last charge was finally able to get up onto the ridge and attack on more level terms. Tradition says, too, that William now instructed his archers to fire high into the air so that their arrows dropped onto the heads of the defenders instead of sticking harmlessly into their shields. No doubt they had been doing this for some time if they had been deployed at all after the first onslaught, since anything else would have stood a good chance of cutting down their own fellows engaged at close quarters with the enemy.

Now, as twilight was already falling, came the decisive moment of the whole long day, the death of the English king. Strangely, although this was a turning point in British history we don't actually know exactly how Harold died. Two different stories have come down to us. The traditional one, known to every schoolchild probably from that day to this, is that he was fatally struck in the eye by an arrow. The *Carmen*, however, gives an altogether different version. In this, as the English shield wall is finally weakening and beginning to break up, William himself spots a chance to dispose of his rival once and for all. Getting together a group of knights, including Eustace of Boulogne, Hugh of Ponthieu and one 'Giffard', he deliberately targets Harold, still in the thick of the fighting and giving a good account of himself, and sets out to hack him to death. Gruesome descriptions are given of how Harold was pierced through with a lance and 'drenched the earth with a gushing torrent of blood', at the same time being beheaded and disembowelled and even having his leg cut off.

Which of these stories is true, we really don't know. William of Poitiers, so full of detail on everything else, says nothing at all about how Harold met his end. It has been suggested that, as a former soldier himself, he found the deliberate ganging up on Harold and the subsequent butchery to be a shameful act, and did not want to tarnish his hero William with such a deed, particularly when the victim was a consecrated king.

The other almost contemporary record, the Bayeux Tapestry, is as unclear as usual. The caption, 'Harold is slain', is spread over two different deaths. One under the word Harold shows a man clutching an arrow apparently stuck in his eye, while the other has a man cut down by the sword of a horseman. The suggestion that both are Harold in a kind of cartoon sequence can probably be discounted. In the first picture he is shown with a shield, but in the second this has disappeared and instead he is dropping a battle axe as he falls. It has also been pointed out that if both were intended to be Harold, he seems to have had time to change his socks in between.

Wace also has the story of an arrow but he places it towards the start of the battle and has Harold pluck it out and carry on fighting. In fact he flatly declares, 'I do not indeed know ... and have not heard say, who it was that smote down king Harold, nor by what weapon he was wounded.' This suggests that a century after Hastings neither story seemed to be regarded as definitive, at least in Normandy.

It is quite likely that there is an element of truth in each. No doubt in that last bloody assault there were arrows aplenty as well as a desperate struggle about the hilltop. We are also told that Harold's body was so disfigured it was hard to identify, which suggests more than just one arrow in the eye. Whether William himself was directly involved we will never know. He certainly never boasted about it.

It was, however, a decisive moment. With the king gone, and probably his brothers too, either at that time or earlier, the English army was left leaderless. The housecarls, true to their calling, fought on valiantly but were eventually overwhelmed, while in other parts of the army no doubt some died where they stood and others took whatever opportunity presented itself to slip away into the darkness of the forest behind.

Even these were pursued by the mounted Normans, cut down and ridden over in an attempt to make the victory as complete as possible. In the dark some of these horsemen themselves came to grief, plunging down what Poitiers describes as a 'steep valley intersected by ditches,' and which others have interpreted as an ancient British earthwork. Here a group of the English seem to have made a stand, their bravery praised by Poitiers. 'In this dangerous phase of the battle,' he says, 'many Norman nobles were killed,' and it seems Eustace of Boulogne only just escaped, suffering a severe wound in the process.

At the end of the day, though, it was clear who had the final victory. Shorn of all detail, the result is recorded with dour precision in the *Anglo-Saxon Chronicle*. 'There was slain King Harold, and Leofwine the earl his brother, and Gyrth the earl his brother and many good men; and the Frenchmen had possession of the place of carnage, all as God granted them for the people's sins.'

9

CONSOLIDATION
OCTOBER 1066–1072

If we are uncertain what happened to Harold in his last minutes when living, we are even more uncertain as to what happened to him after death. By the time William finished his pursuit of the fugitives and returned to the battlefield, it would probably have been quite dark. In the meantime, as depicted in a whole series of cartoons along the lower frieze of the Tapestry, others had been busy gleaning everything they could from the fallen. Armour, shields, bundles of swords, all was taken, leaving the corpses, and no doubt others who were merely wounded, lying naked as they were born. How then was the dead king to be recognised among the pile of bodies where he fell?

There is a story that when women came to claim husbands, fathers and brothers from those left on the battlefield, Harold was so disfigured that it was left to his long-time mistress Edith Swan-neck to identify the body by some mark known to her alone. Next we hear that Harold's mother, Gytha, came asking for the body so that she could take it for proper burial but was flatly refused. Hard political necessity must have overcome William's reputed greed if that is the case, for she is said to have offered his weight in gold in exchange. Instead we are told he gave the body to one William Malet, telling him to bury it secretly on the seashore and adding that since he had guarded the coast so devotedly in life, he could go on guarding it in death.

This rather sour joke of William's shows him in a very poor light, and he seems to have offered none of the respect traditional from a Christian ruler to a fallen foe. Even Cnut fifty years before had allowed Edmund Ironside a Christian burial at Glastonbury and himself honoured his grave. William, by contrast, seems only anxious to heap derision on Harold and ensure there should be no opportunity for his resting place to become a place of pilgrimage for the English. We have no idea whether his order was in fact carried out. If it was then Harold's last resting place is completely unknown, though one tradition says he was buried on a nearby clifftop, presumably in the Hastings area. There are, however, other places that have over the years laid claim to the body of the English king.

One such is the Holy Trinity Church at Bosham, stronghold of the Godwins and relatively easy to reach from Hastings. It has been suggested that Malet was given the task of burial as he was half English. If he wanted to obey the letter of William's order and yet honour a fallen king, this would be a way to do it. The church, later enlarged by the Normans but which Harold would have known well, still stands a matter of yards above the high-tide level. Repairs to the floor in 1954 revealed an elaborate but unmarked coffin of approximately the right date, containing some bones, and positioned at the foot of the altar steps. It is alongside that of a child reputed to be the daughter of Cnut, who drowned in the nearby millstream. Some have claimed that the coffin is that of Harold Godwinson, though further scientific testing would be needed to establish this as a fact. An absence of direct descendants would make DNA testing problematic, though it might just be possible to find some in connections of the old Danish royal family since the twelfth-century Danish monarchs were descended from Harold's daughter Gytha.

A stronger claim is usually made for Waltham Abbey in Essex. Although a religious house had stood here for some hundreds of years, the Abbey was re-founded, rebuilt and generously endowed by Harold in the years before 1066. It is claimed that he stopped here to pray on the journey south from Stamford Bridge and that two canons accompanied him to Hastings. A strong tradition claims that, although William refused money for Harold's body, he did in fact turn it over to Countess Gytha, or at least to the two canons from Waltham who may have supported her claim, and who then brought it back to the abbey and buried it before the high altar. The basis of this claim comes from William of Malmesbury, writing in 1125, and he is backed up by Wace in the 1160s, though Wace adds, 'I do not know who it was that bore him thither, neither do I know who buried him.' In the abbey grounds today there still stands a memorial to Harold, reputed to mark the site of his grave, and this is certainly the nearest the last consecrated Saxon king has ever come to a gravestone. It is recorded, though, that when on one occasion the grave was excavated it was empty. Perhaps that would not be surprising if we were to believe another legend, recorded in a *Life of Harold* also written at Waltham, that gives a completely different end to the story. According to this Harold survived the battle of Hastings and in fact lived for many years after. This legend and the evidence for it will be explored more fully in Appendix 1.

If Harold got any kind of proper burial he did better than many on the English side at Hastings. Though the Normans reputedly buried all their fallen, the bodies of the losers, apart from those immediately claimed by their loved ones, were apparently left to rot where they lay, a situation that William of Poitiers describes as 'justice'.

One account declares that Duke William actually camped for the night on the battlefield itself, despite the fears of his supporters that among the corpses were likely to be many who were only wounded and who might rise in the night and murder him. In all probability the whole army remained very close to the spot, too exhausted to seek any other lodging in the darkness that followed close on their victory. The next day, a Sunday, was spent in burying the dead and then William withdrew to his camp at Hastings. True he had, by the skin of his teeth, won a great victory, but had he won the war?

It has been suggested that he should have realised by the sheer bloody-minded tenacity of the English in battle that it would not be as easy as that. In fact, he waited five days at Hastings, expecting submissions from those English leaders still remaining and yet none arrived. These five days were also needed, no doubt, for the recovery of what was left of his army. One calculation suggests he may have lost up to a third of his men in the battle, and those surviving would have had a severe mauling in the hand-to-hand combat. At the end of this time, however, they would have been forced to move on.

This was an army living off the land and they had now been more than two weeks in the same area. Food supplies would have been running out and they would have to go somewhere else to find more. London might be William's obvious target, but barring his way was the heavily forested Andredsweald which might hide who knows how many armed enemies and provide little in the way of food. He also wanted to remain near the coast, having sent to Normandy for reinforcements and wanting their numbers before moving inland. It was along the coast to Dover that he went first, then, receiving the submission of that town and immediately setting about fortifying it for his own purposes. Canterbury, too, surrendered and with it the chief men in Kent, swarming in, as the *Carmen* puts it, like flies to an open wound.

At this point William suffered a setback that, in other circumstances, could have ended his whole enterprise. While at Dover a sickness broke out among his men that has generally been identified as dysentery. No doubt their good French wine had run out and they were reduced to drinking water, while camping in less than sanitary conditions. The duke himself fell ill and for a matter of weeks all progress was stalled. Had there been any leader of stature left in southern England at the time, a swift attack now could have changed the course of history.

The only strong, experienced leader, however, had been taken out of the game at Hastings and his loss was being deeply felt among the survivors now gathered in London. There a teenaged prince, two earls in their early twenties, an elderly archbishop and another archbishop already under a cloud of disapproval were all that England could now muster by way of leaders, and none had the necessary power and authority to land a decisive blow. The *Chronicle* records that Archbishop Ealdred and the people of London now offered the crown to young Edgar, 'as was his true, natural right', but there was no hurried coronation. No doubt other matters were more pressing. Earls Edwin and Morcar also promised they would fight for him, but, in a possibly unconscious echo of some fifty years before, the *Chronicle* declares that, 'in that degree that it ought ever to have been forwarder, so was it from day to day later and worse; so that at the end all passed away'. Certainly the opportunity passed, William recovered and his campaign continued.

Although the English recorded that William ravaged everywhere he went, an attempt was made in the late nineteenth century to establish by means of the values in the Domesday Book that in fact his army was only taking what it needed from day to day. Though this is no longer taken as definitive, still it lets us follow his footprints as he travelled in a wide circle around London without making a direct bid for the city itself. Some five hundred cavalry were sent to try their luck over old London Bridge, but when they were repulsed by spirited defenders they merely burned Southwark and moved on. London had withstood many such attacks in the previous hundred years and William was not going to waste his time there when there were other ways of forcing submission.

He moved on through Wessex, threatening Winchester, and Queen Edith, widow of Edward, who held the old capital surrendered it without a fight. More than just a moral victory, this gave William his first really tangible reward. Though others submitting had offered gifts, the royal treasury was lodged in Winchester and William lost no time in taking it over. At almost the same time he received reinforcements to replace those killed, fallen ill or left on garrison duties, and with these he moved north again to the Thames, crossing at Wallingford.

The old Anglo-Saxon burgh here had been a major base for housecarls but now there was no resistance. In fact it was here that he received the first indication that the nerve of the English might be on the verge of cracking. Archbishop Stigand arrived. Possibly originally sent as an envoy from London, in fact he submitted to William and paid him homage in return for confirmation in his post. At around the same time Edwin and Morcar apparently withdrew their men to the north, having already sent their sister, Harold's pregnant widow, to safety in Chester. Their desertion of Edgar has been condemned by many as rank treachery but it also made sound sense at the time. If they and all their forces were to be trapped inside William's iron circle around the capital, there would be no possibility of any further resistance. Moving at least kept their options open, however slim their chances of success might appear to be.

William's policy now seemed to change. As he and his men moved on, swinging round to the north of London, their destruction became more widespread. With Harold's estates as particular targets, the aim was now to strike terror into those who resisted, the same tactics William had used repeatedly in his earlier Continental campaigns. When, in early December, he turned back south to Hertford and Berkhamsted, within striking distance of a now encircled London, it was the end of the road for 'King' Edgar and his supporters.

Now all the leading men met with William at Berkhamsted, and Edgar, 'having no means of resistance', as Orderic Vitalis records, formally submitted to him. The same source tells us that William then 'affectionately embraced him, and treated him all his life with the regard due to a son', which, considering that his relationships with his own sons were often less than cordial, may well be true.

So Edgar, elected king a matter of weeks before and never consecrated, was now 'un-kinged', but where did that leave William? Poitiers declares that it was the English who now urged him to take the crown because they were accustomed to obey a king. For the Normans (but not the English) this meant William should immediately have a coronation, but the man himself showed a becoming modesty. He had so far only reduced a small corner of the country to submission. Surely he should complete the job before obtaining formal recognition, and anyway he wanted his wife to be crowned with him. The arguments of his supporters won him over. They too wanted to serve a king – especially one who would be generous with the spoils of conquest – and if he had the title and honour of a king, surely this would encourage other parts of the country to submit more quickly. A coronation was therefore arranged.

By some reports, even now when the Normans first marched into London they were met with resistance, and one of the new king's first acts was to direct the building of a fortress near the river in the eastern part of the city where the Tower of London now stands. Nor, it seems, did he trust himself into the hands of the Londoners but lodged instead in Edward's palace at Westminster, close to the new abbey where the coronation would be held.

Those who believed in omens, which William firmly declared he did not, would also have had a field day with the coronation itself. On Christmas Day 1066 Westminster Abbey was packed with English and Normans, with one of each, Ealdred, Archbishop of York, and Geoffrey, Bishop of Coutances, presiding. The ritual followed the usual English form with the exception of a question put in both English and French to the congregation – did they want William as their king? The wild acclamations that followed this reached the ears of the numerous armed guards outside, who, thinking some kind of riot was beginning, immediately set fire to the buildings around the abbey. What the purpose of this was no one has quite explained, though there were suggestions it was simply an excuse for more looting. Now those inside heard the hubbub outside, smelt the smoke and saw the flames, and immediately rushed out in a panic, leaving William still uncrowned and almost deserted. According to Orderic Vitalis, 'The bishops only, with some few of the clergy and monks maintained their post before the altar', while William trembled from head to foot, though whether with anger or fear, we don't know. If this 'omen of future calamities' as Vitalis called it did indeed foreshadow things to come it was strictly accurate, since fire and panic were to feature for quite some time in the reign of the new king.

Eventually the ritual was completed and William was consecrated and crowned, but not before Ealdred had extracted from him the customary promise to rule the whole nation justly according to the laws of his predecessors. To this, however, William added the proviso, as long as the people remained loyal to him.

Initially it seemed as if this bargain might be kept on both sides. Certainly Edgar and the surviving earls were treated with surprising leniency, the existing sheriffs and clergy remained in post, as did the royal clerks now serving the new regime. William even made an attempt to learn English. There was, of course, a distribution of lands and spoils to those who had travelled hopefully with him, but the confiscated lands of those who had fallen at Hastings satisfied the initial cravings of these land-hungry men. Even the Pope was included in the distribution, receiving Harold's priceless golden banner of the Fighting Man, together with a selection of treasures from the English churches and treasury.

Those who had submitted to the conqueror were confirmed in their landholding, although they had to pay for this privilege and no doubt grumbled about having to buy back their own lands. There was another difference, too. All lands, whether given to English or Normans, were now held from the king in return for specific military service and a personal oath of fealty. William was from the start asserting his absolute control in a way he had never yet been able to do in his own duchy, where of course the French king was still his overlord.

It was during this time of apparent peace and goodwill that Edwin and Morcar came to submit themselves to the new king. They too were allowed to redeem their lands and initially at least retain their earldoms. The earldom that had belonged to Harold's brother Leofwine was now given to William's half-brother Odo, Bishop of Bayeux, together with Dover and its new castle. William Fitzosbern was rewarded with the Isle of Wight and extensive lands in Hampshire, including Winchester, where another castle was now begun. He also became at this time Earl of Hereford, Gloucester, Worcester and Oxford, taking over much of Harold's old earldom on the Welsh Marches in land as yet unvisited and unconquered. The implication was that he would take a leading part in bringing these areas under firm control.

Odo and William Fitzosbern were now left in charge as William's regents as the new king returned home to Normandy in March 1067. Needless to say, he received a rapturous welcome. With him, officially as guests but more in the way of hostages, he took all the leading men in England who might possibly act as figureheads for revolt. So Edgar, Edwin, Morcar, two English archbishops and even young Waltheof followed in the train of William's triumphal progress, rather in the way notable foreign captives were displayed in ancient Rome by returning generals. With him too went large quantities of what can only be described as loot.

William remained in Normandy for most of 1067 and in his absence we have two startlingly different accounts of what was going on in England. According to William of Poitiers, Odo and Fitzosbern were each burning with a desire to bring peace and justice to the people under their rule and to bring former enemies into friendship. Orderic Vitalis, however, with his usual willingness to present the English point of view, declares that these regents were twin tyrants: 'Meanwhile the English were oppressed by the insolence of the Normans and subjected to grievous outrages by the haughty governors...' They would not listen to any complaint or give any kind of justice to the English, but 'screened their men at arms who most outrageously robbed the people and ravished the women'. The *Anglo-Saxon Chronicle* tends to go along with the latter version.

Certainly, if the new king thought he had removed all possibility of rebellion he was mistaken. Throughout the year there were rumblings which from time to time burst into actual violence. In Herefordshire a leading thegn known as Edric the Wild repeatedly attacked the new Norman garrisons installed in the existing castles built in earlier times by Earl Ralf. Eventually he formed an alliance with two Welsh princes to ravage across much of the county.

Surprisingly, the people of Kent even approached Eustace of Boulogne to help them overthrow Odo and seize Dover castle. Eustace had had a fairly chequered career since his run-in with the people of Dover some fifteen years earlier. At one time he had been involved in an attempt to overthrow William of Normandy, but then joined his invasion force in 1066 and played a prominent role in the Battle of Hastings. Now, however, he seemed willing to take part in another rebellion. Perhaps his rewards had been less than he'd expected. This, though, was a short-lived revolt. Although Odo was away from his castle the defenders quickly scattered the forces assembled against them. Eustace escaped back to Boulogne and some time later became reconciled once again with William.

In Northumbria, too, there was trouble. Before he left for Normandy the king had granted at least the northern part of Morcar's earldom to Copsig, who had been Tostig's hated lieutenant in the area before the rebellion of 1065. This land had always been held by a local family and Morcar had wisely granted it to one of them, a man called Oswulf. Copsig lasted a mere five weeks before being ambushed and murdered by Oswulf, who himself might have been a figurehead for a northern uprising had he not in turn been killed in the autumn of the year.

More worrying for William than all of these, however, were the rumours beginning to reach him in the autumn of 1067 of activity centred on Exeter. Here it was the name of Godwin that caused his alarm. Countess Gytha, mother of Harold, had retired to her lands at Exeter and here she was joined by the sons of Harold's 'handfast' marriage to Edith Swan-neck. The elder of these, Godwine, Edmund and Magnus, would probably have still been in their teens, roughly of an age with Edgar Atheling, but all were clearly ready and willing to avenge their father. Despite the loss of much of their lands the family was apparently still wealthy and well able to finance a rebellion, and throughout the autumn of 1067 support was actively being rallied in the south-west of England.

On 6 December 1067 William returned to England, and after passing Christmas in London he immediately turned his attention to Exeter. A demand was sent that the citizens of that city should formally submit and swear fealty to him, and when that was refused he took an army west to obtain what he wanted by force. This was, incidentally, the first occasion when he called on the military service now owed to him by his English as well as his Norman subjects, an early test of loyalties which, as much as anything else, would tell him how the land lay in his new kingdom.

The newly fortified city of Exeter held out for eighteen days under repeated attacks that, according to Vitalis, cost William's army dear. In the end the collapse of a section of wall, possibly undermined by the Normans, led them to negotiate a surrender. By this time, though, the Godwins had escaped, Gytha and a group of noble ladies to the island of Flatholme in the Bristol Channel, and the boys, like their father before them, to Dublin. Still endeavouring to buy loyalty, William's terms may have been fairly generous, though the *Chronicle* declares he 'promised them well and performed ill'. It also adds that the city fell because 'the thegns betrayed them', though whether this refers to the flight of Harold's family or the failure of the local English to support them is not clear.

By the Easter of 1068 William seemed confident enough of his position in England to bring over his wife Matilda. At Whitsun she was duly crowned Queen of England in Westminster Abbey, with Archbishop Ealdred again presiding. At about the same time two things occurred that would have significance in the future. Gospatric, the cousin of Oswulf, approached William offering a large sum of money in exchange for the earldom previously and disastrously bestowed on Copsig. Again it seems to show William's policy of reconciliation that he agreed to this. However, one who was not prepared to rely on the goodwill of the conqueror was Edgar, who now managed to slip away with his mother and two sisters to Scotland, where King Malcolm gave them all shelter at his court.

In fact the Scottish king soon became smitten with Edgar's sister Margaret, and despite her protests that she wanted to become a nun he was clearly in a position to insist on having his way. The *Chronicle* declares that, 'The king married her, though against her will,' but that her ways worked such a change in him that he 'thanked God who had given him such a wife,' and 'turned himself to God.' As well as achieving an improvement in Malcolm, however, this marriage ensured that the leaders of English rebellions against William of Normandy could now be sure of sanctuary and material assistance from the King of Scotland. Very soon after, this would be put to the test.

'It was then told the king that the people in the North had gathered together and would oppose him there.' This statement in the *Chronicle* rather undersells the alliance that now formed against the conqueror. Edwin and Morcar were the likely instigators, seeing their earldoms and power bases shrinking as more and more was carved off and given to those supporting the new king. They were joined, though, by their nephew the Welsh Prince Bleddyn, son of their sister Eadgyth and her first husband Gruffydd, and more surprisingly by William's new appointee Gospatric. In addition Harold's man Maerleswein, who had been put in charge of York after Stamford Bridge, now appeared at their side, and finally Edgar Atheling himself arrived, with a promise of backing from the King of Scotland.

William's response as recorded in the *Chronicle* sounds rather casual. He went to Nottingham and built a castle and then on to York. In fact, we know from other sources that it was a great deal more destructive. Gathering his forces, he went first to Warwick and threw up a new castle there, presumably allowing his men the usual licence to harry the land all around as they went. One source at least suggests that this was so impressive that Edwin and Morcar had submitted and made peace with him before he even reached Nottingham. York was surrendered without a fight, while Edgar, Gospatric and Maerleswein fled to Scotland. Then, pausing only to throw up another castle there and negotiate a peace settlement with Malcolm, he returned to the south, planting further castles along the way at Lincoln and Cambridge.

If this anti-climax was dispiriting for the English, they would have been further depressed to hear of an attempted strike at the city of Bristol and later at Taunton by the Godwinson boys being beaten off by local forces. Either the name had lost its potency or the reputation of the conqueror had superseded it in the minds of those in the south-west of England.

The north, however, did not remain cowed for long. Late in 1068 William appointed yet another Earl of Northumbria in place of Gospatric. The new earl, Robert of Comines, was on his way to Durham in January 1069 when he was warned of the presence of a rebel army nearby. Being backed by between nine hundred and a thousand soldiers, he no doubt felt himself safe enough and continued to Durham where the usual plundering and violence took place. Early next morning, however, according to the account of Simeon of Durham, the Northumbrians entered the city and scoured through the whole area, killing not only the earl but the entire force he had with him.

Now once again the exiles returned, attacking York and laying siege to the castle. Only the swift arrival of William with an overwhelming force saved the day, but in the violence that followed much of the city was ravaged. 'He also profaned St Peter's minster,' declares the *Chronicle* in tones of deep disgust. Still the English leaders managed to escape, and by now it must have been clear to William that despite all his efforts he was not yet the master of all his new kingdom. A second castle was begun in York near to the River Ouse, and William Fitzosbern left in charge to try and subdue the area, but there were further attacks as soon as the king returned to the south.

The situation in England was becoming something of a vicious circle. The more unrest there was, the more castles were built and garrisoned to contain it, but more castles meant more men to be paid or rewarded with lands. This meant heavier taxes or more seizures of estates which led to more unrest – and so on. Sending

Matilda home to Normandy in the first half of 1069 is somehow symptomatic of William rolling up his sleeves and settling down to the hard and dirty process of stamping his control on the land that nominally at least called him king.

And now there was to be a new player in the game. In the summer of 1069 the sons of Harold Godwinson came again in force to the West Country and were again beaten off with heavy losses on both sides. This time, however, they turned to their father's cousin Sweyn Estrithsson in Denmark for help. Even before this, Sweyn had been urged to launch his own attack on the country his grandfather and namesake had conquered. Now he finally decided to listen to that advice. In early 1066 he had held back, not wanting to face the well-organised English army led by the formidable King Harold. The fate of Hardrada's expedition suggests he was right to do so. Now, however, with Hardrada's threat to Denmark also removed, the situation was altogether different. He would have watched the turmoil of the past two years and have been plausibly persuaded that at least half the country was likely to rise in his support. In northern parts a Danish king was greatly to be preferred to a Norman one. He also remembered, or some say borrowed from William of Normandy, the claim that Edward had at one time promised England to him. As a result he spent the summer of 1069 preparing a fleet of something like three hundred ships and crews, and in late August sent them on their way to England. It still suggests caution on his part that he did not lead the expedition himself. Instead, command was given to his brother Osbeorn, with lesser roles for Sweyn's sons Harold and Cnut.

Vitalis suggests the fleet spent some time raiding along the south and east coast of England, giving William an opportunity to warn his men in York to expect an attack. There is no evidence, though, of him sending any assistance at this time. The *Chronicle* simply records that the invaders arrived in their time-honoured way at the mouth of the Humber soon after the death of Archbishop Ealdred on 11 September. There they were met by Edgar, Gospatric,

Maerleswein and 'all the landsmen, riding and marching joyfully with an immense army'. A new addition to the list of English rebels is Waltheof, son of Siward of Northumbria, who had submitted to William early on. Although confirmed in his lands he had, willingly or not, remained at William's court until 1068 when he was around eighteen years old. Now he joined with this mixed force of English and Danes in their march on York.

The defenders there had begun to take precautions, setting fire to wooden houses near the castles so their timbers could not be used to bridge the moat. Unfortunately the fire then got out of hand and consumed much of the city including the minster, causing the *Chronicle* to suggest that these hated Frenchmen had caused this loss deliberately. When the attackers reached York, however, the Normans were much less effective. Inexplicably, they came down from their castle to engage with the invaders and were overwhelmed. Hundreds were killed and more taken prisoner in what was the greatest defeat suffered by the Normans in the entire conquest. Then, having plundered what was left of the city, the Danes withdrew to their ships.

William raised an army largely of mercenaries and marched north, but by the time he got there the Danes had retreated over the Humber to the Isle of Axholme in Lincolnshire. Now a whole series of rebellions broke out around the country which, if they had been in any way coordinated, might have had a chance of success. Instead they could be tackled separately and put down with great savagery. An attack on the castle at Montacute in Somerset, together with another on Exeter were sufficiently serious for William to send Fitzosbern and Count Brian of Brittany to deal with the situation. Great slaughter and mutilation of prisoners was enough to discourage further outbreaks.

In the Midlands Shrewsbury came under attack from a combined force of Welsh and men from Cheshire and Shropshire led by Prince Bleddyn and Edric the Wild. Failing to take the castle, they moved on into England and met the king himself in fierce fighting at Stafford. Though many were lost here the leaders escaped to the west again, while William withdrew to Nottingham. He had left his half-brother Robert of Mortain to hunt down the rebels around the Humber, but while on his way to rejoin him heard that they had again visited York, attacking the garrisons left there and destroying the castles. Earl Waltheof is said to have played a prominent part in this action.

Once again, by the time William got there the attackers had gone. The *Chronicle* records that the fleet lay on the Humber throughout the winter but the king was not able to reach it. It was time for a change of plan.

By this time it was nearly Christmas, and the fact that the king spent the feast at York, probably in some discomfort, may be taken as a statement of intent. It was the third anniversary of his coronation, and he sent for his crown and regalia and wore it defiantly on Christmas Day. Then immediately afterwards he put into action his two-pronged attack on the rebels.

Somehow making contact with the Danish leader Osbeorn, he made terms with him that they could remain undisturbed throughout the winter if they agreed to leave in the spring, taking with them the plunder they had already amassed. There is some evidence that the Danes were already separated from the English rebels, with Edgar and his men in the Holderness north of the Humber and the Danes in the fens of Lincolnshire to the south. Osbeorn readily agreed to the terms, perhaps because, as was later claimed, William also paid him a large bribe to do so.

The second part of the plan was to hunt down the English rebels and their supporters in such a way that they would have no place to hide and no resources to live on. The Roman Vegetius wrote, 'It is better to overcome the enemy by famine, raids and terror than by battle,' and this was the idea now adopted by William. It became known as the 'Harrying of the North'. The *Chronicle* simply records that 'the king ... went northward with all the troops he could collect, and laid waste all the shire'. Orderic Vitalis gives us more graphic details. Over the whole region from the Humber to the Tyne, he tells us, 'he levelled their places of shelter to the ground, wasted their lands and burnt their dwellings with all they contained ... he ordered the corn and cattle, with the implements of husbandry and every sort of provisions, to be collected in heaps and set on fire till the whole was consumed, and thus destroyed at once all that could serve for the support of life in the whole country lying beyond the Humber.' What followed, in the depths of a harsh winter and in the months and even years after, was a famine that killed tens of thousands, young and old alike, across the north of England. So much property was destroyed that seventeen years later the records in the Domesday Book read for place after place in Yorkshire, 'and it is waste,' while Northumberland was omitted altogether from the survey. The anger and disgust of Vitalis at this action comes down to us clearly across the centuries. 'I am more disposed to pity the sorrows and sufferings of the wretched people,' he writes, 'than to undertake the hopeless task of screening one who was guilty of such wholesale massacre by lying flatteries,' and further, 'Such barbarous homicide could not pass unpunished. The Almighty Judge beholds alike the high and low ... punishing the acts of both with equal justice.'

Nevertheless the policy achieved its aim. Once more the rebels fled north, Edgar and Maerleswein to Scotland, while Gospatric and Waltheof both submitted to William and again received their titles back, although from now on with no real power and with a great deal of suspicion attaching to them.

William could now turn his attention to the Midlands, where Chester was still a hotbed of rebellion and Shrewsbury Castle was once more under siege. To get there involved a journey across the top of the Pennines in bitter winter weather, where threats and bribes alike only just kept the army from mutiny. The Norman chroniclers tend to blame this on the Bretons and French, but it is likely that many Normans too had had nearly enough of the constant cold, discomfort and stomach-turning violence that had attended this whole campaign. Nor was the harrying yet finished. With Chester taken and Shrewsbury relieved, still a trail of destruction accompanied all their movements until it was felt the west was secure and they could turn again to the south.

It was March before they came finally to Salisbury and now the bulk of the mercenaries was to be paid off. Having already bled the country almost dry with taxes, a new source of money was needed for this, and William Fitzosbern is credited with coming up with the idea that had been put into practice in the preceding weeks. In the dangerous times they were living through, many men had entrusted their wealth to the local monastery for safe-keeping, reasoning that these places were the least likely to be disturbed. Now, however, William authorised the scouring of the monasteries for this wealth, with any that was found being seized and rendered up to his treasury. It is highly likely that Church treasures too were scooped up in this way by not too discriminating officials, and that a good deal of this booty was used to reward those mercenaries who had fought through the last long winter campaigns.

The second part of William's plan had been a complete success but the first part was proving less so. Instead of going home in the spring the Danes remained in Lincolnshire and were now joined by Sweyn Estrithsson himself. It is likely, however, that as soon as he saw them he abandoned all plans for a conquest of England. They too had suffered in the winter from hunger and cold and their numbers and condition were greatly reduced. Nevertheless they set up camp at Ely, which was then an island in the fens, and were joined there by a number of disaffected English. One of these has a name that has echoed through the years, Hereward, afterwards known as 'the Wake'.

Although he features in a number of later accounts, including a *Gesta Herewardi* or *Deeds of Hereward*, not all of these are reliable and his appearances in the *Chronicle* are few and not entirely complimentary. He seems to have been born in southern Lincolnshire and to have come from a noble family, although a claimed descent from Leofric of Mercia and his wife Godiva is unlikely. The story is that he was outlawed at the age of eighteen, which might have been any time between 1053 and 1063, and was out of the country at the time of the Battle of Hastings. Returning, he found his brother had been killed and his estates seized by the Normans and he took to the fens to fight back.

Perhaps his most famous exploit recorded in the *Chronicle* is the raid on Peterborough Abbey in early June 1070 in company with a party of Danes. Hereward and his 'train', says the *Chronicle*, had heard that Peterborough was to have a new abbot, a Norman called Turold, and were determined that he would not have all the rich treasures it contained. It is only fair to say that the account is contained in the version of the *Chronicle* written at Peterborough, and though it records the above noble aim it does so with scepticism and clearly regards the raiders as no better than robbers. The monks themselves put up considerable resistance until driven out by fire, and then the raiders ransacked the place, taking 'so much gold and silver and so much treasure in money, robes and books, that no man can compute the amount'.

Possibly Hereward had thought to preserve this treasure or maybe use some of it to pay an army to fight against the Normans. If so he was swiftly disillusioned. On returning to Ely the Danes laid claim to it as recompense for their efforts in England, and when shortly after Sweyn made his peace with William and they all sailed away, the treasure sailed with them. Very little of it actually reached Denmark, however, as the fleet was scattered and largely sunk by a violent storm. Some few pieces even made their way back to England and eventually were returned to Peterborough itself.

Hereward remained at Ely as a last post of defiance against the Normans and over the following months a steady trickle of English resisters joined him there. One was Athelwine, formerly Bishop of Durham, who had joined the northern uprisings in 1068/69 and who felt he had little left to lose. Another, early in 1071, was Earl Morcar. Though he and his brother had nominally retained their earldoms after the rebellion of 1068 it seems likely they had been under some form of restraint, possibly a kind of house-arrest, ever since. Now somehow they had managed to slip away to try once more to raise the country against William. They had been gone too long, however, and the circumstances had changed. While Morcar joined Hereward at Ely, Edwin tried to make his way to Scotland but was betrayed by his own men to a group of Normans and met his death at their hands.

The outlaws in the fens, meanwhile, kept up a steady kind of guerrilla war against the local Normans, robbing, ambushing and killing where they could, then melting away back to their island fastness. The arrival of Morcar, however, and rumours that an ever larger and more dangerous force was gathering there, now prompted William to act. All manner of stories abound of the king's attempts to get to the island, usually thwarted by the daring or trickery of the heroic Hereward. Some of them may even be true. The *Chronicle* simply records that he called out the land force and the ship force, surrounded the area, built a causeway and went in. One tale most likely to be true is that someone showed him one of the few trackways through the marshes, enabling him to get close enough to launch an effective attack.

No doubt many rebels were killed but many more were captured, and these 'he disposed of … as he would'. Some lost hands and eyes, many were imprisoned, among them Bishop Athelwine and Earl Morcar. The good bishop died the following year, but Morcar was still languishing in prison at the time of the conqueror's death some sixteen years later. As for Hereward, he 'led off with great valour' a small band of followers and vanishes from the *Chronicle* forever. Various different accounts are given of his end. He either made his peace with William and lived happily ever after, or was about to make his peace when he was killed by a group of over-zealous Normans, or he disappeared into exile somewhere in Europe, as did many disinherited Englishmen at this time.

The conquest was almost complete. All fight had been crushed out of the English, and when William marched boldly north into Scotland the following year, Malcolm too was intimidated into making terms, giving hostages for good behaviour and agreeing to become the vassal of the English king. One of the terms of this 'Peace of Abernethy' required the expulsion of Edgar Atheling, still sheltering at the court of his brother-in-law, and with the departure of that young man for Flanders, William at last found himself the undisputed king of England.

William the Bastard had finally become William the Conqueror.

10

A CONQUERED LAND

Fifty years before Hastings another foreign invader had come to England, fought against a newly crowned king and on his death was proclaimed King of England. He had a lot in common with William of Normandy. Both came from a people accustomed to fight hard for what they wanted and with an aggressive policy of expansion. His takeover was quicker, and at least as complete as William's and he ended with an empire far greater than anything the Norman achieved. Yet we don't talk of Cnut the Conqueror. Only William was given that title, which may or may not be seen as complimentary.

The comparison between the two is instructive. Cnut was younger when he made his takeover and maybe more open to new influences. Possibly Archbishop Wulfstan was more subtly persuasive than Ealdred. The men he led may well have had different expectations from those of their later counterparts, and their loyalty was generally to Cnut himself rather than to an idea of power to come. In the final analysis England may have been more accustomed to Danes and Danish ways, particularly in the northern and eastern areas. In more ways than one they spoke the same language. What is certain is that within a very short period of time Cnut had dismissed the bulk of his forces and settled down to rule as an English king, with English laws, customs and advisors. He seems to have been seduced by the English and they by him, more especially as he gave them peace and prosperity after a period of turmoil.

It is fairly clear that the same love and respect never existed between William and his new country. There is evidence that, initially at least, he tried to establish an Anglo-Norman state, as Cnut had established an Anglo-Danish one, but his efforts were met with implacable hatred and any opportunity to overthrow him was eagerly seized on by the leaders of the English. Had they been more strongly led or better organised they may well have succeeded for the bulk of the population seemed to be behind them. Indeed, William of Malmesbury, writing for a grandson of the Conqueror, tries to put the blame for all the violence on the English. 'The conduct of the king,' he writes, 'may reasonably be excused if he was at any time rather severe against the English, for he scarcely found any one of them faithful.'

William did have certain disadvantages. Although descended from the same Danish stock, the Normans had firmly turned their backs on their heritage and become thoroughly Frenchified. The fear shown at the thought of crossing the narrow seas of the English Channel is evidence of how far they had moved from their seafaring ancestors. Although Edward and his mother before him had introduced some French and Normans into areas of English life, particularly in Church appointments, the attitude of the *Chronicle* represents the standard English view, stamping them all equally as 'foreigners'. Their customs, language, even their clothes and hairstyles therefore made them wholly alien to the English, a great deal more alien than the Danes had been for centuries past.

Nor were the men William led in any way comparable to those of Cnut. In general the Danes were happy to take their money and go home, or at least go away and raid somewhere else. Those that remained soon became farmers. The area of the Danelaw around Lincolnshire had a higher proportion of independent free farmers than anywhere else in the country.

In no circumstances were William's followers going to be farmers. They were soldiers. They came for land and power, especially power. The lands they won could be farmed by others but they would be ruled by Normans and squeezed dry to provide the greater glory and status for their masters. For the first time a great gulf would be stretched between the rulers and the ruled. It is indicative of the different mindset that at one point before the invasion William of Poitiers has the duke rallying his men by pointing out that Harold had not dared to promise a single acre of Normandy to his followers if they should be victorious. It did not seem to occur to either duke or chronicler that the English king and people might be happy with what they had already got.

It was violence after peace that the conqueror brought, then, not peace after violence. Even Malmesbury noted the difference from the gentleness of Cnut in 1016, 'who restored their honours unimpaired to the conquered'. In the years after 1066 it would be conquest pure and simple. Over the next twenty years the English would lose their nobility, their land, their Church and even their language.

The first and most obvious sign of the new order was the building of castles. There are suggestions that pre-fabricated sections were even brought over from Normandy with the invaders to speed up the erection of these fortifications. Certainly the chronicles suggest that the first were operating at Pevensey and Hastings within weeks of the initial landings. Orderic Vitalis goes so far as to declare that the English lost because they had no castles, which is probably an over-simplification, but as used by the Normans they certainly helped to exert control over a conquered people. The English way had been to fortify a town to protect the local population. The Normans built castles within the towns to protect themselves *from* the local population.

Within the lifetime of the Conqueror dozens of castles were built in every Anglo-Saxon town of any size, and in other strategic places by roads and rivers where new towns would soon grow up. To begin with they were simple earth-and-timber constructions of the motte-and-bailey type. The motte was a great mound of earth with some defensive structure on top into which the garrison could retreat at need. The bailey would be one and sometimes two enclosed courtyards, surrounded by wooden palisades with sometimes a rampart and water-filled ditch outside.

Within this area would be crammed all the necessities of life, kitchens, stables, dormitories, armouries and all those needed to keep them going. There would be little comfort and, certainly in the early years, very little mingling with the local population. Indeed, in most areas no Norman would venture outside the walls of his castle without an armed guard.

The building of these structures caused further resentment on the part of the English. It is unlikely any Norman hand shovelled earth to form the mighty mounds when forced labour was available, and earthworks of around two hundred feet in diameter and forty or fifty feet high would take some shovelling. Nor was that the only cost. If the castle was to be in an existing town, space would be made for it by demolishing houses. The Domesday Book clearly records the effect of these operations. In Shrewsbury, for example, the English burgesses complain that they are expected to produce the same amount of taxes for the king when the site of fifty-one dwellings out of an original two hundred and fifty-two was now occupied by the earl's castle. In Norwich the castle, begun as early as 1067, occupied the site of eighty-one dwellings, while in Lincoln the figure was a hundred and sixty-six.

The remains of these structures, often with later stone-built additions, can still be seen throughout the country, from Cardiff in the west to Norwich in the east, Launceston and Totnes in the far south-west to York in the north. The latter, surviving as Clifford's Tower, remains indestructible though the fortifications around it were twice destroyed and rebuilt within half a dozen years of the invasion. The castle at Windsor was once part of a ring around London approximately twenty miles apart (one day's easy ride) and twenty miles from the capital itself. Garrisoned and strongly held, it was this iron fist that held down the bulk of the country while the conquest was still gathering its strength, and Orderic Vitalis had no doubt that it represented the greatest loss of freedom for the English. Nor does he mince words about the arrogance of those ruling from the castles. They 'treated the natives, both gentle and simple, with the utmost scorn and levied on them most unjust exactions'. It was this immediate and uncontrolled repression, he believed, that led to the repeated but ineffectual rebellions, perpetuating the cycle of violence for many years.

The loss of the English nobility was felt just as keenly. Great numbers of these had fallen at Hastings and in the earlier battles of that momentous year, but it was not only the numbers but the seniority of the dead that caused the greatest difficulty for those who survived. Not only the king but all the leading earls of southern England were wiped out at a stroke, and these were men seasoned in battle and in leadership. The northern earls and the newly nominated king were babies in comparison, a fact well demonstrated by their disorganised and uncoordinated attempts at resistance. Furthermore, by dating his reign to the death of Edward with the claim that it was Harold that was the usurper, William could declare that all who had opposed him were rebels and traitors, and that therefore their lands and titles would all be forfeited.

As we have seen those who submitted quickly would be allowed to retain their birthright at a price, but the earldoms handed back to Edwin, Morcar and Waltheof were merely shadows of their former rights. Certainly after 1068 the former earls of Mercia and Northumbria were simply puppet figures, held close to the court of the conqueror while real power lay elsewhere. This may explain his unusual mercy in pardoning their rebellions.

In their place came flooding in the followers and adventurers who had crossed the sea in expectation of reward and advancement. They got their reward in the form of lands and titles but there were conditions attached. For every piece of land granted, duties were required, in particular the provision of a specified number of knights for the service of the king. This number was fixed by the king himself and bore no connection to the size or value of the holding, the aim being solely to provide the king with a large body of well equipped, well trained professional soldiers for any campaign he might undertake. Nor was it full ownership of the land that was granted. Instead the man receiving the grant became a tenant-in-chief of the king, whose land could be taken back for any failure to fulfil his duties, and in any case needed the king's permission to pass on to his heirs. There were to be no little kingdoms formed within the realm of William the Conqueror. Having achieved the powers of a king, he exerted greater control over his lands in England than he had ever been able to achieve in the Duchy of Normandy.

Initially the need was for defence and consolidation and to this end blocks of land were given to his most trusted followers, most of Kent to Odo and the Isle of Wight amongst other holdings to William Fitzosbern. The so-called Rapes of Sussex were created, north/south blocks of land dividing the county into five parts, guarding the coast and the essential means of access to Normandy. These were granted to the Counts of Eu and Mortain, William de Warenne, Roger de Montgomery and William de Braose and each was expected to build a castle and control administration of their area, ensuring it was solidly held for the benefit of the invaders.

Thereafter landholdings were generally more scattered, especially in the central areas, with leading men holding estates in many different shires. Around the border lands, though, the need for a unified defence led once again to more concentrated power bases, and we find the beginnings of the great Marcher holdings with Fitzosbern in Hereford, Robert de Mortain in Shrewsbury and Hugh d'Avranches in Chester. After the downfall of Waltheof the earldom of Northumbria was bought by William Walcher, the first of the so-called 'Prince Bishops' of Durham, while Brian of Brittany held Cornwall for a time before that too passed to Robert de Mortain. Estates in the east of England, an area most likely to be targeted by any Scandinavian attack, went to Alan the Red of Brittany (brother of Brian), who held lands in Yorkshire, Lincolnshire and East Anglia and who built a mighty castle at Richmond in the Swale Valley of Yorkshire.

We have all these details of land holdings from a unique document, the so-called Domesday Book, commissioned by William in 1085.

Although by no means complete – large towns such as London and Winchester are missing, along with Northumbria and the Isle of Wight – it gives a mass of information about the condition of England both before and after the conquest. Not only are land, houses and people covered, the Little Domesday covering Essex, Norfolk and Suffolk even counts the cows, pigs and sheep in those shires.

William, of course, was not compiling this information for the benefit of historians. He seems to have had several motives and one of these was to airbrush the reign of Harold out of history entirely. The survey questions compare the land at the time, in 1086, with its condition 'tempore regis Edwardi', 'in the time of Edward'. Harold's short reign in between does not get a mention and he is referred to, when dealing with his own landholding, as 'Earl Harold'. Anyone reading the entries with no previous knowledge would assume, as they were intended to do, that William had taken over from Edward on 5 January 1066 instead of some eleven months later.

A second and more important motive concerned the raising of money. William must have been delighted to find that when he took on the powers of an English king, he inherited one of the finest tax-raising systems in Europe. This was the mechanism that year after year had raised thousands of pounds to pay the Danegeld, and now it would be used to raise thousands for the new king and his duchy. By 1085, however, he had already been to this well many times, also raiding the monasteries to pay his army, and still his need for money was pressing. A main aim of the survey, therefore, was to establish what wealth was yet untapped in the country he 'owned', and what else it could produce for his support.

It was a very thorough survey. The country was divided into seven 'circuits' and in each a panel of commissioners asked the same set of questions, a copy of which is still preserved. For each hundred the sheriff of the shire, the priest, the reeve and six leading villeins had to give information on oath concerning the name of the estate, who held it in Edward's time and now, how large it was, the people, livestock and equipment, how much pasture and woodland, how many mills and fishponds, the value of the estate in Edward's time and now, how it had been assessed for tax, and finally, the killer question, could it pay more.

It took around a year to collect all the information and to collate and summarise it, and astoundingly the manuscript book that resulted seems to have been entirely written by just one man. Some have suggested he might also have been the originator of the scheme. It was not officially called the Domesday Book. That was the name the people gave it, for not only did the questions seem an examination worthy of the end of time, but it also became the absolute judgement on who owned what throughout the land. Nor was it just a record of fact. Disputes were raised and settled by the king's officers in the course of the survey, and some have seen in this the seed of the system of itinerant justice dispensed by the king's officers that later became such a feature of the English legal system.

What the survey revealed was the completeness of the takeover by the king and his followers. Around one-fifth of the land in England was held by the king directly, another quarter was held by the Church in one form or another, and around a half was held by those Normans, Bretons and Flemings who had followed William across the Channel. In shire after shire the same names appear in the list of landholdings – the Count of Mortain, Roger de Montgomery, William de Warenne, Count Eustace of Boulogne, Count Alan the Red of Brittany, Hugh d'Avranches and the Count of Eu. In fact it has been calculated that the majority of this land was held by just eleven men, while others, Roger Bigod in Norfolk and Suffolk, for example, were big fish in smaller ponds. The majority, of course, were Normans though other 'Frenchmen' were also favoured, particularly Eustace of Boulogne who seems to have been fully forgiven for his momentary lapse in 1067. Significantly, at the end of most shire lists come a selection of 'King's thegns', a leftover list of English names holding one or two hides each. Formerly the backbone of English society, they were now of no account at all in the land of their birth.

The revolution in landholding is reflected too in the revolution that took place in the English Church at this time. William had clothed his invasion with the appearance of a crusade and was expected to make good on his promise to bring the Church in England more into line with the Pope's reforming agenda. He had championed this cause in Normandy but in the course of doing so had made sure that it in no way undermined his own authority. His approach in England would be very similar.

When complaint was made about the English Church the first name mentioned was usually that of Stigand, who had been Archbishop of Canterbury since the flight of Robert of Jumièges in 1052. His position was suspect in a number of ways. First his predecessor had not been formally deposed and nor was his appointment initially approved by the Pope. He did not go to Rome for his pallium but simply kept the one left behind by Robert. When eventually Stigand did receive a pallium it was from a pope, Benedict, who had been irregularly appointed and was himself deposed shortly after. Worse than all of this in the eyes of the reformers, however, was the fact that Stigand, when appointed archbishop, did not give up his previous bishopric of Winchester but kept both offices together. As a result of these flaws he had been regarded as something of an outcast by the English Church even before the conquest. Bishops refused to be consecrated by him and, despite claims to the contrary in Norman accounts, Harold did not receive his crown from him.

In spite of this, however, he remained archbishop for over three years under William. He was useful as a figurehead, in the same way as the former earls were figureheads, and he even consecrated a new Bishop of Dorchester, a monk from the abbey of Fécamp in Normandy, in 1067. By 1070, however, his usefulness was over. It may be that the death of Archbishop Ealdred of York the previous autumn was the trigger for action, or possibly the crushing defeat of the northern rebels meant William could dispense with his

Anglo-Saxon archbishop. For whatever reason, William now invited Pope Alexander to send a legate to England to inquire into Church affairs, and at a Council at Winchester attended by the king himself Stigand was formally deposed. His fall was timely for William in another way. Accused of crimes of misusing Church property, the former archbishop was thrown into prison and all his considerable wealth confiscated by the king, which no doubt came in very useful when he had just used the money from the monasteries to pay off his army.

Nor was Stigand the only bishop to fall at this time. His brother Aethelmaer, Bishop of Elmham, was also deposed, along with Bishop Aethelric of Selsey, who was suspected of having links with the Godwin family and who was also imprisoned. In fact the Pope ordered a review and reinstatement of the latter the following year but William ignored it and Aethelric remained in prison until his death, as did Stigand.

The replacement archbishop appointed in August 1070 was Lanfranc, one of the major figures of the reforming Church. Born in northern Italy, he became a teacher of theology, logic and rhetoric, and in 1039 was master of the cathedral school at Avranches in Normandy. In 1042 he became a monk at the famous abbey of Bec. His teaching became so famous that pupils flocked to his school at Bec from all over Europe, but he may have first come to the notice of William of Normandy when he opposed his marriage to Matilda. Indeed it is claimed William intended to exile him for this but a chance meeting between the two gave Lanfranc a chance to talk his way into the duke's friendship. It may, in fact, have been Lanfranc that finally persuaded Pope Nicholas to give retrospective approval for the union. Thereafter the relationship seems to have become close and sincere. Lanfranc was William's choice as first abbot of his Abbey of St Stephen in Caen, and in 1066 he was offered and turned down the archbishopric of Rouen, the highest position in the Norman Church.

He was equally reluctant to accept Canterbury but no doubt a winning argument was the good he might do in spreading his reforming ideals in England. When he arrived, however, he found an immediate problem. The whole of Normandy was subject to the Archbishop of Rouen, but in England there were two provinces and two archbishops. William had recently appointed Thomas of Bayeux, his former chaplain, to replace Archbishop Ealdred, but when he came to be consecrated by the new Archbishop of Canterbury, Lanfranc refused to do this unless Thomas gave him a promise of obedience first. Thomas gave the promise but only under protest, pointing out that it had not been required from his predecessors. When the two of them travelled to Rome the following year for their palliums he raised the issue again with the Pope, who decided it was a matter for the English Church to settle for itself.

As a result another Council was held at Winchester in May 1072. Before this Lanfranc had assembled an impressive amount of evidence on his side, some relating back to the writings of the Venerable Bede and some based on earlier papal letters. In fact, though, the letters were clear forgeries, probably manufactured by the monks of Canterbury. History has generally excused Lanfranc from complicity in this. He was surely too sincere, too upright to engage in such tricks. Nevertheless he won his case and the Accord of Winchester declared once and for all the primacy of Canterbury over York, giving Lanfranc a free hand in 'Normanising' the English Church.

A look at the list of bishops who witnessed the Accord of Winchester shows how this was done. Few were left of those appointed by Edward and of these only Wulfstan of Worcester and Siward of Rochester were English. Death and deposition had cleared the way for an almost complete change of leadership in the Church. William, Bishop of London, a Norman brought in by Edward, would be succeeded in 1079 by another Norman. No less than four of the new appointments in 1070 – the bishops of Winchester, Elmham and Selsey, together with Archbishop Thomas – had been chaplains to King William. The new Bishop of Exeter was Osbern Fitzosbern, brother of William Fitzosbern and also related to the king. So, too, was Osmund who would in 1078 replace the Flemish Hereman, Bishop of Sherborne and later of Salisbury. A similar clearout took place among the abbots and priors of monasteries so that by the end of William's reign there was scarcely an Englishman left anywhere in the higher reaches of the Church. As William of Malmesbury noted, they 'appointed diligent men of any nation, except English'.

Nor were these replacements necessarily of a higher quality than their predecessors. Bishop Aethelmaer of Elmham, allegedly removed because he was a married man, was replaced by a married Norman. Abbot Turold of Peterborough was more a Norman knight than a churchman, while Abbot Thurstan of Glastonbury fell out so violently with his monks that on one occasion they hid from him in the abbey church and he sent in armed men against them, killing three and wounding eighteen. Two bishops of Normandy also had a great influence in English affairs. Odo of Bayeux and Geoffrey of Coutances were presumably approved by the reformers in the duchy, yet Odo became bishop while still a teenager, and both were fully involved in the battle of Hastings. The claim is made that they did not actually strike a blow, but they certainly did everything else. 'Here Bishop Odo with his staff encourages the boys,' reads one of the captions in the Tapestry. Lanfranc himself may have been a scholar and an exemplary churchman but he may have been the exception rather than the rule.

Nor was it only the personnel that changed in the English Church. In 1072 it was decreed that cases involving churchmen would be withdrawn from the ordinary hundred courts and heard instead in ecclesiastical courts set up by the bishops and archdeacons. Even the dioceses were altered. The Council of London in 1075 decided that bishops should be based in major towns, resulting in a number of significant changes. The Bishop of Dorchester, a small place on the banks of the Thames in Oxfordshire, moved across country and became Bishop of Lincoln. The Bishop of Lichfield became Bishop of Chester, and Bishop Herfast, who had already moved his bishopric from Elmham to Thetford, now moved again to become

Bishop of Norwich. All these moves, while maybe improving the economic situation of the bishops concerned, also brought them within towns that were firmly under Norman control.

There were, however, limits to William's policy of advancing the Church in England. Ideas such as the celibacy of priests and improved morality of the clergy in general were acceptable, but when Hildebrand, now Pope Gregory VII, issued the *Dictatus Papae* in 1075 there were a number of provisions he was not prepared to countenance. Hildebrand's aim was for the Pope to be recognised as sole head of the universal Church, able to depose kings and emperors who did not obey his decrees, and to allow subjects to renounce their fealty to such rulers. No medieval monarch could stomach such a rule, and in fact it was the conflict between the Pope and the Holy Roman Emperor that let William ignore some of the other unpalatable suggestions, such as the further demand that all appointments of bishops and archbishops should be made by the Pope alone. Since these clergy were also major landowners with great secular influence within the country, it was inconceivable that William would allow any such power to the Pope, and after taking advice from Lanfranc he told him so. This prompted a demand that William should rule England as a vassal of the Pope and swear fealty to Gregory for the kingdom. The grounds for such a demand are not immediately apparent though they may relate back to Pope Alexander's support for William's invasion. Since they were delivered verbally to the king, we will never know. The answer, though, was clear. 'I have not consented to pay fealty, nor will I now because I never promised it.' No fealty was ever paid and William continued to appoint bishops as before, a situation that was later to lead to the so-called Investiture Controversy.

Not everything in England was overthrown by the conquest. As mentioned above, the remarkably efficient tax system was adopted wholesale along with the whole bureaucracy of the royal court that administered the existing institutions of central and local government. That such a machinery existed and was accustomed to serving the king in fact made the takeover of the country so much easier. Things ran as they had before but with two main differences. First the official in charge became Norman rather than English, and second over a fairly short period of time transactions that had formerly been carried out in the native English language were now done in French or Latin. There is some evidence that William attempted to learn English but gave it up as being too difficult. English therefore became a second-class language and anyone who wished to aspire to any position at all in the land had to abandon his native language and learn French instead.

Nor was the Englishman to draw comfort from familiar buildings and townscapes. Fire and sword had done much to clear the old architecture and what was left was now largely demolished to make way for the new. Within two generations William of Malmesbury was contrasting the 'mean and despicable houses' of the English with the 'noble and splendid mansions' of the Normans. An idea was put about that the Saxons had lived in hovels and worshipped in mean wooden churches, and so little was left it was difficult to refute it.

A great wave of building took place. 'You might see churches arise in every village,' said Malmesbury, 'and monasteries in the towns and cities, built after a style unknown before.' Some of this was down to guilt. The so-called 'Penitential Ordinance' of 1070, approved by the papal legate Erminfried, fixed a scale of penance for all the Normans and their allies (but not the English) that fought at Hastings and in the years after. At a rate of a year's penance for every man killed in the battle and three years for every man killed while plundering, some would have been doing penance for life. Building and endowing a church or abbey, however, would do instead. William, in fact, endowed two abbeys, one on the site of the battle itself and another at Selby in Yorkshire where his youngest son was born. Many other churches would have been similarly inspired.

Likewise the new bishops wanted to make their mark, especially when the diocese was now moved to a new town. The mighty structures we see today at Canterbury, Winchester, Lincoln, York and Durham were all begun within twenty years of the conquest. It would be a mistake, however, to take these as examples of superior Norman building since almost all were substantially rebuilt and enlarged in later centuries, leaving only fragments or foundations of the earlier buildings. Durham is probably closest to its Norman original.

Nor can we judge how much grander were the new buildings. The lines of the earlier Saxon church laid out alongside Winchester Cathedral reveal a structure probably two-thirds the size of the new building, bearing in mind that something over a hundred feet were added to the length of the new cathedral in later centuries. Similarly a number of surviving Saxon churches, at Wareham and Bosham for example, though subject to later alterations, do not seem to bear out the idea of shabby wooden buildings.

The land, the Church, the language itself, in every way the Englishman was reminded he was now a conquered subject, while around him in the form of castles, churches and fortifications the conquest was day by day being built in stone. Ordéric Vitalis comments that the Normans had forgotten that 'not by their own strength but through the providence of God … they had conquered … and subjugated a nation greater and richer and more ancient than their own'. Within twenty years of the conquest they had done their best to completely obliterate all trace of its achievements.

11

THE LAST YEARS OF THE CONQUEROR
1072–1087

'As the ocean never remains in a state of complete rest, but its troubled waves are always in motion ... so this world is in a constant state of turmoil from the tide of events, and is always presenting new forms of sorrow or joy.' So wrote Orderic Vitalis before launching into the events of the final years of William the Conqueror. Clearly with the benefit of hindsight he could see that the tide of events that had allowed William a space of years in which to invade and conquer England was now on the turn. Though the king in 1072 might feel he had at last achieved some measure of peace in his new kingdom, in fact he was to spend the rest of his life defending his two lands from those trying to encroach on his territories or indeed sweep him from power altogether.

By 1072, when Orderic declared that 'tranquillity prevailed in England', the happy coincidence of events on the Continent that had hamstrung William's enemies for so long was already passing away. The death of his father-in-law Baldwin V of Flanders in 1067 had not disturbed the friendly relations between Flanders and Normandy, but the new ruler Baldwin VI, William's brother-in-law, ruled less than three years before his untimely death in July 1070 left Flanders with a succession crisis. His two young sons, Arnulf and Baldwin, were only in their mid-teens, while Baldwin himself had an ambitious brother known as Robert the

Frisian. The intention was that Arnulf should have Flanders and his brother Baldwin his mother's land, Hainault, and that both lands would be ruled by their mother Richildis until they came of age. Robert swore he would support his nephews in this but the moment his brother died he seized Flanders for himself.

Richildis appealed for help to the boy's overlord Philip of France, and also to William in England. It was arranged that William Fitzosbern would go to her assistance, and would in fact marry the widow himself, thus cementing Flanders ever closer to the interests of Normandy and England. Vitalis, however, claims he went off 'as if he was only going to a tournament' and took with him only ten men at arms, which if true seems to have been a monstrous under-estimate of the seriousness of the situation.

A battle was fought at Cassel in February 1071 in the course of which both William Fitzosbern and young Arnulf were killed, while the widow Richildis and Robert the Frisian were each captured by their enemies. It was clear, though, that Robert's forces had won the day, and after a negotiated prisoner exchange he became the new Count of Flanders while Richildis and her younger son were allowed to depart for Hainault.

The loss of his closest friend and most trusted lieutenant was a serious blow for William in England, though Vitalis, half-English as he was and a monk to boot, saw the death of Fitzosbern as a fitting judgement on one he called the 'first and greatest of the oppressors of the people of England'. Worse than the loss of a friend, though, was the loss of a friendly country so close to Normandy itself. Robert the Frisian showed from the first that he would not be favouring his sister's lands. Instead, the following year he married his stepdaughter Bertha to Philip of France, thus establishing an alliance of William's enemies.

Philip himself was no longer the biddable child he had been. He came of age in 1073 and though Baldwin of Flanders had been his guardian for so long, he seems to have failed entirely to pass on any of his friendship for William and Normandy to the young king. No doubt the fact that William was now a king himself was something Philip found hard to swallow. Theoretically it meant his vassal was now his equal as well, a complication that would cause friction for centuries to come.

It was to Flanders, then, that Edgar Atheling fled when turned out of Scotland in 1072, and though he returned to Scotland as soon as William was busy elsewhere, in 1074 it was Philip of France that offered him a castle and lands in France from which he would be able to attack and continually harass the duchy of his enemy. On this occasion it was literally the tide that came to William's aid, Edgar and the supporters he had raised in Scotland being shipwrecked off the English coast while on his way to take up this offer. Though many were drowned Edgar himself survived and managed to make his way back to Scotland, but this alliance of his enemies was bad news for William and was probably instrumental in the negotiations that now followed. Whether it was Malcolm or William that made the first move we don't know, but now a settlement was patched up between the king and the Atheling. Sufficient guarantees must have been given for Edgar to feel able to travel to Normandy, where William was at the time, to formally submit to the king and be restored to favour. He was accompanied on his journey by the Sheriff of York, possibly to ensure the mutual promises of goodwill were kept, but all went well, the submission was made and the reconciliation accomplished with promises of lands and honours in England suitable to the Atheling's situation.

The reason for William's presence in Normandy related to another shift in the Continental tides. His occupation of Maine had been made simpler by the succession struggle that followed the death of Geoffrey Martel, but by 1072 that struggle was over. Fulk le Rechin, sometimes translated as Fulk the Ill-Tempered or Fulk the Quarrelsome, had overcome and imprisoned his brother and was now firmly in control as Count of Anjou.

Even before this, however, the citizens of Le Mans, the most important city in the County of Maine, had started to throw off the Norman yoke. In 1069 an attempt was made to restore the family of Herbert 'Wakedog' in the form of a nephew of Count

Hugh IV, whose sister, Gersendis, had married a powerful Italian nobleman. The Norman governor was killed and his forces expelled, and the fourteen-year-old Hugh, son of Gersendis, was proclaimed Count Hugh V. When further revolts threatened his rule, appeal was made to Fulk le Rechin for armed support and the ambitious count was happy to oblige, invading and occupying Maine in the name of Count Hugh.

This was a situation William of Normandy could not allow to continue. In theory at least, his son Robert was Count of Maine, a title he had obtained when still a child in 1063. As soon as William could safely leave England, he gathered an army notable for its mixture of English and Norman troops, and set about the re-conquest of the county. Though this was largely accomplished by the end of 1073 he was not able to lay hands on Count Hugh, and Fulk le Rechin was to be a thorn in his side for many years to come.

While William was busy consolidating his rule on the Continent, however, trouble was once again brewing in England. This time, though, it came from a surprising source. Vitalis gives us a picture of English and Normans beginning to settle down and live amicably together, and he should know being himself born in 1075 of a Norman father and English mother. It was not the English that would rock the boat this time, however, but the Norman lords put in place to rule over them.

Ralph de Gael was in fact a Breton by birth but his father had served William well and been rewarded with the earldom of East Anglia. Roger de Breteuil was the second son of William Fitzosbern and took over his father's titles and possessions in England. These two young men, becoming respectively Earl of East Anglia in 1069 and Earl of Hereford in 1071, now became the visible signs of discontent even among the victors of 1066.

In the spring of 1075 Roger's sister Emma married Ralph, and it was at this bridal feast that a plot was hatched to depose the King of England. 'There was that bride-ale the source of men's bale,' as the *Chronicle* puts it. The cause of their dissatisfaction is hard to pin down. It has been suggested that William had forbidden the match and the wedding was in defiance of him, though this is clearly refuted in the *Chronicle* record. Vitalis, putting words in their mouths as usual, throws the book at William in his list of complaints. He was a bastard and therefore unworthy. He was involving England in endless quarrels overseas and with his children – which claim would make the earls clairvoyant since the troubles with his children had not yet arisen. More to the point he had not rewarded his followers properly, some being given barren land to farm and others having their honours reduced. This last is most likely to be the crux of the matter. The first earldoms given by William matched those pre-existing in the country before 1066. Latterly, though, the new earldoms were considerably smaller and it is likely that both Roger and Ralph had had their expectations trimmed when they followed in their fathers' footsteps.

There is evidence, too, that this plot was intended to be part only of a wider uprising that would attack the king on all fronts. The Bretons were not over-popular with the Normans generally, and it is likely Ralph was in touch with Philip of France and possibly with Flanders and Anjou as well. Certainly an appeal for support was sent to Denmark and a promise of ships and men received from King Sweyn. What was needed was a suitable figurehead for the English part of the plan and the only Englishman of any standing still available was Waltheof.

This son of the old Earl of Northumbria had been younger than his fellow earls at the time of the conquest. Some accounts say he became friendly towards William in the time he spent at his court and it may well be that the king felt he had inspired some measure of loyalty in the young man. When in 1072 Gospatric was finally stripped of his earldom and fled to Scotland it was Waltheof who became Earl of Northumbria in his place, and it may be that it was then he married the king's niece Judith. Possibly William felt that this was his last chance to make some kind of bridge between his Norman rule and the rebellious northerners.

For a time it seemed to work. Waltheof reputedly worked well with the Norman Bishop of Durham, and only a perpetuation of an old blood feud with a rival Northumbrian family disturbed the peace in what was, in any case, an area still recovering from the devastation of a few years before. The plot dangled before him at the bridal feast of Ralph de Gael, however, may have been a temptation too far.

We don't actually know how closely involved Waltheof became. The *Chronicle* declares he was one of the plotters though not the leader, while Vitalis claims he refused to join the group and his only treason was a failure to let the king's regents know at once what was going on, his silence being due to an oath forced on him by Roger and Ralph. In either case it was not long before he got cold feet.

The generally accepted story is that he confessed his part to Lanfranc, who sent him straight over to William in Normandy to repeat his confession and throw himself on the king's mercy. This he did and the *Chronicle* records that 'the king let him off lightly' – at first. Lanfranc was also quick to reassure William that his presence in England was not needed and that the local forces could cope very well, as indeed they did.

The bridal feast over, Roger returned to his earldom to raise forces, intending to rejoin Ralph as soon as this was done. When he led his men as far as the River Severn, however, he found himself opposed by an army led by the bishops of Worcester and Evesham and his part in the uprising was quickly snuffed out, he himself being taken prisoner. Earl Ralph fared no better, being routed in a battle at Swaffham in Norfolk, though he managed to escape to his castle in Norwich and thence back home to Brittany. The *Chronicle* emphasises that 'the garrisons of the castles ... and the inhabitants of the country came against him' and that this rebellion was therefore put down by Normans and English acting together. Clearly by this time the whole population preferred a little peace to the violence of the previous decade.

Earl Ralph's quick exit, however, had left his new wife on her own, holding his castle at Norwich. There she withstood a three-month siege before calmly negotiating a surrender on terms that she and her household could depart with life and limb intact to join her husband across the Channel. Lanfranc then reported to William that his kingdom had been 'purged of its Breton filth'. Rather late in the day some two hundred ships duly arrived from Denmark, led by Sweyn's second son Cnut. Finding no ongoing revolution, they contented themselves with the traditional raiding up the east coast and burning York before departing again with their plunder.

For the other plotters judgement came with the return of William to England towards the end of the year. We are told he did with the rebels as he pleased, some being blinded and some exiled, while Earl Roger was imprisoned for life according to Norman law. Now, however, Waltheof also found himself on trial, with his own wife giving evidence against him. At first the judges failed to agree on his involvement and a retrial was needed before he was finally declared guilty of treason and, under English law, sentenced to death. Vitalis suggests this verdict was in fact given because his judges hoped to get their hands on his land, and furthermore gives a bizarre version of how the sentence was carried out.

Waltheof had been held at Winchester, and his executioners were afraid the English townspeople would cause a riot if they saw him beheaded. As a result, very early in the morning on 31 May 1076 they took him up St Giles hill just outside the town to carry out the sentence. He begged some moments to say a final prayer and began the 'Our Father'. When he got to, 'Forgive us our trespasses,' however, he broke down in tears and spent so long weeping that, losing patience, the executioner drew his sword and beheaded him there and then. Whereupon the severed head calmly completed the prayer, pronounced a firm 'Amen' and expired.

Earl Ralph and his wife, however, had escaped all of this and, safe in Brittany, had begun to make links with other enemies of William. He now faced the prospect of his duchy being completely encircled by foes and in September 1076 took an army to Brittany to try and prevent this happening. Settling down to besiege Ralph's castle at Dol, however, he was in for a surprise. Out of the blue Philip of France arrived with sufficient forces to lift the siege and send William scurrying back to Normandy. The *Chronicle* gives few details other than the fact that William lost 'both men and horses and much treasure.' Vitalis specifies the loss of tents, baggage, arms and utensils to a value of £15,000. Clearly this was a comprehensive rout, the first major setback of William's adult career, and for the first time he was forced to negotiate for a peace treaty rather than imposing his own terms. Even then it was noted that 'it lasted only a little while'.

Vitalis has no doubt as to the cause of this catastrophe. With all the advantages of hindsight he points out that William never won a battle or took a castle by siege after the execution of Waltheof, something that he clearly regards as unjustified judicial murder. Be that as it may, the sudden change in William's circumstances seemed to be confirmed when soon afterwards Simon de Crépy, Count of Amiens, announced he was entering a monastery and handed over that useful buffer state the Vexin to Philip of France. Simon had been brought up at William's court and at one point seemed set to marry William's daughter Adela. Now, however, his actions allowed Philip to occupy the land right up to the original borders of Normandy on the River Epte, and William could make no move to prevent him.

It has been suggested that the unusual number of significant church dedications in Normandy in the year 1077 was either William's attempt to get back on the right side of his God, or simply the creation of opportunities to show off how powerful a ruler he still was. On 14 July the new cathedral at Bayeux was formally consecrated, and this may well have been the occasion for unveiling the tapestry that now bears its name. Even more important, on 13 September, was the dedication of the church of St Stephen in Caen, William's own foundation and still incomplete. This seems to have been attended by everyone of note in England and Normandy, including lords, bishops and both English archbishops. The heaviest blow of the year, however, was yet to fall.

By this time William's eldest son Robert was in his early twenties. He has come down through history with the nickname 'Curthose', which might be translated as 'shorty', though another name 'Gambaron', possibly *jambes ronde*, has been given as 'fat legs'. Neither name is particularly complimentary and if bestowed by his father, as has been suggested, might indicate that the relationship was not a close one. In fact there had been friction between them for some time.

As we have seen, Robert had been nominally Count of Maine since 1063, and before embarking on his great adventure in 1066, William had maintained the traditional Norman practice of nominating his successor and having all the lords swear fealty to him. By some accounts Robert had even been accepted by Philip of France and done homage for the duchy. In the years since, however, he had not been allowed the smallest measure of authority in either land. Even when William was away in England it was Queen Matilda rather than her son who acted as regent in Normandy.

As usual Orderic Vitalis plays up the situation with a long conversation between Robert and his father where Robert demands money and power and William replies that his request is 'not convenient,' or simply 'quite preposterous', declaring, 'I will never while I live relinquish the government.' There is a suggestion too that Robert was not the most responsible character, and that when he was given money he wasted it on a gang of flattering followers who constantly wanted more and pointed out the gap between his father's immense wealth and his own comparative penury.

In fact there was probably something deeper at play here. A whole generation had grown up since the conquest, sons as ambitious and thrusting as their fathers had been, while as yet those fathers had no intention of giving up the power and wealth they had so recently accumulated. When the crisis came in the autumn of 1077 – sparked by a prank involving Robert's younger brothers soaking him with the contents of a chamber pot – the king's son was supported by a whole swathe of the younger generation, including the eldest sons of Roger de Montgomery and William Fitzosbern. The night following the prank, when the king had failed to satisfy the righteous anger of his eldest, Robert and his followers took themselves off and tried to seize the castle at Rouen. The *Chronicle* says he rebelled 'because his father would not let him govern his earldom in Normandy, which he himself and with his consent Philip of France had given to him'.

Their plan failed. The castellan resisted them and immediately sent word to William, who in a rage set off after them with an army. Robert fled, first to his uncle Robert in Flanders and then to Philip of France who, seizing the opportunity to make mischief, set him up in a castle at Gerberoy on the borders with Normandy. From there Robert spent a considerable amount of time raiding his father's duchy until in January 1079 William could tolerate the situation no longer and besieged the castle.

Even now he could not get the upper hand. A succession of lively sorties by the garrison within culminated in one where father and son unknowingly faced each other in violent combat. The *Chronicle*, though cutting short its account of the engagement, states that William was wounded in the hand and had his horse killed under him. A man bringing another horse was also killed, and the end of the story, as supplied by another account, says that Robert, recognising his father by his voice, was suddenly appalled at what he had done, gave William his own horse and told him to ride away at once.

This incident seems to have given everyone a jolt. The *Chronicle* says Robert withdrew again to Flanders and on all sides attempts were made to patch up some kind of reconciliation. It is likely that Matilda played the largest part in this. William's pride, severely damaged in coming off worst against his son, took another knock when it appeared his queen had been secretly supporting her son with money throughout his exile. Nevertheless by the Easter of 1080 at the latest, Robert was back again at his father's side and peace was restored again in the family and in the duchy. Perhaps to reinforce this, at a Church synod held at Lillebonne at Whitsun that year the Truce of God, which seemed to have been forgotten for some time, was once more imposed upon Normandy.

William's long absence in Normandy, however, had given rise to opportunities for mischief back in England. In the late summer of 1079 Malcolm of Scotland had broken the Peace of Abernethy and raided into England as far south as the Tyne, killing and plundering far and wide and going home laden with booty. The failure of the Prince-Bishop Walcher of Durham to protect his people may have contributed to his own downfall the next year, though the immediate cause of that seems to have been a blood feud between two of his servants.

The murder of one of these, a Northumbrian by descent, and the failure of the bishop to deal adequately with the other sparked a threat of rebellion in the area in the spring of 1080. Walcher agreed to meet the discontents at Gateshead, though the fact that he took an armed guard of a hundred men with him suggests he was aware of the danger. They did him little good. His total rejection of the petition of wrongs presented to him provoked immediate violence. Walcher and his men were forced to flee into the nearby church, which was then set on fire, and the whole party either burned to death or were butchered as they tried to escape.

In retaliation William, still in Normandy, directed his brother Odo to deal with the rebels, who had gone on to Durham to try and seize the castle. This the earl/bishop was happy to do, marching north with an army and devastating the area once again. Simeon of Durham declares that he killed innocent and guilty alike and furthermore took the opportunity to plunder the cathedral, carrying off its treasures for himself. Odo, despite being a bishop, seems to have been one of the most war-like and rapacious of the Norman lords, drawing on his kinship with William and the authority given to him to advance his own power and wealth on all occasions. He was, says Orderic, 'generally dreaded by the English people, issuing his orders everywhere like a second king'.

When William himself returned to England later in the year his son Robert was by his side, and it is a measure of the changed relationship between them that it was Robert who was then sent north to deal with King Malcolm. This he seems to have done with great efficiency; indeed no one ever doubted his courage or ability as a soldier and he would go on to fight with honour in the First

Crusade. The terms of the Peace of Abernethy were re-imposed, and on the way home, to help secure these northern lands, Robert founded on the Tyne a 'New castle' which has given the place its name from that day to this.

With Scotland secure William now turned his attention to Wales. The briefest of entries in the *Chronicle* for 1081 records that, 'This year the king led an army into Wales and there he set free many hundred persons.' Some Welsh accounts put this down as a pilgrimage to St David's but it seems to have had a far more war-like basis. Norman policy in north and central Wales had been as aggressive as elsewhere, with castles planted as far as Conwy in the north and Montgomery (named for its founder) in the centre. In the south, however, William Fitzosbern had found it beneficial to adopt a more conciliatory attitude, and Normans had fought alongside the Welsh king Caradog ap Gruffydd in his battles with his fellow Welsh rulers. The fall of Caradog in a battle near St David's in west Wales led, however, to the rise of a new ruler, Rhys ap Tewdur, and it is likely he was the target for William's advance into south Wales. We don't know if there was actual fighting or if the show of force in itself was enough to impress his authority on the new man. It is likely that homage was demanded and given, and that the men freed were either prisoners from the wars or possibly slaves en route to Ireland from the vigorous slave trade still carried on in Wales and the West Country of England.

Once again, while the king was busy in one part of his lands trouble broke out in another. This time it was Fulk le Rechin who was taking advantage of William's absence to attack Maine, and as before the king had to cross the sea with an army to re-impose his authority. On this occasion, though, it seems that before battle could be joined the intervention of the clergy led to a negotiated settlement, though the peace that followed was to be relatively short-lived.

In the meantime William was to suffer a number of hammer blows in his personal life. The first of these came with the abrupt fall from grace of Bishop Odo in 1082. No details of this were recorded at the time other than that, late in that year, the bishop was arrested, taken to Normandy and tried before the king, before being imprisoned at Rouen. Everything else comes from later, possibly unreliable accounts, chiefly those of Orderic Vitalis and William of Malmesbury. Both agree that the main reason for his arrest was that he had gathered a group of knights around him and was planning to leave England with them and travel to Italy to make himself pope. A rather more charitable interpretation has also been suggested, that he was in fact going to Italy to defend the pope who was at the time under attack from the Holy Roman Emperor. Either way it was a high-handed action that his brother would not tolerate. Famously, Vitalis records that when arrested, Odo declared that as a bishop he could not be tried by anyone without the consent of the Pope, to which William is said to have replied that he was not arresting a bishop but an Earl of Kent he had himself created. Again the half-English Vitalis adds greatly to the charge sheet in his account of the crisis, with William accusing his brother of oppressing the English, stealing from the Church and having 'dangerous ambitions'. William declares that he had entrusted the government of his kingdom to Odo and 'he should render an account of the stewardship'. The outcome was that the mighty Odo would spend the next five years in close custody in the castle at Rouen, though it is noticeable that he was not deprived of his lands.

It was late in 1083 that perhaps the greatest personal loss was suffered by the king. In October of that year his beloved wife Matilda fell seriously ill and she died on 2 November. Almost immediately Robert once again deserted his father, suggesting that his earlier reconciliation had been only skin-deep, perhaps as a favour to his mother, and her death had left him free once more to join the king's enemies. To be fair, this time he did not go straight to Philip of France, spending time travelling in Italy and Germany, but that is certainly where he ended up, opposing his father to the last. In the meantime the ever-loyal second son William, known as 'Rufus' or 'the Red', took his place at the side of a king who was beginning to cut a rather isolated figure.

William was not left long to brood, however. First a renewed rebellion in Maine demanded his attention in 1084, and then a far more serious threat drew him back to England the following year with an enormous army of mounted men and infantry, the equal at least, so the *Chronicle* declared, of any that had previously been seen in the land. The occasion for this was a severe and prolonged threat of invasion from Scandinavia.

Cnut had had one look at England already in 1075. Then he was only a king's son, and from 1076 the new king's brother. The death of Harold of Denmark in 1080, however, had seen the throne pass to Cnut himself. No doubt he had liked the look of the land he had visited, and marrying the daughter of Robert of Flanders, long-time enemy of William, gave him an added incentive to revive the old claims of Sweyn Estrithsson to the crown of England. The fleet he prepared was massive, allegedly a thousand ships with a further six hundred to be supplied by Robert of Flanders. No wonder William came rushing to England with the biggest army he could muster.

This was a mercenary army, so William of Malmesbury tells us, and the first thought recorded in the *Chronicle* seems to have wondered who was going to feed all these people. In fact William solved this problem by dispersing them throughout the country. To put it kindly, he reinforced the garrisons of every castle and town. More bluntly, he billeted this mighty force on whoever could take them, magnates and towns alike, so that in some places the complaint was that the towns were so full of foreign troops there was no room for their own citizens. Around the coast, too, areas of land were laid waste so that invaders would find no food to sustain them. All in all, the *Chronicle*'s declaration that 'the people suffered much distress this year' seems no less than the truth. The palpable tension would have been 1066 all over again.

Cnut, though, had troubles of his own. Delayed from day to day by a threat of action from the Holy Roman Emperor to the south, eventually his men were threatening mutiny. They wanted to go home and get in the harvest and finally asked Cnut's brother

Olaf to make this request on their behalf. Olaf was immediately arrested and sent under guard to Flanders, but then Cnut gave in to necessity and the invasion was postponed until the following year.

This news only reached England late in the year. Some of the mercenaries were sent home but many remained, and it was against this background that, at his Christmas court at Gloucester, William set in motion the survey that was to result in the Domesday Book. Not a survey of land but a survey of landholding, the collection of information went hand in hand with the collection of a heavy tax. Through the early months of the following year, still waiting for signs of an invasion, the returns of the survey came in to William, building up a picture of the resources of his realm and the people he could call on in case of need. What he also needed, of course, was an assurance of their loyalty.

By the middle of the summer the situation was greatly improved. The death of Cnut was reported, killed by his own men on 10 July apparently for levying fines over the previous year's mutiny. Clearly there would now be no invasion. Equally welcome was the visit of the Viscount of Le Mans, come to confirm a peace settlement ending the trouble in Maine. Neither of these, however, changed the plan that William must already have formulated as a logical conclusion to the work of the Domesday survey.

On 1 August, in the vast open space of Old Sarum hillfort in Wiltshire, he called together 'all the landholders of substance in England, whose vassals soever they were', and required from each a personal oath of loyalty. It is probably an exaggeration for John of Worcester to suggest that every bishop, archbishop, earl, baron, sheriff and knight in the country was there, but certainly with his new information to hand the king is likely to have summoned every tenant-in-chief and a good proportion of the wealthier subtenants, maybe a few thousand people in all. Then in a ceremony unprecedented in England or in Normandy, each swore that 'they would be faithful to him against all others', an oath taking precedence over any previously sworn to an overlord.

Strangely, the significance of this oath is passed over completely by the nearest contemporary writers. Even the *Chronicle* passes straight on to the king collecting another heavy tax 'upon every pretext he could find, whether just or otherwise', before leaving England and returning to Normandy. It then devotes a great deal more space to the terrible weather and the various diseases of men and cattle that afflicted the land in that and the following year than to anything that befell the king when he reached his native land.

For now Robert had once again appeared at the court of Philip of France, and the French king was encouraging raids from the Vexin into Normandy itself, overrunning the Evreux area and plundering with very little opposition. There is in fact a suggestion that William was ill in the early months of 1087. William of Malmesbury carries a story that he was taunted by Philip that he was 'lying in' and 'keeps his bed like a woman after her delivery'. The taunt would be the more pointed since by this time the king had grown very fat, with a belly like that of a woman in the late stages of pregnancy.

He was far enough recovered by the end of July, however, to lead an army into the Vexin himself to sack and burn the town of Mantes from which the raids on Normandy had been launched. The *Chronicle* points out that he was now attacking his own overlord, and furthermore that in the course of the action he destroyed all the town's churches, killing two anchorites or holy recluses who were burnt to death there.

In doing so, however, he brought about his own downfall. Vitalis says he rode too close to the heat of the burning town and was overcome by it, falling seriously ill. William of Malmesbury gives an alternative: that as his horse leapt a ditch, the pommel of the saddle was driven into his over-large belly, causing serious injury. Whichever is true, it was to prove fatal. Taken back to Rouen, his condition worsened. He could not stand the heat and noise of the city and so was moved to the Priory of St Gervase outside the walls, where it quickly became apparent that the king was dying.

Although emphasising that William was in constant agony, Vitalis then gives us page after page of purported speech from him, recalling in some detail his entire career and confessing freely to every accusation Vitalis could throw at him, in particular the persecution of the English 'beyond all reason'. More believably, the final dispositions of the king are also given.

Money was to be given to the poor and for building churches, especially to replace those so recently burned down in Mantes. Prisoners were to be freed, including Morcar, Roger de Breteuil and even Wulfnoth, son of Earl Godwin, whom William had held for over thirty years. The one exception to this generosity was William's brother Odo. The king clearly intended that Odo should remain in prison but he was eventually worn down by the persuasion of his brother Robert of Mortain and the other magnates gathered at his bedside. Nevertheless he warned them, 'You ... are bringing on yourselves a serious calamity.'

As for the two lands over which he ruled, Normandy had to go to Robert though he was even now at the court of William's enemy. The land had been granted long before and the king declared the grant could not be annulled, though he described his son as a 'proud and silly prodigal'. England was another matter. According to Vitalis William stated, 'Having ... made my way to the throne of that kingdom by so many crimes, I dare not leave it to anyone but God alone.' Nevertheless he immediately indicated that he hoped God would favour his son William Rufus with the land, and furthermore gave him a letter to take to Lanfranc confirming the choice and sent him on his way at once. William Rufus was actually at the coast about to take ship when he heard his father had died.

To his youngest son Henry he bequeathed £5,000 in silver, and again Henry went off at once to see it properly weighed out. So in fact none of his immediate family were with the king when he finally breathed his last early in the morning of 9 September 1087. The aftermath, if Vitalis is to be believed, was truly bizarre.

Everyone who had been watching at the king's bedside 'became as men who had lost their wits', with all the magnates immediately rushing off to secure their own lands and all the lower servants stripping the body and the royal apartments of everything of value they could lay their hands on. Nor was this the end of the humiliation for the dead king. With all others fled, only a country knight could be found to arrange the preparation of the corpse and its transportation to Caen for burial. On the way into the city a fire broke out in a nearby house and everyone left the hearse to help extinguish it, and during the funeral itself in the Abbey of St Stephen a loud protest was made by a man who claimed the church had been built on his father's land and he had never been properly compensated. As a fitting finale the grave had been made too small, and in trying to cram the body in, the stomach burst, filling the church with an 'intolerable stench' and bringing a rapid conclusion to the proceedings.

Vitalis declares that he carefully investigated the details of the king's death and burial and had given 'not ... a well-feigned tragedy ... nor a humorous comedy ... but a true narrative ... for the perusal of serious readers'. He then pronounces a touching and rather pathetic epitaph for the end of a great king.

A king once potent and warlike ... lay naked on the floor, deserted by those who owed him their birth, and those he had fed and enriched. He needed the money of a stranger for the cost of his funeral. He was carried to the church amidst flaming houses, by trembling crowds, and a spot of freehold land was wanting for the grave of a man whose princely sway had extended over so many cities, towns and villages ... There is but one lot for rich and poor ... Trust not then, O sons of men, in princes who deceive, but in the true and living God who created all things.

12

WINNERS AND LOSERS OF 1066: A PERSONAL VIEW

In looking at the events that made up the Norman Conquest the overall winner is not hard to find. William the Bastard, known after his death as William the Great and later William the Conqueror, would probably have been happiest with the second of those titles. He always insisted he was no conqueror but the rightful king of England. Those who lived through his takeover would, no doubt, have begged to differ.

Certainly advancing from bastard to duke to king might argue for greatness at least in achievement, but whether he deserves all the other accolades thrown at him as a great general and great strategist might be harder to justify. Energy, determination and utter ruthlessness are the hallmarks of his victories rather than any superior military thinking. 'I was bred to arms from my childhood,' he is said to have declared, 'and am stained with the rivers of blood I have shed.' When faced with a military impasse, therefore, his answer was simply to hack off limbs as at Alençon, or devastate an entire area as with the Harrying of the North, rather than innovate some more imaginative solution. Even the famous 'feigned retreats' at Hastings were not an original idea.

The coincidence of dates in the late summer of 1066 might at first glance suggest a brilliant strategy. However, even if it is allowed that he might have known when Harold stood down his troops, his attempt to take advantage of that very nearly ended in disaster and it is unlikely he was aware of the northern invasion until after he had landed in England. Would he really have been keen to take on Hardrada with his mighty reputation and his land and sea forces if that king had been victorious at Stamford Bridge? Nor is it conceivable that either would have agreed to share the land. William's behaviour at the time seems a very clear indication that he did *not* know of the invasion. In fact he seems to have had very little strategy at all once he had crossed the sea, skulking near the coast, throwing up basic fortifications and waiting for something to happen. Had he really been aware of the situation in England he would surely have struck out against some important or strategic town, Dover perhaps or Canterbury, or even Winchester or London itself, while the major part of the English army was engaged elsewhere. As it was, he appears to have been terrified of being cut off from his easy line of retreat to Normandy.

In fact his whole campaign seems to have been characterised not by supreme strategy but by supreme luck. He was lucky to be able to land his forces unopposed – those few who landed accidentally further along the coast and were massacred show that he could easily have fared much worse. If Pevensey was deliberately chosen as a place least likely to be defended, he was still lucky that he had the time to clear his men out of such a place by the one available track before anyone arrived to block his exit.

He was lucky again that the English forces were depleted by two fierce battles in the north, and that the core of the army was forced to make two long journeys in the weeks before they faced him. In the battle itself he was lucky that the ill-discipline of some of the less experienced men Harold was forced to rely on allowed him to thin out the ranks of the opposition, and then the ultimate stroke of luck that not only was Harold himself killed, possibly by one random arrow, but so were his brothers, wiping out all the experienced leaders of both family and country.

Of course William's luck began well before that. Had his major opponents on the Continent not died just a few years before, he could never have hoped to launch any kind of attack on England.

Nor could he have expected Harold to fall into his hands in the way he had and be forced to swear an oath of allegiance – assuming, of course, that the Tapestry and the accounts that back it up were not just superb pieces of Norman propaganda.

Propaganda was something the Normans were good at, declaring that something was so and persuading others to believe it. The Victorians in particular were happy to believe that William and his followers brought peace, prosperity and good order to a backward people, something that they themselves were claiming to do in many parts of the globe at the time. In reality, though, William brought nothing new to England. The peace, prosperity and efficiently working institutions were all here before he arrived and the institutions simply taken over wholesale by the invaders.

The different obituaries of William found in different versions of the *Anglo-Saxon Chronicle* are instructive summaries of his impact on the land. A kinder one claims, 'We will describe him just as we have known him, we who have looked upon him and who once lived in his court.' It calls him 'a very wise and a great man', more honoured and more powerful than his predecessors and 'mild to those good men who loved God'. Even then, though, it declares he was 'severe beyond measure towards those who withstood his will', and the only positive action recorded is that he built churches and filled the land with Benedictine monks.

An alternative version is not so kind. Here he is, 'a very stern and a wrathful man so that none durst do anything against his will', putting earls in chains and deposing bishops. It attempts to give him credit for imposing peace and justice and then breaks out again: 'Truly there was much trouble in these times and very great distress.' When these different summaries are set side by side as in some translations the effect is very odd.

No doubt William would claim, as Malmesbury did, that he intended to rule the English well but they wouldn't let him. This really cannot excuse the barbarity of his actions. Nor could he honestly expect to be welcomed with open arms by a nation when he had slaughtered its king and most of its nobility and stolen the land and its treasures. In describing the opening of the battle of Hastings, Poitiers likens it to the prosecution opening the case in an action for theft. No doubt he meant to imply that Harold was on trial there, but in fact it was William who was the thief, taking a land to which he had no shadow of a right. That his aim was theft pure and simple is backed up by all the accounts that agree his besetting sin was avarice. 'He was given to avarice,' says the *Chronicle*, 'and greedily loved gain.' He took great quantities of gold and silver, 'with or without right and with little need'. 'He used to drain the country of money,' says William of Malmesbury.

Again the claim has been made that it was the Norman lords rather than the king that did the worst of the damage in England, people like William Fitzosbern and Odo who rode roughshod over the people and took whatever they wanted. These were the king's men, however, and he did nothing to stop them acting in this way. It is quite clear they could not have done it without his express or implied approval. However it might be dressed up, William was a tyrant and people did not cross him with impunity. The *Chronicle* is quite explicit. 'They must will all that the king willed if they would live, or would keep their lands, or would hold their possession, or would be maintained in their rights.' Even his brother Odo found this out in the end. With this attitude William took whatever he wanted and allowed his friends to do exactly the same.

Even his own contemporaries did not regard William as a noble bringer of peace and order and the braver and more honest of them said so. A Norman monk, Guitmond, with a reputation for learning and spirituality was invited to England by William with the intention of offering him a high appointment in the English Church. After looking round for a while, however, Guitmond turned down the offer, telling the king, 'I look upon England as altogether one vast heap of booty and I am afraid to touch it and its treasures as if it were a burning fire.' When he returned to Normandy, Vitalis tells us, word soon spread that he had 'in the presence of the king and his nobles stigmatized the conquest of England with the character of robbery'.

What a coat of whitewash, then, was applied to the Conqueror and his reign before the Victorians could hail him as the real founder of England's greatness. Exaggerating the good and ignoring the bad, attaching to him their own ideas of virtue and vice, he became a strong, wise leader, a faithful husband, a firm ruler, invading England for England's own good and only reluctantly using force against people who stupidly (though romantically) rebelled against his good order. A history primer of the early twentieth century, under the heading, 'William's Excellent Rule', declares, 'The English had good cause to be grateful to William in spite of his faults, and to regret him when he died in 1087.' Truly William must be accounted one of history's winners.

Another clear winner was the Duchy of Normandy itself, vastly enriched both economically, culturally and in status by the conquest of England. The plundering of the resources of the rich and fertile island for the benefit of the duchy has been likened by one writer to the plundering of Europe by the Nazis during the Second World War. Immeasurable quantities of gold, silver, books, tapestries and other treasures were stripped out and carted away across the Channel. Not only individuals but families, whole regions and the Norman Church in general were boosted by this wealth. Vitalis writes of 'ignorant upstarts driven almost mad by their sudden elevation' while William of Malmesbury extols the benefits to monasteries throughout the duchy in this way: 'Their poverty was mitigated by the riches of England.' It is difficult to judge his attitude to this. 'I perceive,' he adds, 'the mutterings of those who say it would have been better that the old should have been preserved in their original state, than that new ones should have been erected from their plunder,' but he makes no further comment on the matter.

The fact that the duchy's ruler was now also a king would have made a difference to how it was viewed by its neighbours on the Continent, though this would not have been an unmixed blessing. It would be clear that its ability to defend itself should be greatly enhanced by now having the resources of England to call upon.

On the other hand it might now be seen as a threat to others, leading former allies to fall away. Philip of France in particular would be keen to find any way to undermine his now over-mighty vassal. William had certainly hoped to keep his two lands together under one rule, and we can only speculate as to what might have followed if that had occurred and Normandy maintained the dominant position it had had in his affections. The defection of his son, however, cut short this interesting situation and the duchy's dominance was in fact short-lived.

The other winner as a result of the conquest might at first sight seem surprising. Edward the Confessor had in most estimations been a nondescript king and a nondescript man. Had there been a smooth and unchallenged transition of the crown to Harold and his sons, he might have occupied no bigger place in history than Edmund I, Edwy or even Edward the Martyr. The little claim to the throne that William had, however, rested on his nomination by Edward, so it was in the interests of the Normans to emphasise his importance. He therefore has a prominent role in the Bayeux Tapestry and in the Norman accounts of the conquest and his reign is the starting point for all the listings in the Domesday Book.

His claims to sainthood were equally shaky and these too were promoted by the Normans, although not by William himself. There seems little idea at the time of this death that Edward was in any way particularly saintly. His obituary in the *Chronicle* contains only the usual platitudes that he was pure and blameless and true in faith. Nor does the *Vita Edwardi* in its original form seem to make any such claim, though an early addition, perhaps seeking a happy ending to a story originally intended to glorify the Godwin family, does mention some apparently miraculous cures carried out by the king.

Much is made of Edward's founding and endowing Westminster Abbey and this is certainly the most prominent act for which he is remembered. The original Benedictine abbey was founded on the site at Thorney Island beside the Thames by King Edgar and St Dunstan in 960, but Edward's new building seems to have been intended from the start as a burial place for English kings. There is a suggestion that he wanted to distance himself from Winchester, where Cnut, Harthacnut and Edward's mother Emma were buried. The idea that he devoted himself entirely to the project in his last years to the neglect of his kingdom and everything else, though, seems to be an exaggeration. He certainly did not neglect his hunting and seemed active enough at the time of the Northumbrian crisis in the autumn of 1065. Some accounts say it was after this that he gave himself over to the abbey project, but that had been begun at least ten years earlier. There is no denying, however, that he gave close attention to the progress of the building, endowed it generously and was undoubtedly at least as pious and attentive to his religious duties as the average nobleman of his time was expected to be.

There was a brief revival of interest in English traditions when William's youngest son Henry I married Edith of Scotland, niece of Edgar Atheling and great-great-granddaughter of Athelred, in 1100. The stories of Edward's celibacy, of miracles performed by him and obtained by praying at his tomb, and death-bed prophecies now apparently come true, were all revived and added to at this time. His tomb was opened in 1102 and the body found to be uncorrupted, taken as a sure sign of sainthood, but this flare of notoriety seems to have been short-lived. By the early 1130s there even seems to be some confusion among the monks of Westminster as to exactly where Edward was buried, suggesting it was not a particularly popular place of pilgrimage.

A good deal of the credit for the revival of the cult of Edward must go to Osbert of Clare, a prior of Westminster later in that decade. His revised version of the *Vita Edwardi* again played up the holiness of the king, turning it into a standard saint's life complete with celibacy and miracles in life and after death. One motive for his interest might be that at that time Westminster had no mighty saint or holy relics attached to it, and thus it was losing out to other great churches which were becoming avid collectors of such 'holy bones'.

The way to sainthood by now involved official recognition by the Pope, a formal 'canonisation', so in 1139 Osbert, with the backing of King Stephen, went to Rome to seek this official sanction for Edward. Stephen himself was a disputed king at the time, and either that or Osbert's lack of convincing evidence led Pope Innocent to turn down his request. Some twenty years later, however, Edward's cause was picked up by a new abbot of Westminster, and with strong backing from Henry II, this time it was successful. A bull for canonisation was issued in February 1161 by Pope Alexander III. It is only fair to mention that Pope Alexander was at the time disputing the papacy with another claimant backed by the Holy Roman Emperor, and that Henry II of England was one of his main supporters.

Even then St Edward might have slid into obscurity had King Henry III of England not claimed him as a patron, rebuilding Westminster Abbey and providing him with a much larger and grander tomb. Another Chapel of St Edward was built at Windsor Castle, but when Edward III adopted St George as England's patron saint it was later re-dedicated as St George's Chapel. By then, though, Edward's position as an English saint was secure.

Turning now from winners to losers, once again we have an obvious candidate for first place. The Norman Conquest deprived Harold Godwinson not only of his crown and his life but also of his reputation. As far as possible written out of history entirely, all that is left in Norman accounts is a man who bullied and dominated an elderly king, usurped a throne, broke an oath sworn on holy relics and recklessly led ill-prepared troops into a battle where he was repeatedly outwitted.

Nothing is said of his talent for administration displayed over many years, though even William of Malmesbury was forced to concede that 'Harold would have governed the kingdom with prudence and with courage'. He received his first earldom when only just into his twenties, and following the death of his father became more and more involved in the government of England as a whole. Nor do we find rebellions against him by those he had charge over. Instead the *Vita* records that he ruled with patience and mercy, and the years of peace and settled government before 1066 stand witness to his obvious abilities.

Similarly, his depiction as a military fool is a travesty. As a soldier and commander of forces his record is at least the equal of William's and achieved with considerably less brutality. His expedition against the Welsh leader Gruffydd was a classic pincer movement involving land and naval forces and was a complete success, while the victory at Stamford Bridge matches anything William could show in the way of rapid movement and swift mastery of an unexpected opportunity.

The difference between them was that Harold preferred peace to war, using diplomacy at every opportunity to avoid unnecessary bloodshed. A supreme example of this is his peace-making role following the Northumbrian rebellion in 1065. It might be thought that with Earl Tostig expelled, his brother would be the last person likely to work to achieve a peaceful settlement. It was Harold the diplomat, however, Harold the realist, who patched up a deal between the rebels and their king when Edward was quite prepared to use force against them.

With a lifetime of service already to king and country and a record of acting consistently for the peace and well-being of the realm, it is tempting to think how well the country might have been served by a reign of King Harold lasting longer than nine troubled months. That he is persistently seen solely as the man who fell before the might of the Conqueror shows how cruel history can be to those it perceives as losers.

As it was, the other big loser was England itself. It was not just the plundering, spoilation and subjugation of the land, though that was bad enough, but the fact that the whole character and outlook of the country was changed by the conquest. The roots of its Anglo-Saxon culture stretched back some six hundred years, as long as the duration of the Roman Empire. It had been interrupted but not overthrown by the coming of the Danes, and indeed had in the end absorbed and benefitted from some aspects of Scandinavian culture, while itself giving much of value to the northern lands. By the mid-eleventh century the mingling of English and Danish names in families across the country shows England as one of the most successful multi-cultural lands in Europe.

This long, slow period of development had borne fruit in sophisticated institutions of government and law, as well as in a rich and varied range of artistic achievements. England was famous for its jewellery and treasures worked in gold and silver, for its tapestries, and for its beautifully illustrated books heavy with gold lettering. This was the English treasure that Poitiers said was squandered, possibly taken for granted by the English nobility. The Normans, having no such treasures of their own, no doubt felt they could do better with them.

Nor was it only worldly treasure that England produced. To many it seemed an island steeped in holiness. 'Does not the whole island blaze with such numerous relics of its natives that you can scarcely pass a village of any consequence but you hear the name of some new saint?' So wrote William of Malmesbury, acknowledging how the blending of Celtic and Roman traditions had produced throughout the land a bumper crop of acknowledged holy men and women. These too, however, did not match up to the Norman view of things. They belonged to an earlier time when the common definition of a saint was someone who had led a notably holy life and who would be acclaimed and venerated as a role model by their local community. A new idea of sainthood had begun on the Continent, a more formal idea that a saint had to be 'proved' and indeed accepted by the Pope before such a title could be used. Beginning in the ninth century and growing increasingly strong as the Pope claimed more authority in the eleventh century, it was this new idea of canonisation of a saint by the Pope that the Normans embraced.

By some accounts whole swathes of English saints were dismissed from the calendar by Lanfranc, although recently the suggestion is that this was more a critical review than a wholesale attack on established English cults. Many relics were certainly lost, though, in the rebuilding of churches, and the fact that the Normans saw fit to challenge such long acknowledged sanctity in such a way caused outrage among the already beleaguered English clergy and people. Nor was any new saint permitted to be recognised without the express sanction of the archbishop. England may have gained one saint of doubtful sanctity, but it is likely it lost many more, worthier of the name.

In at least one established measure of civilisation, England was far ahead of Normandy, and indeed of Europe in general. Though its language was still growing and developing, absorbing and adapting in particular from Scandinavia, it had for centuries been a written language as well as a spoken one. In Scandinavia tales and legends were still handed down by word of mouth. In Europe chronicles and religious works were recorded in Latin. England, though, had all of these and more besides written in its own native tongue. Epic poems such as *Beowulf*, tales of war such as *The Battle of Maldon*, saints' lives, stories from the Old and New Testaments, the *Anglo-Saxon Chronicles* themselves, all these were available to anyone who could read his own language, and there is evidence that literacy went considerably deeper in England than just the clerical class. English inscriptions on rings, armbands and other items suggest that craftsmen too were masters of the written word. The range of this native literature is also surprising. An extraordinary poem, *The Dream of the Rood*, describes the crucifixion from the point of view of the wood of the cross, while another, *The Ruin*, compares the ruins of ancient Roman buildings with their early splendour. At the other end of the scale the Exeter Book contains a collection of riddles, of which the Anglo-Saxons seemed extremely fond.

Once again we see the myth that the Normans brought an advanced level of civilisation to backward England. Not only did they have nothing comparable to this rich flow of language and imagination, but their coming and the down-grading of the native tongue to a second-class language meant that nothing similar would be produced for centuries until once again Geoffrey Chaucer made writing in English acceptable.

The other major change brought to England by the conquest was a new attitude of belligerence. William of Malmesbury makes a strong contrast between the native population and the invaders. The Anglo-Saxons, he says, when they first arrived 'were barbarians ... warlike in their usages', but after converting to Christianity and enjoying years of peace gave up their warlike ways, 'regarding arms only in a secondary light'. On the other hand the Normans 'are a race inured to war and can hardly live without it'. Fighting came as second nature to the Normans: the sons of the ruling classes were bred and trained for nothing else. It almost seemed that when they had no one else to fight they fought each other. This was the attitude that now held sway in England – the attitude of the rulers if not of the ruled – and it not only boded ill for their neighbours in Wales and Scotland but also meant that England would be involved for centuries in troubles and wars on the continent of Europe that it had previously shunned.

The claim has traditionally been made that England benefitted from the conquest by way of a more advanced civilisation and culture, beautiful buildings, Church revival and a more ordered way of life. Clearly these things were present already in the conquered land, and by and large the benefits flowed all the other way. It is much more likely that the English civilised the barbaric Normans, while the development of their own culture was stopped in its tracks. On the balance sheet of the conquest, then, it seems obvious that England comes down on the losing side.

Three kings ruled in England in 1066. One was a saint, one a soldier and one a Bastard. As so often in the flow of years, it was the Bastard that came out on top. It is possible that, just as carbon and iron are both needed to make steel, it was the blending of two very different peoples that eventually led to England's greatness in the world. Those who lived through the forging, however, may have felt they paid a very high price.

APPENDIX 1

DID HAROLD DIE AT HASTINGS? THE LEGEND OF THE HERMIT OF CHESTER

In 1753 a collection of ancient documents known as the Harley Collection was sold to the newly founded British Museum to be preserved for the nation. Among them, catalogued as Harleian MS 3776, was a group of manuscripts from Waltham Abbey. One of these we now know as the *Waltham Chronicle* and another was titled *Vita Haroldi* or *The Life of Harold*. Almost a hundred years passed before this latter document was translated from the original Latin into English by Walter Birch, Senior Assistant at the Department of Manuscripts at the British Museum. What it then revealed was an extraordinary story that could overturn everything we think we know about the death of Harold II, last Anglo-Saxon king of England.

The manuscript appears to be an early fourteenth-century copy of an original work from the late twelfth century, written by a secular canon of Waltham Abbey. This in turn claimed to be based on a shorter primary source from someone with direct personal knowledge of the facts alleged. The story it tells is quite simply that Harold survived Hastings, that another body was wrongly identified as his, that he was slowly nursed back to health, went abroad to try and raise help to dislodge William, failed in that, became a pilgrim and eventually returned to England to live out his life at Chester as a hermit. Extracts from the manuscript itself, as translated by Birch, will expand on this story.

To begin with, it explains why and how the manuscript was written. 'Your fatherly authority, then, orders, and your brotherly love begs me to take every watchful care,' says the writer, indicating that it is his abbot who has ordered the story to be written. 'For you do truly desire that a work ... cast in the form of a single book and compiled from various records written by our fathers ... concerning the praise of the glorious God-bearing Cross, with the memorable deeds of your founder, ... should be rendered famous.'

It then explains how Earl Harold first came to be associated with the abbey and its famous Holy Cross. Harold, at some unspecified point in his life, was suffering from a serious illness and his physician, 'a trustworthy and prudent man', frankly admitted he could not cure him. 'At that time a stone figure of our crucified King had recently been revealed and discovered by the heavenly direction, which, having been brought by God's desire to Waltham, was famous in that place for its miraculous virtues.' Harold's physician, therefore, recommended him to pray to the Cross. 'Nor was the mercy of the Saviour long wanting to him who asked for health with a faith unfeigned, for soon the pain and weakness of his body grew less ... And thus restored in a short time to perfect health, he proved by acts of magnificence how indebted and devoted he was to the medicine by which he had regained his health.' Harold, in fact decided to rebuild and endow the monastery in gratitude for his cure.

> This excellent man, eager to exalt the place and its worship with all classes of its worshippers, proposes to build there a new temple, to increase its number of attendants and to augment their revenues ... Foundations of a large church are rapidly laid, the walls rise, lofty columns at equal distances unite the walls with interlacing arcades or vaults, a roof of leaden plates keeps out the wind and the inclemencies of the weather. The number of clergy is increased from a shameful two to the mystic twelve of the company of the Apostles ... He also, with a splendid liberality, endowed them with estates and possessions, that they might have sufficient for their necessities.

Probably by the time of writing, the generosity of their founder is in danger of being forgotten, or at least downplayed by the Norman rulers. The writer is determined that it should not be lost forever so he adds:

> But lest the account of his munificence should be lost altogether ...
> – and it is known that a violent jealousy has aimed at this – it is

worthwhile to endeavour ... to make known to those who wish to consider them, the shadows, so to speak, of the facts. We have therefore thought good to insert ... an account of those things which, through the jealousy of Harold, were abstracted from the Church of the Holy Cross by William, the first Norman king of the English, and carried off to Neustria.

An impressive list follows of treasures carried off to Normandy, including three gold and four silver-gilt shrines full of relics and precious gems, four 'books of Holy Writ' ornamented with gold, silver and gems, gold and silver candelabra, crosses worked in gold, silver and precious gems, chalices, censers and richly ornamented priestly vestments. Clearly the loss of these had stung through more than a century.

The writer continues then with a brief survey of Harold's elevation to kingly status and his victory over Hardrada, before moving on to the most important part of the story, Hastings and its aftermath.

As, then, the English army was beaten and overcome at the first attack of the Normans, King Harold, pierced with numerous blows, is thrown to the ground amongst the dead: yet his wounds, many and deathly though they were, could not altogether deprive him of life. Thus, as the enemy's host departed from the scene of the slaughter, he who the day before was so powerful, is found stunned and scarcely breathing by some women whom pity and a desire to bind up the wounds of the maimed had drawn thither. They act the part of Samaritans by him, and binding up his wounds, they carry him to a neighbouring hut.

From thence, as is reported, he is borne by two common men, franklins or hinds, unrecognised and cunningly hidden, to the city of Winchester. Here, preserving the secret of his hiding place, in a certain cellar, for two years, he was cured by a certain woman, a Saracen, very skilled in the art of surgery, and with the co-operation of the medicine of the Most High, was restored to perfect health.

The writer later acknowledges that a number of other stories exist about what happened to Harold's 'body' after Hastings, and in particular the general understanding that it had been carried to Waltham Abbey and buried there, becoming a place of pilgrimage. He therefore offers the following explanation as to how this misunderstanding came about.

This horrible report had reached the ears of the private domestic canons of the King at Waltham, seeing that nearly everyone was saying that the king had fallen at the battle of Hastings. The clerks … not unmindful of the devotion due to their most generous patron, sent a certain woman of a shrewd intelligence, Edith by name, to the district where the battle had been fought, that she might carry away the limbs of their dead lord to be buried reverently in their church. She seemed a more suitable person to make the attempt insomuch as the weaker and less favoured sex would be considered less an object of suspicion to the cruel officers in authority, and more an object of compassion. But this woman seemed more fitted than all others to carry out this affair because she could more easily discover amongst the thousands of corpses him she sought, and would handle his remains more tenderly, because she loved him exceedingly and knew him well, inasmuch as it was clear that she had been frequently present in the secret places of his chamber. But when she reached the ill-omened spot she heard from many Normans who were everywhere boasting that the King of the Angles was ignominiously beaten, with his cross broken in halves, and that he was lying on the battlefield killed amongst the slain.

But let the reader see what turned out to be a truer account. For others thought that they who had carried off the King half dead had set about this report, foreseeing that it would be dangerous to them and to him and would prove their certain destruction if the enemy should hear that he was alive. We must not therefore wonder at the mistake of the woman who, unable to discern the features of the body – hacked about as it was, covered with blood, already becoming black and decomposed, since she could not find one which she could be certain was the King's – seized hold of and carried off with her another man's mangled corpse to satisfy the public estimation. And this was the body which was received in all reverence by the Canons of Waltham, without questioning the truth of the matter, and was handed over for burial in the Church of the Holy Cross.

After two years, then, Harold is restored to health and his first thought is to set about regaining his lost kingdom.

> On regaining his strength thus he thought he would prove by great deeds the courage of his royal spirit which his soul had not lost in the overthrow of his body. Already had the nobles of his kingdom, as well as the people, bowed their necks to the yoke of the conqueror; already had nearly all his chiefs either perished or been driven from the country, leaving their ancestral honours to be divided and possessed by strangers.
>
> ... He crossed over, therefore, to Germany, the home of his race, with the intention of proceeding to Saxony, but grieves to find that already the miserable overthrow of his nation is common talk in all quarters. He earnestly begs his kinsfolk to lend their assistance to one of their own stock: ... he importunes the Saxons as well as the Danes, whom he visited with an equal anxiety, to secure their help in driving out the invaders from his kingdom. But when he saw that their interests were directed into other channels, he ... gave himself up to the agitations of a great anxiety. For he who was now King of the English as well as Duke of the Normans, in his foresight for his own security had been thoughtful and prudent enough to anticipate Harold by hastening to ally himself ... in friendship with the King and nation of the Danes as well as with the neighbouring countries, and to conciliate their favour.

Now comes Harold's second life-changing moment, when he decides to give up the world and become a man of God.

> Harold, coming at length to himself, and returned as it were from a fantastic dream, is completely changed in his heart. He perceives, though late, that it was God who was opposing him ... and the eyes of his understanding being opened, he sees that he must choose another kind of warfare, and that other kinds of defences would be required. He begins, then, to see his errors and to lament the faults of his sins and wrong-doings in the sight of Him who sees all things. He begins to find that the path to a more blessed kingdom is far easier, and to have a foretaste of his opportunity. He is fixed in his

mind to become an imitator of the Cross which he had loved, to bear his cross daily, to come after the crucified One and to follow him. ... Thus the outward appearance and inward disposition of Harold are both suddenly changed. The hand which he was wont to arm he supports with a spear shortened into a staff. Instead of a shield, a wallet hangs from his neck. His head which he was wont to equip with a helmet and adorn with a diadem is shaded with a head-dress. His feet and legs, in the place of sandals and greaves, are either altogether bare or encased in stockings.

In hunger and thirst, in cold and nakedness, in prayers, in watchings, in insults and wrongs; in a word, in every toil and hardship the flesh is weakened, the spirit strengthened, the soul rejoiced. ... He delights that he has been conquered by man, since by conquering the world and himself he has, though conquered, learnt how to achieve a more glorious victory over the devil.

Therefore ... he leaves all his friends who had seemed to cleave to him up to that time, he deserts his kinsfolk, he retires secretly from all who had known him ... This man, now a noble man indeed, departed then to a far distant country to visit Sacred places in order that he might pay honour to relics of the saints in their own homes and shrines ... intending after that to return to his own country ... And if we are unable to accompany him to every place and on every single day as he wanders through many countries of Christendom and spends so beneficially his time, or if we do not know and cannot relate every single thing he did or suffered on his long pilgrimage, let us at all events, following him as he is now already a long way off from our shores, go and meet him as he returns to us with all speed.

At last, then, Harold came back to England to live out his old age as a hermit. For a time he lived in a cavern near Dover 'not far distant from the spot where he had formerly lost his earthly kingdom by nearly meeting his death'. Then he moved to Wales and spent a number of years living among the Welsh and praying for those he had once fought against. In England and Wales, of course, there was the danger that he might be recognised.

But as he was going into a land ... where he was once known, he concealed both his features and his name, wearing always in public the veil of a little piece of cloth before his face ... If, then, his name was asked he would say that men called him Christian. He indeed disguised both his face and his name because his name was known to all and his face to many ... But it was not to be feared that, even if he were betrayed by his enemies, he would be treated in a hostile manner, leading such a life and behaviour as he was doing, or put into closer restraint than he had put himself. ... For who would not show all the reverence and honour he could to such a man, when he saw how lowly minded and mild, how kind-hearted and gentle, how indifferent to worldly things he was.

Finally in old age Harold 'begs that God with his wonted kindness will grant him such a resting place, where he may pass the remainder of his life in the quiet of much desired repose, and there end his days by a happy death'. He is led to Chester and directed by angelic voices to a hermitage by the church of St John where the previous occupant has recently died. There he lived another seven years, apparently becoming well known for his wisdom and piety, and it seems that some who visited him there may have begun to suspect the truth of who he was.

And as he abode there, when he was frequently asked by those who came to visit him ... whether he was present at the war when King Harold was said to have been killed, he replied, 'I was certainly there.' But to some who suspected that perhaps he might be Harold himself, and who questioned him more closely than was right, he would sometimes thus speak of himself, 'When the battle of Hastings was fought there was no-one more dear to Harold than myself.' With such ambiguous words ... he did not so much confirm the truth of the facts as refuse to strengthen them in their doubtful conjectures.

'But now my story pleads for an ending,' says the narrator. Instead of continuing himself, however, he hands over to another, 'that the pen of those who know these things more fully may narrate what it is necessary to be known concerning Harold'. Before he leaves us, though, he begs that the reader 'may grant pardon for the garrulousness of the writer of this present work when he sees how very difficult it was to patch up and make new again the materials at his command, torn and misplaced as they are by the studies of former authors'.

The last part of the *Vita Haroldi* purports to be the narrative of the hermit who succeeded Harold in the hermitage at Chester, who explains how he came to know the truth of what he says.

'Now this same noble man had formerly an attendant named Moses, who, when I the present writer, was confined in the same place at Chester where the Lord Harold ... died, attended me also for two years. And I will tell you briefly and faithfully ... the events which follow according to the account of Moses and other faithful men.'

He then gives an account of the last days of the former king.

He rarely quitted the chapel but was constant in continual prayer ... In front of his eyes he hung at all times a cloth which covered nearly the whole of his face so that when he wished to walk at all far he required the hand of a guide. Why he did this his attendant did not know, but perhaps he did it to hide the appearance of the wounds upon his gashed face ... or else it was that he might not be recognised and venerated by any who had known him in former times.

Now as the day of the death of the venerable Harold drew near, and as that last moment of extreme necessity arrived when the holy man demanded the consolation of the Holy Sacrament, a priest whom I knew well, named Andrew, came and visited the sick man and administered to him all that the Christian rite requires. But as he was listening to his last confession he asked him of what station of life he was. To whom he replied, 'If you will promise me on the Word of the Lord that as long as I live you will not divulge what I tell you, I will satisfy the motive of your question.' The priest answered, 'On peril of my soul I declare to you that anything you shall tell me shall be preserved a secret from everyone till you have drawn your last breath.' Then he replied, 'It is true that I was formerly the King of England, Harold by name, but now I am a poor man, lying in ashes, and that I might conceal my name I caused myself to be called Christian.' Not long after this he gave up the ghost, and now, conqueror over all his enemies, he has departed to the Lord. But the priest at once told them all that the man of God had confessed to him in his last words, that he was indeed King Harold.

This is the story, then, set down and preserved at Waltham Abbey until after the Dissolution of the Monasteries in the sixteenth century, when the manuscripts passed into the hands of various noble families and finally made their way to the British Museum. It was certainly no secret. Gerald of Wales, writing of a visit to Chester in 1188, recites the story fairly fully, saying that the city claimed Harold was buried there. He brackets this, however, with another claim that the Holy Roman Emperor Henry V was also buried there, which is clearly untrue, so perhaps he did not put much faith in the local story. It is mentioned again regularly through the centuries, though usually as a 'Romance' or 'Legend', a work of fiction rather than fact. It may even have influenced Sir Walter Scott in the writing of his famous story *Ivanhoe*. The question must arise, however, as to why a religious house would either produce or preserve such a fiction.

The account was almost certainly written at the end of the twelfth century. In 1090 the church built by Harold, and filled by him with the treasures described, had been demolished and replaced by a Norman structure, partly based on the foundations of Harold's church but extending much further eastwards. At that time the *Waltham Chronicle* records that the body of Harold was disinterred and reburied in the choir of the new building. The author of the *Chronicle* declares that he had himself seen the body during its reburial when he was a young boy, and had been told its history at the time by an elderly sacristan who had seen the original burial. The new church was completed in 1150 and most of what survives today dates from that rebuilding.

Soon after, however, in 1177 the secular canons were removed and the church re-founded as an Augustinian Priory, and it is to this period that the *Vita Haroldi* seems to date. One suggestion given for its publication is that the 'cult of Harold', leading people to make a pilgrimage to his supposed burial place, was embarrassing to the Norman clergy now in charge, and they wished to downplay Harold and emphasise instead the wonders of their Holy Cross. A great deal of revenue for the Church was generated by those pilgrims, however, and another suggestion is that the story was written as a kind of 'sour grapes' by one of the ejected canons in order to cut off this lucrative source of money for his successors in the priory. If that is so, it would seem surprising for the Augustinians to carefully preserve the document and spread the story far and wide. The place was certainly a major pilgrimage site throughout the Middle Ages – even Henry VIII and Anne Boleyn visited – and of course pilgrims did not have to be explicit as to why they came.

If we look at the story itself, it is certainly plausible enough. The total absence of any hard evidence, or even a coherent and consistent account, of what happened to Harold's body after Hastings leaves a large gap at the end of the traditional narratives, and the misidentification of a corpse in such circumstances would be an easy mistake. The story gives a lot of circumstantial detail which is impossible to corroborate at this distance, such as Harold's attempts to raise support on the Continent and his years of pilgrimage around various holy shrines. There is an interesting coincidence of dates for both Harold and his mother leaving England around 1068, though there is no evidence of contact with her or any other member of his family, and surely if he had done so it would have formed a focus and raised the profile of any future attempt to overthrow the conquerors. Possibly by then it was all too late and well enough was left alone.

The places identified as stopping places for Harold in England are again plausible enough. Dover would probably be too close to King William for comfort, but Wales and Chester would be suitably remote. By repute Harold's son was born at Chester soon after the Battle of Hastings, but he seems to have disappeared from the record long before Harold himself reportedly arrived there.

The writer is careful to detail the sources for his tale, claiming that, certainly in the later years, it comes from direct eyewitnesses. Although full of pious sentiment and sermonising, as one might expect from a cleric of the time, the story as told is consistent and psychologically plausible. If it was intended to dissociate Harold from Waltham, it had the opposite effect, seeming to tie him in the popular mind even closer to the site. There has even been a suggestion that Harold's body may eventually have been returned to Waltham, and was possibly that which the writer of the *Waltham Chronicle* saw reburied there when the new Norman church was completed.

Hastings, Chester or Waltham? 1066 or sometime between 1090 and 1150? Harold, last Anglo-Saxon King of England, died and was buried, but how, when or where we may never know.

APPENDIX 2

WHERE WAS THE BATTLE OF HASTINGS FOUGHT?

Those seeking out the battlefields of the past sometimes have a very difficult task. Roads, even rivers, move, forests disappear, towns and villages come and go and railways and motorways slice up the landscape. By and large, though, those places fought over in the three battles of 1066 are relatively easy to find.

Fulford, it is true, has largely disappeared under houses, with the remaining open part (tracked down via a name on a map and the assistance of a local dog-walker) is about to suffer the same fate. The only indication that any fatal encounter ever took place there is a road sign, and even those just a few miles away in York are very vague as to the actual site of the fighting. Stamford Bridge fares better with a memorial stone in the middle of an enclosed and well-maintained space, though what Harald Hardrada would have thought of the tasteful, expensive houses lining the approach to this place of carnage is anybody's guess.

And of course we all know that the Battle of Hastings took place not in Hastings itself, but a few miles away at the place called Battle. Or do we?

If we had to rely on the descriptions in the various accounts of the battle we would have no hope of finding the place. It was 'by the ancient apple tree' according to the *Anglo-Saxon Chronicle*, 'nine miles from Hastings' according to John of Worcester, 'on a hill abutting the forest through which they had just come' according to William of Poitiers, while the *Carmen* adds 'the ground was untilled because of its roughness'. Fortunately we have a better guide than these, a landmark that has guarded the spot from that day to this and has been known throughout the centuries as St Martin's Abbey at Battle.

Our evidence for this comes mainly from the *Chronicle of Battle Abbey*, written around 1180 by an anonymous monk from the abbey. This claims to explain the history and origins of the abbey, 'having at hand certain records concerning the site and establishment of our place' and using information 'from verbal statements and from documents written by our predecessors'. In other words, although written over a hundred years after the event, it claimed to be based on documents and oral traditions much closer to the time.

By this account the origin of the abbey lies in a vow made by William of Normandy immediately before the battle itself, in order to encourage his men and possibly also in the hope of striking a bargain with God for a victory. 'Wherefore now,' declared William, 'secure of His aid, and in order to strengthen the hands and courage of you who for my sake are about to engage in this conflict, I make a Vow that upon this place of battle I will found a suitable free Monastery for the salvation of you all, and especially of those who fall.'

Among the crowd of men hearing this vow was a monk called William Faber who came from the Abbey of St Martin at Marmontier near Tours. He had once served the duke before he became a monk, and now was one of the many assorted clergy accompanying his expedition to England. After the victory he reminded William of his vow and four monks from Marmontier were brought over to form the nucleus of the new abbey, which was also to be dedicated to St Martin, a very popular saint at the time.

According to the *Chronicle* the fighting had occurred 'at the place which is now called Battle' and it was King William himself who had caused it to be named as such. Further, he had marked the place where the English standard had stood, where Harold had in fact been killed, and that was the place where he wanted his abbey to be built.

There was a certain amount of argument about this, however. The monks declared that the site was unsuitable. In particular it was 'upon a hill with a parched soil, dry and destitute of water'. They began to put up some buildings at a 'lower place on the western side of the hill', at a place identified by the name 'Herst' and a thorn tree. This compromise did not at all suit King William. When he found out, 'The king grew angry and commanded them with all haste to lay the foundations of the temple on the very place where he had achieved the victory over his enemy.' Arguments about the lack of water and local stone were brushed aside. William would endow the place so that 'wine shall be more abundant here than water is in any other great abbey' and after a 'vision', suitable quantities of stone were located nearby. Recognising the truth already noted, that 'they must will all that the king willed' the monks then set-to to build the abbey and its church in the right place, and 'they wisely erected the high altar upon the precise spot where the ensign of King Harold ... was observed to fall'.

That would seem to settle the matter beyond dispute – and yet, more especially in recent years, doubts have arisen as to whether in the end the place so honoured was in fact that where the battle was fought. One reason for this is the almost total absence of any archaeological evidence for a battle on that site.

It would be thought that, in a place where thousands fought and died in the course of a whole day, the ground would be full of evidence for their passing. Perhaps arrowheads, points from lances, a knife or two or a stirrup might be found, or even ancient bones of those fallen, especially since some accounts claim many were never properly buried. Certainly, on later sites of civil war battles, finds are fairly easy to come by. Battle, though, has offered up almost nothing.

It must be remembered that the battlefield would have been thoroughly looted and anything of value removed. Recycling is not a modern invention. Also the clearing and levelling of the land for the abbey and its surrounding buildings would have taken away layers of topsoil that might have included artefacts. Even recent digs in 2011 and 2012, however, failed to find anything that could be dated to 1066, though these were small-scale and hampered by the contamination of the ground by the many modern re-enactments that take place there. A proposed further dig may possibly reveal some more substantial evidence.

Possibly harder to explain away are a number of accounts of the battle which contain descriptions of a place nearby where countless Normans came to grief while pursuing fleeing English warriors. Orderic Vitalis gives the fullest account of this, saying, 'They fell unawares into an ancient trench, overgrown and concealed by rank grass, and men in their armour and horses rolling over each other were crushed and smothered.' Later he describes the place as a 'mouldering rampart and succession of ditches' while Poitiers also describes 'a steep valley intersected with ditches'. Both of these seem to suggest the 'trench' was man-made, possibly part of some ancient fortification. On the other hand the *Battle Abbey Chronicle*, describing the same incident, calls it 'a dreadful precipice caused either by a natural chasm of the earth or by some convulsion of the elements', 'of considerable extent', 'overgrown with bushes or brambles'. Not only does it name this feature, but it says it is 'still called Malfosse,' an 'evil ditch'.

The problem here is that there seems to be nowhere in the vicinity of Battle that matches these descriptions, neither man-made rampart nor natural feature, and nowhere that today bears the name of Malfosse. In a footnote to the *Battle Chronicle* at this point the translator notes that some have suggested the precipice was to be found somewhere along a stream then called the Asten, and now possibly Powdermill Stream, that rises in the west of Battle Park and flows below Crowhurst and through Bulverhythe to the sea. His objection to this is that the English would be unlikely to be fleeing in this direction.

A local historian has recently suggested, however, that by moving the battlefield a few miles south, this objection can be overcome. Crowhurst itself is the place identified as the most likely site. This builds on the premise that Duke William's ships lay not in the present town of Hastings but on the tidal creek that then existed behind present-day Bulverhythe, at around the area of Upper Wilting Farm. A route inland from there would pass Crowhurst, which has all the attributes given to it in the accounts – a hill with a ditch or 'fosse' at its foot and mostly marshy land around, and a steep drop into another stream along the edge of Rackwell Wood. It is claimed that artefacts have been found in this stream, although they have not yet been fully dated.

One argument in favour of this is that Crowhurst was Harold's own manor. Had he been heading in this direction it is possible the two forces could have met unexpectedly here and battle ensued. Certainly in the Domesday Book it is recorded as being laid waste. On the other hand if Harold believed William was in Hastings – and the accounts suggest his fortifications were there – he is more likely to have followed the ridge from Caldbec Hill to Hastings, passing well to the east of Crowhurst. A complicating factor is that on that ridge, two miles to the east of Crowhurst and near Crowhurst Park, a large mound beside the road is by local legend the burial site of the Normans who fell in the battle.

Closer to the traditional site is the place where a recent survey for a television programme established a new position on the now famous 'Battle roundabout'. In this area, it was claimed, artefacts have been found which have been dated to the correct period. This would only involve moving Harold's line a little further eastward, however, or maybe stretching it a little more than previously thought.

It would also fit quite well with the third alternative site for the battle, which is Caldbec Hill itself. This would involve swinging Harold's line anti-clockwise through forty-five degrees or so, to face down another steep hill which again has a stream and formerly marshy land at the base. Behind them now would be Kingsmead, the place where by repute they had spent the previous night, and there are other indications, too, picked up by the Victorian translator of the *Battle Abbey Chronicle* which could be fitted to the site. Should the fleeing English have passed through Kingsmead, which is likely if they had left horses and other gear there, the land drops away quite steeply behind there to another stream which could well have been the 'Malfosse' at the bottom of the 'dreadful precipice'. In 1279 land called Wincestrecroft in this area referred to as 'Mainfosse' was handed over to the abbey, and in 1851 Winchester Croft was still there, although it has now disappeared from the map. In addition that part of the hill itself was known as 'Montjoie', now 'Mountjoy', and the name was believed to derive from a cairn of stones built there by the Normans as a monument to their victory. This explanation would, of course, also fit well with the traditional site.

Reading the various accounts of the battle, it seems clear that it took place probably unexpectedly and at a place that previously had no name. Although known as the Battle of Hastings, no one has ever suggested it was fought in or even very close to that town, and it is suggested that had it taken place at Crowhurst it may well have been known by that name. Similarly, it would seem perverse to name a place Battle if the actual battle occurred somewhere else. As to where in Battle the front line was drawn, a great deal more investigation would be needed before that could be established beyond doubt. To a large extent it would depend on exactly where the forces were when they sighted each other, and whether Harold had the time and the inclination to come down from Caldbec Hill onto the ridge where the abbey now stands.

As for the abbey itself, it was not completed until after the death of the king, and the *Chronicle* says he was never able to visit the site while the work was in progress. Certainly it would be far easier to build on its present site than at the top of Caldbec Hill, but it would have been a brave monk that would have dared defy the explicit orders of William the Conqueror.

APPENDIX 3

A NOTE ON SOURCES

The period before and after the Norman Conquest is richly covered by contemporary and near-contemporary sources in both Latin and English, together with the pictorial source comprising the Bayeux Tapestry. The following have been referred to extensively in this book.

The Anglo-Saxon Chronicle
Written almost entirely in the English language of the time, this is in fact a collection of chronicles forming a continuous thread from the beginning to the end of our period and beyond. An original chronicle of the ninth century was copied and distributed to monasteries around England. These copies were then added to using available information on national and local events well into the eleventh century and in one case up to the death of King Stephen in 1154. Seven of these manuscripts survive in more or less complete form, along with two fragments. The oldest is the so-called Winchester Chronicle (also called the Parker Chronicle as it is part of the Parker Library at Corpus Christi College, Cambridge). This was begun in the later days of King Alfred and continues up to 1070. Others come from Abingdon, Worcester, Peterborough and Canterbury. The Worcester Chronicle seems to be based on an older northern version, possibly compiled at Ripon or York. The Canterbury manuscript appears to have been written and abridged from an earlier source similar to the Peterborough Chronicle, and is written in both Latin and English.

These chronicles are the most important source of information for the period they cover, although they are not all consistent as regards the dates and events they describe. In many cases they are the closest contemporary account and therefore little affected by the benefit or otherwise of hindsight. Many of those writing later accounts used the Chronicles as source material. In particular much of the work of John of Worcester is very similar to the Winchester Chronicle.

Encomium Emmae Reginae (The Encomium of Queen Emma)

This was written specifically for Queen Emma, probably between 1041 and 1042, by an anonymous monk of St Bertin's Abbey in Flanders. It is written in Latin in a style that aims at the classical, and gives a clear but very biased account of the conquest of England by Swein Forkbeard and the reign of his son Cnut. It is a major source for the story of the death of Alfred, though its aim of glorifying Emma and exonerating Godwin makes it unreliable. It ends just before the death of Harthacnut.

Vita Edwardi Regis qui apud Westmonasterium Requiescit (The Life of King Edward Who Rests at Westminster)

This is another work commissioned by a queen, this time queen Edith, wife of Edward the Confessor. The writer is again anonymous but was clearly a cleric and apparently not English. It is usually said he was a servant of the queen, but neither of those suggested seems to have held any obvious position in her household. Goscelin was a monk of St Bertin's Abbey in Flanders who came to England probably in the late 1050s and joined the household of Herman, later Bishop of Ramsey. Folcard, again a monk of St Bertin's, came to England to join the Abbey of Christ Church, Canterbury. Some unspecified trouble there caused the Archbishop of York to involve the queen in the issue. It is known Folcard then wrote a life of St John of Beverley for the archbishop and he may have written the *Life of Edward* for the queen.

It is a strange work in two rather disjointed parts. The first and longer part seems to have been written during Edward's lifetime, though the star is not Edward himself but the family of the queen. The second part, probably completed soon after 1066, focuses on the holiness of Edward and is clearly an attempt to pick up the pieces after the disasters of that year for the Godwins. It is this latter part that is developed and elaborated on later by Osbert of Clare. Neither part can really be regarded as an objective narrative of events.

Heimskringla – Snorri Sturlusson

Snorri Sturlusson was an Icelandic politician, poet and historian of the thirteenth century. Born into a wealthy family, he was brought up by a relative of the Norwegian royal family, and later his reputation as a poet led to him being invited to visit Norway as a guest of the young King Hakon. The collection of sagas he put together, which was later known as the *Heimskringla*, is the history of the kings of Norway. Written in Old Norse, it claims to be based on older sources such as family registers of the pedigrees of kings, poems of the 'skalds' or Viking poets, and on oral traditions. He would have been well placed to have access to such sources and, as he says, he cannot guarantee they are true, only that old and wise men believed them to be so.

As might be expected, it is better on Norwegian events than English, and more reliable on later happenings than those in the distant past. The Saga of Harald Hardrada is a useful source in that it covers his entire career, including events in Russia, Byzantium, Denmark and his death at Stamford Bridge.

Gesta Normanorum Ducum (Deeds of the Norman Dukes) – William of Jumièges

William of Jumièges was a monk of the Abbey of Jumièges in Normandy. He entered the monastery not later than 1025 and so would have been on the spot to get first-hand knowledge of the career of Robert of Jumièges both before and after his ill-fated time in England. His *Gesta* was an extension of an earlier work on the Dukes of Normandy which he revised and updated from the 1050s to 1070. He was therefore writing of contemporary events and his style is concise and matter-of-fact with no elaborate detail. His main drawback is a lack of experience of life outside the monastery, in particular military life, and he is, of course, firmly on the side of the Normans.

Carmen de Hastingae Proelio (Song of the Battle of Hastings) – Guy, Bishop of Amiens

This is probably the earliest account of the events of 1066 from a Norman point of view. It is a poem in Latin intended to be spoken or sung aloud, and was probably prepared rather hastily in 1067 for presentation to King William on his return to Normandy in March of that year. It is therefore a nearly contemporary source for the story that Harold was hacked to pieces in the battle and thereafter gathered up in a purple cloth and buried on a cliff top.

The only manuscript copy of the poem disappeared some thirty years after it was written and was only rediscovered in 1856, leading to suspicions that it was a forgery or some much later work derived from earlier writers. Now, however, it is generally accepted as authentic and the author is named as Guy, Bishop of Amiens, an uncle of Guy of Ponthieu, the captor of Harold Godwinson. The aim seems to have been to get himself and his friends and relatives into favour with William, and it must have worked well as Bishop Guy was chosen to accompany William's wife Matilda across the Channel to England for her coronation the following year. The *Carmen* may well have influenced those designing the Bayeux Tapestry, although the Tapestry clearly does not accept all the *Carmen*'s pro-Norman sentiments.

Gesta Willelmi ducis Normannorum et regis Anglorum (Deeds of William, Duke of the Normans and King of the English) – William of Poitiers

We would know much less about William of Poitiers were it not for Orderic Vitalis acknowledging what he called 'a valuable work' of 'unquestionable truth' on which he drew heavily, though sometimes selectively, for his own account. William was a Norman from a good family, becoming a soldier before turning away from that life to enter the Church. He studied at Poitiers, becoming, according to Vitalis, more learned than his fellows, and later became chaplain to Duke William and Archdeacon of Lisieux. He did not accompany the expedition to England but would have been well placed to hear directly from those who did, while his military background enables him to deal with matters such as tactics and manoeuvres. His *Deeds of William* was written in the 1070s and is full of detail including lengthy speeches put into the mouths of the main players, which he claimed he was recording accurately. It is the first full biography of William, though the beginning and end are now missing, and Vitalis says Poitiers was prevented from continuing the story to the king's death because of 'adverse events'. Possibly reflecting his sources and military background, his account is highly coloured and triumphal in tone. He declares, for example, that it would only be justice if the English dead at Hastings were left to be eaten by wolves and vultures. His aim was clearly to glorify William and 'to ensure for him eternal fame', and he quickly glosses over the less reputable parts of his story.

Chronicle of John of Worcester

The *Chronicon ex Chronicis* (*Chronicle of Chronicles*) was an account of world events from the creation of the world begun by an Irish monk known as Marianus Scotus. A copy of this was brought to England and at the request of Bishop Wulfstan of Worcester the monks of Worcester priory copied and supplemented it with much additional, particularly English, material. For a long time, due to a comment in the chronicle itself, it was thought that up to 1117 it was written by a monk known as Florence of Worcester. Now, however, it has been compellingly attributed to another monk called John. Not the least of the reasons for this is that Orderic Vitalis saw what he called John's chronicle when he visited Worcester. Much of the work closely follows the *Anglo-Saxon Chronicle* with some local additions, though when it gets to John's own time it becomes more expansive.

Historia Ecclesiastica – Orderic Vitalis

Orderic Vitalis was a product of his age, a child of a Norman father and an English mother. Born at Atcham near Shrewsbury in 1075, he was sent to the monastery there at the age of five, and then six years later to the Abbey of Saint Evroul in Normandy. It was in Normandy that he acquired the name Vitalis as they claimed they could not manage his English name, and his championing of the English point of view in his writing perhaps reflects the 'stranger in a strange land' feeling that he never quite lost. His *Historia Ecclesiastica* was originally commissioned as a history of his Norman monastery, but Vitalis had a talent for getting side-tracked and the work eventually grew to eight books. Of these, Books 3 to 6, covering among many other things the Norman Conquest and the activities of the Conqueror and his sons, were written between 1123 and 1131. Acknowledging his debt to other writers, he still has many original (and imaginative) stories to tell, not the least being the talking severed head of Earl Waltheof. Endearingly human, at one point he writes, 'It is now winter and I am suffering from the extremity of the cold,' before concluding Book IV. Certainly he is not always reliable on facts, but he does offer an English corrective to other heavily pro-Norman accounts of the times.

Gesta Regum Anglorum – *William of Malmesbury*

Born around 1095, William, like Orderic, had a Norman father and English mother, but he spent his adult life as a monk at Malmesbury Abbey in his native Wiltshire. He was reputedly a great scholar and lover of books, particularly history books. Inspired by the works of Bede, he aimed to write a similar objective, factual account of the English kings from AD 449 to 1120. Completing this in 1125, he later added a second volume extending it to 1142. He declared he was aiming to achieve credit for diligence in his work, and would not include anything for the more recent years at least unless he had seen it himself or heard about it from a credible authority. Nevertheless he is taken to task by the author of *Vita Haroldi* for his introduction to the section on the Norman Conquest where he says he will 'steer a middle course' between the Norman writers who 'praised to excess' King William, and the 'undeserved reproach' of him by the English writers. Malmesbury says he will 'openly proclaim' the good deeds, while 'his bad conduct I shall touch on lightly and sparingly'. The *Vita* author says he should instead have just written the truth.

Roman de Rou – *Wace*

Wace, sometimes called Maister Wace or Robert Wace, was born on Jersey, probably to a good family, and was brought up at Caen in Normandy. His *Roman de Rou*, written between 1160 and the mid-1170s, was commissioned by King Henry II of England and was intended more as an entertainment than a serious history. It does, however, cover the whole career of William of Normandy from the time he became duke until his death, continuing some way beyond that. It makes much use of earlier sources such as Poitiers and Malmesbury, but also claims to include information passed down in his own family traditions.

Other important sources used in this book are the *Vita Haroldi*, the Bayeux Tapestry and the Domesday Book, but these have already been discussed in some detail in their appropriate places.

SELECT BIBLIOGRAPHY

Primary Printed Sources

Anglo-Saxon Chronicle, ed. and trans. J. A. Giles (London: G. Bell & Sons, 1914)

Bayeux Tapestry, Lucien Musset, trans. Richard Rex (Woodbridge: Boydell Press, 2005)

Carmen de Hastingae Proelio, Guy of Amiens, ed. J. A. Giles (London: 1845)

Chronicle of Battle Abbey: from 1066–1176, ed. and trans. M. A. Lower (London: John Russell Smith, 1851)

Chronicle of John of Worcester, trans. Thomas Forester (London: Henry G. Bohn, 1854)

Chronicle of the Kings of England, William of Malmesbury, ed. and trans. J. A. Giles (London: Henry G. Bohn, 1847)

Domesday Book: A Complete Translation, ed. A. Williams and G. H. Martin (London: Penguin Books, 2002)

Ecclesiastical History of England & Normandy, Vols. 1 & 2, Orderic Vitalis, ed. and trans. Thomas Forester (London: Henry G. Bohn, 1853)

Encomium Emmae Reginae, ed. Alistair Campbell (Cambridge: Cambridge University Press, 1998)

English Historical Documents 1042–1189, ed. David C. Douglas and George W. Greenaway (Oxford: Routledge, 2001)

Gesta Normanorum Ducum, William of Jumièges, ed. J. Marx (Rouen: SHN 1914)

Gesta Willelmi ducis Normannorum et regis Anglorum, William of Poitiers, ed. R. Foreville (Paris: 1912)

Heimskringla, Snorri Sturlusson, ed. E. Monsen and A. H. Smith (Cambridge: 1932)

Journey Through Wales, Gerald of Wales, trans. L. Thorpe (Harmondsworth: Penguin Books, 1978)

Roman de Rou: Chronicle of the Norman Conquest, Wace, trans. Edgar Taylor (London: William Pickering, 1837)

Vita Edwardi Regis qui apud Westmonasterium Requiescit, ed. F. Barlow (Oxford: Clarendon Press, 1992)

Vita Haroldi, ed. and trans. Walter G. Birch (London: Elliott Stock, 1885)

Waltham Chronicle, ed. L. Watkiss and M. Chibnall (Oxford: OUP, 1994)

Secondary Sources

Ashley, M., *The Life and Times of William I* (London: Book Club Associates, 1973)

Ashley, M., *Mammoth Book of British Kings & Queens* (London: Robinson Publishing, 1999)

Barlow, F., *Edward the confessor* (New Haven & London: Yale University Press, 2011)

Barlow, F., *The Godwins* (London: Pearson Education Ltd., 2002)

Bennett, M., Bradbury, J., DeVries, K., Dickie, I., Jestice, P. G., *Fighting Techniques of the Medieval World AD 500–AD 1500: Equipment, Combat Skills and Tactics* (Staplehurst: Spellmount, 2005)

Brook, C., *From Alfred to Henry III 871–1272* (London: Sphere Books, 1969)

Carter, M. E., *The Groundwork of English History* (London: University Tutorial Press, 1908)

Douglas, D., *William the Conqueror* (New Haven & London: Yale University Press, 1999)

Harvey Wood, H., *The Battle of Hastings: The Fall of Anglo-Saxon England* (London: Atlantic Books, 2009)

McLynn, F., *1066: The Year of the Three Battles* (London: Jonathan Cape, 1998)

Morillo, S., *The Battle of Hastings* (Woodbridge: Boydell Press, 1999)

Morris, M., *The Norman Conquest* (London: Windmill Books, 2013)

Rex, P., *1066: A New History of the Norman Conquest* (Stroud: Amberley Publishing, 2011)

Rodger, N. A. M., *The Safeguard of the Sea: A Naval History of Britain 660-1649* (London: Penguin Books, 2004)

Stenton, Sir Frank, *Anglo-Saxon England* (Oxford: OUP, 1997)

Trow, M. J., *Cnut, Emperor of the North* (Stroud: Sutton Publishing, 2005)

Walker, I., *Harold: The Last Anglo-Saxon King* (Stroud: Sutton Publishing, 1997)

Wise, T., *1066: Year of Destiny* (London: Osprey Publishing, 1979)

Wood, M., *The Domesday Quest: In Search of the Roots of England* (London: BBC Books, 2005)

Index